Introdu

CW01500873

April 1997. When visiting f own for some minutes while Sue was ... ... herself for the meal we were going out for that evening. I browsed enviously through something that our friends possessed and that we did not aspire to own, nor had we since moving into a new house some months prior. A bookshelf crammed with all sorts of tomes – they were of all shapes and sizes and displayed the evidence of very wide reading, most of which were of too philosophical a nature for my taste except one or two that held my interest. My gaze rested on one in particular, a relatively thin volume entitled A Pennine Journey by Alfred Wainwright, subtitled The Story of a Long Walk in 1938.

Wainwright, as he will be known from this point on (I do not consider that I could possibly be so familiar as to refer to him as AW), has earned the respect of many for his candid and descriptive guides to many walks. Although specialising on walks in the Lake District, he is also recognised as being the provider of the definitive guidebook to the Pennine Way. My respect for the man did not stem so much from the words within these volumes but more from a deep-rooted sensation that he and I shared many innermost thoughts and feelings – a respect that perhaps to read and know all his works might diminish. The slight mystery as to his exact character only served to maintain my belief that we were kindred spirits – the more I knew of him the greater the risk might be of my hopes for Wainwright the 'role model' being dashed. I did know that Wainwright liked his own company, enjoyed the solitude of high places, felt an affinity with nature and was not a lover of larger towns and cities. Where our spiritual paths failed to run parallel was in the fact that he was able to illustrate his adventures with fine pen and ink drawings – my artistic talents extended only to a failed 'A' level in art. I am the proud owner of a watercolour set that comprises a posh wooden case and some sable brushes, all of which are still in pristine condition, not through scrupulous cleaning after use, but just through lack of use in general. I promise myself (and Sue, who bought the set) that one day … one day. I rest easy and tell myself that when I am getting on in years I will take up the brush and palette; Sue is of the firm opinion that I am already getting on in years so when am I going to make a start? Naturally I ignore such comments and consider that the greying hair gives me a look of distinguished experience rather than just that of an old gimmer.

Sue reappeared from the bathroom. We enjoyed a pleasant meal, after which we returned to the house and retired to bed. I had to have a closer look at the book for earlier in the evening I had only had time to skim through its pages. I was smitten in an instant with the idea behind its content. The journey referred to in the title involved a walk that started out from Settle, proceeding initially north-east, then north up the eastern side of the Pennines as far as Hadrian's Wall, and then returned south to Settle following the Pennines to the west. I exclaimed that on our return I would obtain a copy of the book. I could see the look on Sue's face begin to sour; she knew this would mean only one thing. Like Wainwright, I believe that much enjoyment is to be gained from meticulous and enthusiastic planning. Perhaps he was right when he said that women are incapable of enthusiasm, for I believe that while it may be they are capable of mild anticipation, it never reaches the giddy heights of the same sensation felt by men. We chaps are more readily able to return to our childhood and savour the excitement of a much-anticipated event. It has never been the case that a sensible mother would eagerly join a child in playing with dolls, but try and keep an apparently equally sensible father away from the Scalextric or the Subbuteo…

Sue knew that from that moment on, until the day of leaving, I would be as keen as mustard for her to share in my plans, however laborious. She does not differentiate easily between the outpourings of enthusiasm and out-and-out wittering. It has always been the same: I will perceive a perfectly logical need for a

Back to the Wall

The story of a long ramble in the northern Pennines, from Settle to Hadrian's Wall and back, following a route first trodden by Alfred Wainwright in 1938

A. Walker

Published in 2016 by:CM&CK Cocks
Yolanda
Brewery Yard
Stroud
United Kingdom

email: aw@awalker.me.uk
website: awalker@me.uk

Copyright © A Walker, 2016

Designed & typeset by A Lambert
Cover design by iindie Ltd
Printed in the UK

ISBN print: 978-0-9956043-3-9
ISBN ebook: 978-0-9956043-4-6

British Library Cataloguing-in-Publication Data
A catalogue record for this book is available from the British Library

Dedication

This book is dedicated to the two people who have mattered most in my life during the time that it was in the planning, walking and writing. Without Wainwright's inspirational seed there would have been no planning, walking or writing, and without Sue's continued love and support there would have been no water with which to nurture that seed.

Whether posthumously or in life, my thanks go to both, my respects go to both and my love goes to one.

Contents

useful, everyday object such as a garden shed and Sue fails to sense that same urgent need. The result of this is that, from time to time, I will mention, enthusiastically, the aforementioned object to ascertain whether her perception of our needs has changed. I have invariably found that not only has her attitude not positively altered, but that she has somehow developed a hatred for the object that deepens at every mention – as yet I have not been able to reverse this stance as far as clothes are concerned. She and I both knew that my liking for planning would more than likely drive her to distraction, especially when I outlined the timescale for my planned venture. I would undertake the walk sixty years after Wainwright had originally undertaken it, which would mean some seventeen months between first being bitten by the bug and actually removing the sting by setting out.

This planning was made all the more interesting (for me) by the fact that A Pennine Journey was not a guidebook. To retrace the steps involved careful reading while closely studying the relevant map, all points of reference being highlighted in the book with blue marker pen. This operation was carried out in stages, usually with the map spread out over the bed and me marking the book when a point of correlation was identified. I soon realised that the taking off of the pen top was clearly not dissimilar to listening to someone snore or sniff incessantly – you can live with it but why can't they roll over or blow their nose? (That is, rolling over for snoring and blowing their nose for sniffing.) Equally, whenever I needed to make reference to the map, and more especially when I had to refold it to follow the route, there would be a particularly quiet and intricate development to the plot of the television programme Sue would happen to be watching. Worst of all, I suspect, and I am pleased Sue never actually said so, was when at the end of a chapter I would ponder the route, more often than not tapping my front teeth with the pen while, perhaps, estimating a day's mileage. She would know that I was simply itching to be able to show her the route I was considering. I do hope that I have not painted a terribly sad picture of bedtime bliss with one of us eagerly straining to hear the television with the other poring over Ordnance Survey maps. There are times when we live like any normal married couple, arguing or putting up shelves, although, come to think of it, putting up shelves had not been something that had taken priority, for our books were still residing in the boxes in which they had been transported in when we moved. Would our lives be more complete, I wondered, if we set to and erected some shelves immediately? I doubted it and returned to my maps. Not only did Sue's enthusiasm not extend to sharing my near obsession with whatever was the current flavour of the month, but we had learned from an earlier experience during our renovating of a dilapidated cottage that neither did it extend to DIY. It seemed highly unlikely that she would change now, so if I didn't stir and build the shelves, the books would remain in their various boxes scattered about the house. Well, I was far too busy in my mental wanderings to bother about such minor things, so they would either have to wait or we would have to resort to our more usual practice of G-A-L-M-I – Get A Little Man In.

Sue did display a polite interest in my studies and would tolerate my briefly outlining the basic route. She showed an even greater interest in asking just how the hell did I think I was going to walk some of the distances that were required of certain days, for it was, to me, an important part of the planning that I should stay at the same villages as the original. I answered confidently that I was not concerned as to the mileages, although secretly I wondered just how the hell I was going to walk some of the distances required, too. There was, after all, several months in which I would be able to harden my feet to withstand the battering they would undoubtedly receive. I had walked the Dales Way previously and knew only too well that you can be as aerobically and 'cardio-vascularly' fit as you like, but if your feet give out, so do you. Perhaps I could give up smoking but, on reflection, I consider a hand-rolled cigarette to be an integral part of a good walk, and besides, Wainwright was a smoker in those days when it was seemly to be so. So no, I would carry on my socially unacceptable habit at least until it became viewed with the same disdain as had become the owning of a handgun. Apart from all that, acceptable places for a cigarette were rapidly becoming few and far between, but as far as I knew there had been no law passed regarding secondary inhalation of smoke while being entirely alone on top of a hill, and I concluded that I ought to make the most of it while I could.

I digress; I am somewhat prone to digression but I am a strong believer that the art of conversation is all about digression. It would surely be a very boring world if we were to answer all questions with a simple 'yes' or 'no' and keep exactly to the point of order. I often find it amusing to retrace one's steps back over a conversation to find that a current discussion regarding the fundamental roles of man and woman might have actually been born from a conversation as to who, as a child, had the largest Scalextric. It is sometimes difficult to comprehend how for many centuries man could have had the clear lead in decision making when in truth all he really wished to decide was who would have the inside lane with the TR7.

I recognise my character well enough to know that large tracts of this book will be wander into areas of digression, so if you consider yourself to be a person who clings unerringly to the point then stop reading now, put this book down, place it in the box of past belongings for the car-boot sale and go immediately and build some bookshelves. That said, I must return to the matter at hand and my overriding desire to undertake this journey which from the very outset had struck me as not being something that I necessarily wanted to do but, moreover, as a part of my destiny. I perceived it as a mission that must be carried out starting on a Sunday in late September, just as Wainwright had done. I would walk from Settle to Buckden to Muker to Romaldkirk to Blanchland to Hexham to Haltwhistle to Alston to Knock to Soulby to Dent and back to Settle in eleven days, a total of two hundred miles – just as Wainwright had done.

He had led but I was pleased to follow, for I was, after all, following in the footsteps of the master; I was following him back to the wall.

Chapter 1

Settle to Buckden

S ettle, on a fine, warm, sunny morning in September, is a more pleasant place to be than it might have been ten years ago. It is situated on the main day-tripper route from West Yorkshire to the Lakes and, in the days before the bypass, was a horrendous bottleneck for all those wishing for a few days' escape from their crowded and pressured lives in the towns and cities. They would set out earlier and earlier each time they made the journey in an attempt to get ahead of the squeeze – invariably this would fail, for all the others had hatched exactly the same cunning plan. They would, however, finally arrive at their destination, somewhat fraught and not a little frazzled, only to find that they had endured the trials of the journey and landed themselves in the crowded and pressured Lake District. Barely would they arrive when it would be time to make the return journey, suffering the exact same hassles but in reverse order, at the various traffic bottlenecks of which Settle vied with Skipton for being king of the hill.

It is difficult to imagine how the travellers would possibly be able to handle such crowded Settle streets now – incidents of road rage would abound, with fisticuffs breaking out throughout the town as drivers tried to cut-in or undertake by some sly manoeuvre. The scene would become a 1990's spectator sport as bystanders would lay bets on whether the driver of the Astra, drumming his partly clenched fists on his steering wheel, would actually accost the driver in front for not having acknowledged being let in from a busy side street.

The building of the bypass has brought to a halt the tribulations of driving through Settle. All that happens now is that the traffic becomes bottlenecked elsewhere en route, until that is bypassed, and so on, ad infinitum, until all the bypasses are bypassed, and all we will have is a vast wasteland of macadam between West Yorkshire and the Lake District. The only way to enjoy the Lake District is to make the effort to be far from the madding crowd, atop the hills and fells that, even in the summer months, remain relatively peaceful. The majority of the day-trippers make for the valley roads and byways so that, from your vantage point high above, they can be seen and observed as ants are observed, but they cannot be heard. No, make for the hills, but please check that I'm not there first for I prefer to be alone when I am walking.

At eleven o'clock I walked from the centre of Settle bidding farewell to Sue and, in a scene not wholly unlike something out of Casablanca, told her that when I set off down the long straight stretch toward the junction with the Horton road, I would not look back. These first few steps gave me a rather peculiar feeling of being more totally alone than I had envisaged and that perhaps it might have been a better idea to walk with someone else. That had never been a feasible proposition for I had not met anyone who had shown the slightest inclination to want to walk two hundred miles in eleven days and neither could I think of anyone I knew who would be physically able to walk such a distance. In all fairness I had no idea whether I was capable of carrying out this walk, except I expected to be carried by a greater imperative, namely that, for some reason, I felt it was a part of my destiny to complete this adventure. Sixty years to the day had seen Wainwright leave Settle and head, firstly, north toward Horton-in-Ribblesdale – I wanted to tread that same way, which was the route I had been planning for so many months. This was my day; this was the start of my personal journey in which I would be joined along the way by long-dead lead miners, long-dead legionaries and sad and distant memories of old railways and other forgotten dale-dwellers. I might not see them in body, but their spirits would join me as I moved among the ruins and the remnants of their past presence.

Incidentally, I lied earlier; I did look around at least twice. In fact I looked around when so far down the road that, even if Sue had been watching my last steps before disappearing at the junction, I could not have made her out. I turned the corner at the junction with the road to Horton and set off in earnest upon my trip – I saw this very much as my trip all through the whole of the days that I was walking. I was convinced that I would be entirely alone in following this route, which cannot be said for many other long-distance paths. The shelves at the bookstores only need to be scanned to see how popular long-distance walking has become, with several volumes giving slightly differing variations of the same route – the Pennine Way is no exception, with Wainwright's own once solitary guide now joined by many others. There are those that describe it followed north to south and others south to north. The result of this popularity is that it is easy to feel that you exist within a slow-moving procession, and you will see the same walkers day after day as you overtake them when they stop, and vice versa as you rest. I do not wish to come across as a lonesome anorak but I enjoy walking alone, and on this walk I also had good reason to believe that I would benefit from being without companion. En route I wished to discover all I could about Wainwright's course and I wanted to be free to stop when I chose to note specific details. I wanted to find out as much as possible about the people and the places that he stayed in. I wanted to be able to talk with the locals, which is always easier when alone. I wanted, more importantly, to share in the essence of being as one in nature, which can only be fully experienced alone.

As I had approached the Horton road a number of vintage cars passed taking part in the annual Bradford to Morecambe rally. How novel, I thought, that some of these vehicles would have been of the type that would have travelled along the quieter byways in the days sixty years earlier. As Wainwright would have walked along the various roads he would have seen cars such I was seeing as I left Settle. I pondered for a moment on whether in another sixty years we will still be able to hold the rally in modern-day cars and as to whether they would prove as durable as some of these older, more simple and altogether more elegant means of transport. We appear to have entered a phase in society that has almost fully adopted the throwaway philosophy: if something is broken, no thought is given to the viability of repair. We now know that if our iron or our kettle breaks then two trips are required: one to the shop to purchase anew and one to the tip to discard the old. It is a frightening thought that this attitude appears to have also spilled over into our lives in other areas, such as relationships where, it seems, only passing thought is given to the repair and reconciliation of them – it is much easier just to concede and start again. Our sense of commitment to our irons or kettles is, understandably, controlled and influenced by economic factors, but surely there must be something deeper in our more intimate dealings with other people? Perhaps there still is for the present, but what of the future; will our purchase/discard society continue to flourish and what will be the effect of an increase in our throwaway mentality? I sometimes fear for that future.

I had not travelled far along the Horton road when I heard the sound of a train on the railway line that runs largely parallel to the road for much of the way northwards up Ribblesdale. In 1938 I would have heard and seen a great many trains at a great many places along the entire route, but I knew that that would be no more for most of the dales railways had long since been closed and the lines broken up. Hardly a day would pass without my encountering reminders of Dr Beeching and his handiwork of the 1960s. The line now following my route is part of the Settle–Carlisle railway, which itself, in the past, had been seen as being at risk of closure, leaving the only rail link to Scotland one that ran up the eastern side of England to Edinburgh. I paused for moment as the train passed and looked back at the receding view of Settle nestling in the valley of the River Ribble as it exits from its turbulent passage through the steep-sided ravines to the north of the town before commencing a more tranquil and meandering route south of the town. Settle itself doesn't give an impression of outrageous growth for it is not situated in any particular commuter belt and in any case space for expansion is limited by the immediate topography. To the east and west the steep-sided Ribble valley precludes economic development, and the flat valley floor, where it can be, has been developed.

In the days of 1938 the walk along the road north of Settle would have been a roadside stroll of six miles to Horton-in-Ribblesdale. However, in 1998 it has become an unpleasant experience with some parts distinctly dangerous to venture out as a pedestrian. The only points of sanctuary are where, for some distance, a footway has been constructed or a verge has been formed. It was, though, my intention, be it foolhardy or otherwise, to follow in Wainwright's footsteps, by description of the route taken, for as far as was possible. It had been evident from his account that he had passed through Langcliffe and Stainforth, so my way was set for me. Like so many small villages, Stainforth has now also been bypassed by simply straightening the road on a course to the west and the village has now become a rather plush little dormitory serving Settle. It is a village where, I suspected, house prices would have soared as desirable residences were formed from the original workers' cottages. The danger of this type of village development is that while the pub may survive for the locals, other services such as the tearoom where Wainwright would have been tempted to pause had it not been for the crowd of noisy cyclists are forced into closure. There is no passing through-traffic save for, on this day, one sole walker who would probably never call at the village again. Nor were there any cyclists, for no doubt they also proceed passed the village without thought of stopping.

Even if the tearoom was still open I would have passed it by for I would also not allow any thoughts of rest until I had reached Horton, where I would relish the prospect of the remainder of the day being spent on moorland paths and tracks – paths and tracks that would be well away from the rush of cars and lorries and coaches that, for these first two hours, had hurtled passed me as though I were a closed-down tearoom. I would also be away from the roar of powerful motorbikes which raced by me as if the road were an informal Sunday TT. They would bear down on me with such rapidity that there was no warning of their arrival until they were almost alongside with me nearly leaping headlong for the nearest undergrowth.

There were one or two aspects of this part of the walk that rendered the traffic bearable. Firstly, I was walking with a warming sun on my back and I followed my shadow all the way along the roadside. This was the same sun as Wainwright had enjoyed – the passing of sixty years in terms of the sun's life was a mere blink of the eye, yet so much had changed on the earth upon which it shone: man had reached for the stars and had walked on the moon; the computer had been developed to the point where our lives were reliant upon it; the National Health Service was born and developed to a point where our lives should be reliant upon it; and we could travel the world in a matter of hours. All of these things … yet how strange it is that, at the same time, man does not appear to have been able to develop a means of quarrying for rock in a way that does not leave an ugly blot on the landscape. Over to the west of the Ribble valley are the scars left by years of geological vandalism that have changed the face of the landscape forever. This had been carried out in a way that could never be repaired and, seemingly, not in a way where any effort of repair had even been attempted. The quarry was now disused, yet it would leave its mark for all time with unnatural cliffs formed by blasting and wide slopes where the lorries had once removed their bootie.

The second relief from the traffic was the first sight of mighty Pen-y-ghent, spied as I crested the brow of a hill near Helwith Bridge. Pen-y-ghent forms a prominent feature hereabouts and would be within my sight, intermittently, for the greater part of rest of the day, until I would finally drop below the summit on the Wharfedale side of Horse Head Moor. It is a sleeping giant with its steep tiered southern extremity and its more benign slope away to the north over Plover Hill. The distinctive tiers result in the shape and form of its outline appearing to continually change as an approach is made from the south. At first its length cannot be appreciated and the shape is that of a green pyramid standing proud above all else. Its more picture-postcard form is revealed as Horton is reached when the north–south extent is revealed and it becomes a different mountain with a short, sharp ascent usually being made from Horton-in-Ribblesdale. It is an ascent that demands many pauses, all of which are dual-purpose: first to catch breath and secondly to admire the views opening up over Ribblesdale and across to the other two famous hills in this area, Ingleborough and Whernside. These three between them form the Three Peaks Walk, a twenty-five-mile round trip that challenges the walker to mount all three within twelve hours.

My initial view of Pen-y-ghent called for a photograph, which was one of the first of many I hoped to take on my journey and very nearly proved to be my last. I was not, on this walk, going to repeat the mistake I had made three years earlier when I walked the Dales Way. I had decided in my wisdom to carry a medium-format camera on that occasion, with tripod, film backs and the other paraphernalia that had to accompany me. At the end of each day I was exhausted, not so much from walking but from having the weight of the camera rucksack bearing around my neck all day. I had learned my lesson and now I had gone from the sublime to the ridiculous and had with me the smallest camera I could find; so small was it that as I took it from its belt holder it slipped from my grip, and for a few brief but alarming seconds I was left stood above the macadam of the road juggling with it knowing if I didn't ultimately catch hold of it, my means of photographing would be prematurely curtailed. I must have looked a very odd sight patting the camera back into the air first with one hand then the other, in much the same way as when a glass is dropped and desperate measures are taken to try to avoid it hitting the floor, usually causing more damage than had it been left to gravity. Wainwright had suffered problems with his camera on his walk and I had no desire to see a repeat of cock-ups on the photographic front. I did manage to catch a firm hold and avoid mishap and was extremely careful from that moment on.

I was expecting to arrive at Horton at one o'clock but at ten to I had seen no evidence of the appearance of any form of habitation other than the occasional roadside barn. Then, almost as I rounded the very last corner before the village, I saw grey rooftops through the trees ahead of me. Horton is indeed a shy place seeming to want to remain hidden from gaze. The church, which I knew from the map must be there and that lay at the southern end of the village, was even more desirous of not being seen for only when I was very close could I at last see its squat form. The castellated tower at its western end looked as though it had been erected as a fortification, as though the low main building with shallow-pitched roof was added as an afterthought. However, no longer was the whole site rather untidy and unkempt as Wainwright had described it, for the roof had now been recovered in a light-grey sheeting material. Although this had the effect of producing a cleaner look, it also gave the impression of a scout hut having been built to a strict budget – perhaps it had been reroofed by public subscription and, if so, then credit to all concerned. In these days of falling church attendances it was refreshing to think that there does exist a place of worship that attracts a congregation of such numbers to be able to accumulate sufficient funds to carry out works to keep the building in a decent state of repair. Not wishing to be picky, but it was just a shame that the funds could not be found to reroof in a material more in keeping with the natural material used elsewhere in the village.

I rarely pass a church without being reminded of my own wedding day. Accepting that I was keen to marry Sue, I was, nevertheless, crushingly embarrassed to have been heard by the full church to utter 'I will' three times. The vicar, a most pleasant and charming man, was something of a slow speaker and, I thought, was perhaps paying due reverence to the occasion. He had confused me when at the end of 'Do you...', and so on, there was a long pause in his delivery, which appeared to me to be an invitation to answer affirmatively, which I duly did. I was then surprised when he set off again with the 'to have and to hold' part, again followed by another lengthy pause. Again I spouted forth my willingness and noticed that there was some tittering in the gathered throng behind me. They all clearly knew the service better than I for no sooner had I said the words than the vicar broke into voice again and, finally, it was my turn to respond that I would indeed take Sue to be my wife. I was not allowed to live this faux pas down for the rest of the day, and many found great amusement in my embarrassment, particularly as the whole episode was captured on videotape.

Horton church is an idyllic spot with a fine backdrop of Pen-y-ghent standing high above. On a fine day such as this, with blue sky and wisps of white cumulus cloud, the whole scene provided a tranquil few moments before I pressed on with the final few yards to the Pen-y-ghent Café. The café is the focal point for all those keen enough, or mad enough, to have a desire to circumvent the Three Peaks Walk. Most walkers will set off from here and the café has an antiquated timing device that clocks walkers out when they set off and clocks them back in again when (and if) they return. There is a serious aspect to this of course – namely that it provides a safeguard should a walker clock out and not return. This is all carried out voluntarily, although the café is of course assured of many thirsty and hungry visitors across its threshold. I am not sure that Wainwright would have approved of such efficient organisation, and I am fairly sure that he would not have been a regular visitor to these parts now that they had become so very popular. No more could one expect to be a lone walker in these hills for the paths have become so well-trodden that duck-boarding has been put down over the more marshy sections to conserve the moorland peat bogs. Today however, I was a very willing customer as I ordered a pint of orange for I was ready for a sit down in the sun before tackling the stretch up and over Foxup Moor.

Although walking had already become a widespread recreation when Wainwright first discovered its pleasures, the more popular areas were those served by railway connections. If the ability existed to get away from the more common routes, then the walker could expect to meet few others on his rambles. It is also true that in the pre-war days when Wainwright had made his way through Horton-in-Ribblesdale, walking activity would have been more inaccessible for the plethora of paths that now exist on Ordnance Survey maps simply had not been mapped. Horton, in the late days of this century, is one of the centres par excellence for walkers, generally recognised as the start and finish of the Three Peaks Walk and lying also on the route of the Pennine Way. A brief study of the map reveals something of a confusion for Pennine Way followers as there are several paths shown titled 'Pennine Way'; in fact no less than three all heading north from Horton. I can only assume this to be an ingenious conspiracy hatched jointly by the Ordnance Survey and the guidebook writers for clearly a guide needs to be purchased if one is to reliably tread the correct path where the map creates confusion – only the guidebook can resolve it. My way was clear though, and I merely had to find the old vicarage to take me off the made road on to more pleasant stony paths and tracks.

Wainwright had commented that Horton was a Mecca for potholers and enthused as to how a man's passion could be fired by such adventures. He had stressed 'man's' enthusiasm for he espoused that women were far too practical to be able to capture any emotion even vaguely close to unbridled, and yes childish, enthusing; they were tied by convention to more mundane things that doused any spark of inclination toward enthusiasm and certainly could not, or would not, make any attempt to comprehend the keenness of their menfolk's' desires. It seemed rather fitting, I felt, then that at Horton, in this haven where men could feed their fires of excitement, the vicarage was now the 'Old Vicarage', and above the front door there hung a sign reading 'Women's Holiday Centre'. What the vicar would have made of it I have no idea, but I could well imagine that Wainwright would have had one or two choice personal thoughts: for goodness' sake, is there no housework they can be doing?

The track passed the large detached house and led away at right angles to the road so that the sound of engines was quickly left behind. It soon then began to make its way up the valley side, with rearward views opening up of the valley that I was pleased to leave behind, not that there was anything especially unattractive about Ribblesdale, but I was then able to concentrate more on enjoying the walk than dodging cars. The path is an old green road with dry-built limestone walls to both sides, which are not so high as to obscure any of the surrounding beauty of this fine limestone country. Not far from Horton the path turns northwards and follows the western side of a classic dry valley down which, eons ago, would have tumbled a lively stream. Now though, all that remained of any evidence of a watercourse was the white craggy outcrops reaching across the valley where once would have been waterfalls. This would, at some time in the distant past, have been the continuation of Hull Pot Beck for Hull Pot was just a little way further up this valley and marked the end of the evidence of water above ground. I was now walking in the land of swallow holes and springs where water would disappear below the surface without warning, almost unnoticed, and might later reappear equally quietly.

Now I was free, the feelings of loneliness were gone, replaced by a euphoria that comes of being properly alone. It is so much easier to feel desolate and lonely when we are surrounded by people that are unknown to us and all have their own, it seems, single-minded purposes: they are late for their appointment; they are thinking of last night's acquaintance, who they had met but can't remember the name of; they are struggling with 5-across in the crossword; or they are plotting as to how they can get that promotion. They are always engaged in a thought that would not welcome the intrusion of a stranger. Cities always give this sense of 'aloneness', an enforced loneliness that can only be cured by returning to our own hive and feeling safe within a familiar swarm. Here though, on these paths and hills, nature has time not for the taking or intruding for anyone who cares to come here. There is no asking, more a sublime invitation to simply allow the atmosphere to enter the pores and the soul. If the sensation is not all-pervading, then my advice is to return to your city, your hive, your swarm and leave me in peace to savour the ambience of being swallowed by, yet also swallowing, all that is around me. It is a very special companion who does not trespass in such places.

It is an essential part of walking that the greatest gain comes from this sense of being 'at one'. I should not like to give an impression that I sit alone throughout the day, shunning human contact, for at the end of the day I enjoy the convivial company of others, strangers or otherwise. This is, however, not the case at lunchtime, and as I found a very quiet streamside rock, I slung off the rucksack and my waist bag, removed my boots and socks, took out my tobacco and roller and proceeded to relax for thirty minutes with my feet bathing in the cold water of the stream. I sat quietly drawing on my cigarette looking southwards back down the beck toward Hull Pot, which I had passed some fifteen minutes earlier but hadn't tarried there as it was surrounded by swarmers – those people that of all the moor to choose will join a throng rather, apparently, than be alone. I had passed them by with naught but a swift glance at the pot and had found this gloriously silent spot just sufficiently out of earshot and eye-line of those at the pot itself. I lunched with half a dozen sheep, a number of mayflies and an occasional visiting bumblebee.

I couldn't explain why I had had an uneasy feeling throughout this splendid break, and I put it to the back of my mind. As I sat on the flat rock I took out Wainwright's book and read a few pages, having rolled a second cigarette. It was something in the book that was nagging at me: why hadn't Wainwright written as flowingly as did this stream? I soon realised that he had not made any mention of Hull Pot Beck because he hadn't come this way! In my haste to move on from Hull Pot, I had gaily followed the stream whereas I should have turned north-east. At this juncture I took out something that Wainwright and his contemporaries could not have dreamed of – a device that calculates exactly where you are and gives a six-figure grid reference. The gadget – I am a great one for gadgets – is a global positioning system, small enough to walk with and invaluable in situations where visibility precludes compass bearings being taken to triangulate position. It is also invaluable when you are downright lazy and would rather quietly finish a cigarette than fiddle about looking for landmarks and lines on a map. Switching it on and leaving it to its own devices for a min-ute or two, my trusty machine showed my position as being just a couple of hundred yards off-route, which I would correct when I set off again. I went back to finishing lunch.

The weather by now had become really rather warm and I drank the remain-ing water from my bottle. My choice now was either no water or water from the beck. Choosing the latter, I filled the bottle with somewhat brackish water and comforted myself with the fact that it must be iron staining – this was a far more pleasant thought to satisfy myself with than any of the alternatives I was think-ing of. What, at worst, could the staining be I asked myself. Peat perhaps, or sheep's urine. I dwelled on that train of thought no longer and just soaked up the sun on my face instead, for it had been my follower all day so far. Looking into the sunlight the thistles on the opposite bank danced in the slight breeze and the lacy seed heads were illuminated by the contre-jour lighting. The whole scene was simply sylvan.

I revelled in this pleasure for around twenty minutes when I heard voices from the fell to the east. Sure enough there were three walkers descending the Pen-y-ghent side of the shallow valley where I sat and they made their way toward a stile some 50 yards away. I looked away as they crossed the stile in the same way that little boys look away from the schoolmaster in a vain attempt to avoid being the one picked out for some onerous task. It was all to no avail and they marched directly toward where I was sitting. Did I look like I needed company? I thought as they arrived. Greetings were exchanged and I assumed that they would continue on their way up the valley. But no, they paused, they thought about it a little and were soon busily engaged in removing boots also – it was apparent that they were proposing to lunch here too. Why of all the streams in all of Yorkshire did they have to pick mine? Please do not think that I am unsociable when approached in such a way; it is simply that I fall into a mood not dissimilar to the city-dweller thinking about 5-across or that promotion: my isolation would prefer to avoid disturbance. I chatted with the group politely while drying my feet and re-booting. Of the three it was one of two young ladies who did the talking, perhaps, I thought, because she was the only English-speaker – the others were obviously German. Our discussion was affable and she was generous enough to give me a refill of fresh water from her plentiful supply. I inquired of her as to whether her group was on holiday and from where in Germany had they travelled. I was dumbstruck when she replied, with a pronounced German lilt, that she was from Barnsley and that the gentleman was her uncle over from Germany.

Boots back on, rucksack shouldered and waist bag re-strapped, I bade the threesome farewell and set off in an easterly direction to find the path from which I had strayed. My route now had meant I'd left behind the wall-enclosed green road and the path was fast becoming a narrow and obscure way through heather- and reed-clad moorland as I approached the bleakness of Foxup Moor. Many things have changed in the years that span the difference between Wainwright walking this way and my following in his steps, but certain things will always be the same on these moors. The barrenness of them is one aspect that had changed only insofar as there is greater evidence of walkers having been here, with more pronounced pathways. The openness is exactly as it has been for decades prior even to Wainwright being here save for the fact that there now exists the more distinct possibility of encountering other human activity because walking, as a pastime, has become a very popular pursuit for many. Although there may have been those with the inclination to spend time in the hills in around 1938, there were few with the opportunity and even fewer who might have felt the compelling urge to embark on a course such as Wainwright's, hence he met others on only very isolated occasions. The one aspect of this stretch of the walk that must have been similar, judging by his description, was the ground underfoot. Great areas of bog and marsh still exist as wide, long and deep boot-sucking quagmires which try the walker's patience for only very slow progress is possible where these are confronted. The short relieving interludes of terra firma between these bogs are of insufficient length to avoid being able to gain sight of the next morass some yards ahead.

I was not as alone as Wainwright described himself to be in his account, and I greeted several small groups who passed me as they headed toward a more southern destination – presumably Horton. Meeting others can have its consolations however, and I have to confess to gaining considerable entertainment from one particular group, for at an exceptionally unpleasant wet section they appeared to have strayed into the worst of it. Having come some way into the mire, I can only assume that they were not disposed to retrace their steps and steer a wider course over available higher and drier ground. The result of their obstinacy was that they now found themselves lost in a sea of squelching moorland ooze with only small tussocks to act as islands between. The gentleman appeared to be leading the way and was clearly more able to leap from tussock to tussock than his companion, a young lady. She, more than once, attempted the same jump only to find herself calf-deep in thick, black, filth which was very clearly making her more and more annoyed each time. I had been very fortunate in finding a course to the west of this section and continued at a pace, glimpsing sideways sometimes to better observe their predicament. My speedy rate of progress as I passed wide of them can only have served to worsen the lady's blackening mood. I had first come across them as I crested the brow of a low hill, and as I left them behind in the shallow depression (with the lady in an even deeper depression) and topped the next brow, they were still teetering about among the long grass. I never did come to any firm conclusion as to which way they had originally been heading. I did feel somewhat guilty for having taken a wide course for it is such actions that serve to extend these moorland bogs, but with ten days' walking ahead, I did not especially want to endure any more of the walk than was absolutely necessary with soggy, wet boots and socks. I prefer to be comfortable – Wainwright was a believer in getting the feet wet early for it would surely happen sooner or later. I disagree with him on many things, of which this is one.

By the time that Foxup Beck had appeared in the developing valley below me, to my left the moor bogs had been left behind and the path, now a firm grass track, had begun to swing around to the east to give open views down Littondale. The first sights of these upper slopes of this quiet dale reveal a human landscape that had not changed for generations, with isolated farm buildings and the patchwork field systems. No huge, commercially economical, scientifically rotated crop growth here; just small fields laid over to sheep-grazing on the higher slopes and cattle-rearing nearer the base of the valley. Ahead, on the opposite valley side, above the grazing land, lay the more inhospitable moorland of Horse Head Moor rising to over 600 metres. Horse Head Moor was to be my last ascent for the day, which I would be pleased to climb for I was beginning to feel weary and my tired feet were becoming insubordinate. Still, I comforted myself; at least I had secured a bottle of water that was not of dubious origin. The six miles of road walking had taken its toll on my feet and legs and I was looking forward to arriving at Buckden to sink into a hot bath to soothe away any lingering aches and pains. Buckden, I reminded myself, was still six miles distant as I descended toward the hamlet of Foxup. I had covered only ten miles, with still a further three miles of road walking left before this first day would be completed.

Foxup appeared to have been, at least partly, converted to provide accommodation for holidaymakers. I already knew something of the plight in which farmers had found themselves over recent years and would be a witness to more of their difficulties in the days to come. The farm I spied at Foxup was, no doubt, an example of a once proud family of land-workers having to turn their hand to other means to eke out a living from the land. Not satisfied with man-made fibres having taking the place of traditional fabrics such as woollen cloth, we had now added further insult to injury by blighting the British farmer with the legacy of the scare of BSE, firstly in his cattle and, more latterly, in his sheep stock. The experts introduce new systems, drugs, foodstuffs and so on into our lives with apparent scant regard for the consequences. They will say that exhaustive testing has been carried out and, granted that tests are carried out to assess their safety such tests can only be undertaken for those side effects we are able to predict in the light of current technology. It is not possible to check for adverse consequences where the incubation period is a relatively short amount of time and where perhaps the understanding of such effects is lacking – and so developed BSE and thalidomide, and so will develop goodness knows what in a future that we cannot, dare not, even contemplate at the present. We will enter the new millennium totally unaware that a time bomb has been planted within our own society in the name of progress. The dilemma that is currently reserved for farmers will intensify and only when it affects a great number of us will the powers-that-be have the courage to admit their errors. By then there will be no turning back; no U-turns for the damage will have been done and will be irreparable. Too little, too late as so often is the case.

There was little to be gained by the dwelling on such matters, so instead I concentrated on more pleasant things as I approached the buildings at Foxup through a field gate. More pleasant things in this instance were the wonderful smells of barbecuing food that drifted up to meet me from the group sitting around the open patio tending their sizzling feast, laughing and chatting on this very fine afternoon. Pimm's, I thought, with crushed ice, cucumber and a little paper umbrella; how absolutely delightful, but not for me as I pressed on passed them and over the narrow River Skirfare and away from their paradise dale and on toward Halton Gill. The road down the dale from Foxup remains a very quiet byway and, although it is now hard-surfaced, it still leads nowhere other than to the few houses where I had left the barbecuers. Halton Gill is the last village of any size in Littondale and had been on my agenda as a brief stopping point before rising again. My plan was thwarted however, for I had been walking under the misapprehension that there was a pub in the village and not until I approached the jumble of cottages did close scrutiny of the map confirm that the first hostelry was not reached until Litton, a further three miles down the dale. I decided then and there that I would settle for a brief rest when I topped Horse Head Moor and not before because I feared I would be tempted to rest too long if I stopped before the climb. This would make the steep ascent feel much more difficult and I would rather rest only when I had earned it.

As I approached a signpost at the side of the road indicating that my way was up a steep concreted pathway, I knew that I would have earned that rest. Some of these old routes are precipitous and this was a fine example. For the next mile I stopped very often, ostensibly, I told myself, to take in the splendour of the views, but in reality because my legs and lungs refused to carry me any further. Try as I might I could not force myself to keep progressing upwards without these rests. This concerned me as this first day of my journey comprised only sixteen miles and was one of the shortest on the route. The only time I was able to enjoy the view was during these short rest stops for when I was walking I was looking down, concentrating on placing one foot in front of the other, counting each difficult stride as I took it. I was becoming very anxious as to my general state of health and could only put my discomfort down to the fact that I had developed a cold some days earlier. It was coincidental that as I set out on this walk, map in hand and cold in nose, Wainwright had suffered the selfsame affliction. He had described at some length the severity of his running nose and the extreme lengths that he had had to take to seek relief, such as ripping his shirt sleeves to act as makeshift handkerchiefs. It is not my intention to make further reference to my malady other than to stress that, like all men, I was a brave little soldier who would not think of whining or moaning about the severity of my illness. In actual fact the only reason I didn't whine or moan was that there was no one around to listen. If men are brutally honest about their own weaknesses then one must surely be their inability to feel unwell without sharing it with all those around and without expounding that whatever it is, it is clearly very serious. I suspect if men suffered childbirth or period pains, or were more prone to cystitis, then they might think twice before troubling their womenfolk with every little ache and ailment. This, of course, does not apply to me and neither will it to any other man reading this...

The reward for my labouring toward the summit was in the widening views back over Foxup Moor and, gradually, to Pen-y-ghent which began to appear as a grey-brown hazy mass to the south-west. The sun was low in the sky now and the definite foreground slopes of the ascent of Horse Head Moor were silhouetted against the sunlight in the valley below with further hills across to Plover Hill and beyond to Pen-y-ghent and Ingleborough greying with distance. The sunlit lower land between each receding hill provided an illumination to the haze, again weakening with distance. The day was still warm though, and when I finally reached the wall that runs longitudinally along the highest point of the moor, I sat on a rock and was very thankful for the generosity of those kindly Germans who had given me a fresh supply of water. It seemed rather perverse that I was grateful to Germans where Wainwright had been fearful of Germany and her intentions back in 1938 – it was certainly not Hitler's intention to share his water with anyone; he wanted everybody else's water and sufficient numbers within a nation were prepared to follow his rantings. It is a frightening thought to think of the potential consequences of such a zealot being taken seriously in 1998 and the calamity that could now be unleashed if a power-crazed lunatic could beg the ear of enough gullible disciples. We have only the powers of the United Nations to step in to protect our existence from such a maniac, and if their usual speed of action is to be their judge, then while they were still blustering and issuing declarations the aggressor would have made his first of several moves. Appeasement was the undoing of Chamberlain; hopefully blustering and inaction would not one day be seen as the undoing of the UN Security Council. One council is very much like the next – heavy on the ability to talk and to be seen to be talking, but light on actually getting things done.

I rolled a cigarette and took out the last piece of cake that I had been packed off with earlier in the day as a schoolboy is packed off to school with his wrapped and labelled lunch tucked neatly in his satchel. I should not sound sarcastic for I was glad to have this last energy boost before setting off on the final four miles. It was, at least, all downhill from this point, down first to Yockenthwaite and then along the unclassified road through Hubberholme and finally to Buckden. As I rested I smoked my cigarette, drank the remaining water and spent a few moments reading Wainwright's recollections of this particular part of his journey. He had been tired –which I was comforted by – and he had rested at the gate at the very top of the moor. There was only one gate and only one rock, and it was an eerie feeling to realise that I was more than likely sitting on the same rock that he had all those years earlier, the very same rock at the very same gate and enthralled by the very same thrilling views back over the way we had come. This was why I had come: to savour such moments as this where the only separation between us was the span of years that has been and gone. Here, where you could divorce yourself from the horrendous speed of change that dismantled many slow, outdated traditions and conventions of the valleys, towns and cities, all else was the same as it had been so many years before. The ability to be alone was still possible, if only a little harder to achieve.

Unlike my erstwhile walker I had planned my day somewhat more efficiently and, instead of beginning the descent in near darkness, I left the gate at the head of Horse Head Moor at five o'clock. I was able to enjoy the sight of the sun casting lengthening shadows into the valley before me. The valley was Langstrothdale and it coming into view meant that I was in sight of my day's goal. A very stony and ankle-twisting path led swiftly down toward the farm buildings of Ramsgill where I would turn right and proceed for the last three miles along the valley road. Partway down the path from the moor top the silence that had surrounded me for the previous three hours since leaving the Germans (with the exception of the barbecue at Foxup) was shattered as I was approached by three powerful motocross bikes as they roared up the rutted slope. I realised very quickly why the path was so badly deformed with deep-rutted channels that tried at every step to damage ankles or knees. It was not a natural malevolent formation that mother earth had laid down, but was, even here, a sign of the destruction that we cause without a thought, with stones being kicked up at every turn of the wheels and the gashes in the hillside deepening with every pass. There are people who have been very quick to single Wainwright out as responsible for popularising the countryside and the subsequent damage to it caused by walkers. Walkers take care in the country for they, by and large, respect it and in not wanting to cause damage to it would restrict their activity. It takes very few of these screaming machines to render these quiet ways unsafe for the walker, either for the fear of falling over as a result of the damage done by a speeding bike or actually being run over by the speeding bike itself.

Turning right at the farm at Ramsgill was one of those occasions where I was probably so overly purist as to be foolhardy, for although the road is a narrow unclassified byway, it is invariably busy on a Sunday evening with day-trippers returning home after their escapes to the dales. Today was no exception and my desire to follow as closely as I could to Wainwright's route was probably a smidgen unwise, especially as on the opposite bank of the river lay the well-formed 'Dales Way' path which would have provided a far more attractive alternative. Be that as it may, I had decided to follow the road and I would make the best of it, dodging cars as I went along my way. When Wainwright had trodden this way public paths were little-known of for it was only after the Second World War that a commission was set up to determine public rights of way, and from this commission had led, ultimately, to the establishment of many of our long-distance paths. The Dales Way is one such path, stretching through various dales from Ilkley to Bowness (the sign at Ilkley reads seventy-two miles but it is apparently eighty-one miles according to the sign if a reverse journey is made starting from Bowness!). Also, in 1938, Wainwright would very likely not have seen any form of motor vehicle on this road as car ownership didn't start gathering pace until the 1950s and '60s. I had already discovered on the Horton road that this was to prove one of the severe downsides of trying to repeat this walk step for step and remain alive to tell the tale.

My shadow had been ahead of me all day and now, as evening fast approached, my companion was much taller and more slender, stretched out on the road before me. He walked now with a more tired step but was as rapid as I in avoiding the cars that passed me with exacerbating regularity. On a brighter note, I was now amid scenery that I knew, and I could see ahead the domed summit of Buckden Pike, the terraced limestone topography high above Buckden Beck, the flat fertile valley bottom and the cluster of buildings that formed the village itself. Between Buckden and me lay Hubberholme and it was not long before I began to see the first snatches, through the trees, of the picturesque church with its squat tower surrounded by ancient gravestones. These were reminders of former residents of the parish, more than likely farming families and more than likely generation after generation all resting in this Arcadia, this delightful corner of Wharfedale. Hubberholme Church, on a pleasant Sunday evening, provides a lift to flagging muscles nearing the end of a day's walking. It sits within a perfect setting on the opposite bank of the young River Wharfe to the George Inn at the junction where Langstrothdale become Wharfedale. I could imagine that many a reverent churchgoer takes much enjoyment, after the service, from crossing the narrow bridge and gathering for a drink or two. In fact, I could imagine that, for a fair proportion of the congregation, the after-service gathering is the unspoken reason for being at the church service in the first place. Both the church and the George were clearly places of great spiritual refreshment and it is easy to appreciate why J. B. Priestley had developed such an affinity with the place. He was an ardent admirer of Hubberholme and, as I passed by the church, I wondered whether on that evening in 1938 he was attending the service that was taking place as Wainwright had passed. I was planning to walk by this way the next morning, so I carried on down the road toward Buckden, now only one mile distant. There was insufficient time to call at the church for spiritual nourishment and I resisted temptation for refreshment at the George, partly because I wanted to carry on immediately to Buckden and, mainly, because its doors were bolted until seven o'clock.

After sixteen miles I finally crossed the bridge and walked up the gentle incline into Buckden at twenty-past six to discover that I had forgotten to bring with me the address of the guest house. Fortunately I could remember the name of the owners, Mr and Mrs Lightfoot. This gave me the fortuitous excuse, as I approached the Buck Inn, of stopping for a quick drink, before my legs seized up, to obtain directions. Buckden, although much larger than sixty years ago, is not so large that anywhere in its environs is more than a stone's throw away from the inn. There has been development of the village both in terms of new houses and also of refurbishment of the old cottages. The majority of the building work has been centred on one of two activities: either as weekend retreats for 'offcumdens' or as bed and breakfast establishments. Both have served to change the village so as to dilute its close-knit community with a great percentage of transient residents and it now witnesses a melee on summer weekends but must be very quiet during the short weekdays of winter. I wondered whether the clannishness that Wainwright had observed might still exist and doubted it, except for in very restricted corners of the community – it is more likely that the dale folk have themselves become rather more cosmopolitan in their outlook. No longer can there be an assumption that the next generation will follow their fathers and no longer can there be any guarantee of rural work except for the growing need to serve the wants of the tourist trade.

I was fortunate in that Ghyll Cottage was not more than 50 yards from the inn. I approached the door and was shown to my room, very relieved to finally be able to put down the rucksack and welcome the thought of relaxing in a hot bath – sadly as I looked around the jamb I spotted only a shower in the small, but nicely appointed, shower room. A shower it would have to be. I was lucky I thought, for at least it was an en suite room and I could linger as long as I liked, bathing aching feet as best I was able – a feat rather unsatisfactorily achieved first by holding one foot up then the other, which had the effect of reducing the ache within my feet but increasing the grumbling muscles in my legs. I did think of bathing my feet in the washbasin, but this would still involve standing on one leg, which appeared to defeat the object of the exercise entirely. The only other method I considered was to sit on the toilet lid and plunge both feet in the basin, but this theory floundered because the toilet was just too far away from the basin to be able to actually submerge the offending articles.

Rather than trying to arrive at further alternative solutions, I decided that all this thinking had made me ravenous and adjourning to the Buck Inn was fast becoming the next item on my agenda. Without delay, or at least with only the unavoidable degree of delay due to my sore feet, I made my way back to the inn and did what comes naturally: I ordered a pint, rolled a cigarette and sat outside to watch the last vestiges of day fade and disappear behind the western hills in an orange glory. The sky bade well for tomorrow. I had planned to eat at pubs on most evenings, thinking that a good-value meal could be had for relatively little outlay. Not so unfortunately at the Buck Inn – the menu was an awfully grand affair full of all manner of fancy things, most of which I had not the faintest idea of what they were. I wanted pie and chips, or burger and chips, or sausage and chips, even lasagne and chips – anything really, so long as it came with chips. Not a chip to be seen anywhere. I even asked whether there was a bar snack menu, preferably with bar snack prices. No, the menu on the board was what was available. Now, I have tried before now to get by on a liquid diet, but this invariably leads to a horrendous hangover the next day. I did my best to decipher the menu, plumbing the depths of my rudimentary knowledge of French and also plumbing the depths of my pockets to pay for it, and ordered chicken with something – it was very pleasant but I was a heathen. Chicken and chips would have done as well but might not have been so awfully nicely arranged on the plate. In all fairness, the beer was welcome and the pub held happy memories for me for we had stayed there two years previously in a splendid room for the night. Please, I do not mean to do the place down, but it is just that all I wanted on this first night was a commoner's meal to fill an uncommonly large hole.

Bed was not far behind my leaving the inn; it had been calling for the previous half-hour, and I arrived back at Ghyll Cottage at nine o'clock. After a polite but brief chat with the Lightfoots as they made their way out for the evening, I climbed the stairs to my room and retired to bed to write up my notes for the day. The first day of my adventure had been supremely satisfying and I looked forward with zeal to the walk to Muker, eighteen miles away, the next day. Today had been tiring and tomorrow would be more so for I had two dales to cross with wide-open moorland between.

Chapter 2

Buckden to Muker

I have no reason to suppose that I am anything other than what might be described as ordinary. I base this supposition on limited observation of my own abilities compared with the abilities of others. I was always ordinarily average at school, usually attaining examination results somewhere between just scraping through at worst and mid-grades at best. I was always one of those who, after completing an examination, would feel that my performance would astound the assessor and that I had finally prepared a paper that would be the envy of the rest of the class. However, that never proved to be the case, and I remained baffled as to how it was that the students who exited the exam room laden with doubt and fearing they had failed miserably were usually the ones who, at result time, passed with flying colours and top grades. Invariably these doom-mongers were girls – it was rare, in my experience, for the boys to gather afterwards, at the post-mortem, full of woe. It was always the very bright girls who, year after year, performed supremely well but always came out of the silence of the exam and, largely, remained silent and sullen fearing the worst. At least, that's what they appeared to be doing. It might be that they knew they'd probably done rather well but would let the boys make fools of themselves with their boasting as to how they had answered so-and-so question. The problem with these examination post-mortems was that there would nearly always be a point where the realisation sank in that a particular question had been answered entirely wrongly. The girls who remained quiet would equally quietly go off to lunch and be equally quietly confident that all was well with the world. As ever, with the results would arrive my grades varying between, as expected, just scraping through at worst and achieving mid-grades at best. Sure enough, with the same results those quiet girls would receive their accolades of another 'job well done' – Smart-arses.

I have always been very ordinarily average in other things too. I have enjoyed, from time to time, too much beer of an evening and then, for some obscure reason, become convinced that a curry would be a splendid idea and that I could cope with the hottest vindaloo as though it were a plate of mince. Usually, also, after having enjoyed too much beer and curry in such fashion, the morning after, with raging hangover, halitosis and curry emanating from my very pores, I will suddenly feel as though I am sexually irresistible and fail to comprehend why my advances are met with a firm refusal.

In most things I have little evidence to put me anywhere other than on an average footing. The only area where I appeared to have excelled was in my ability to run fairly rapidly, although in this I was usually propelled by a desire for self-preservation. When an especially mean-looking rugby player was clearly proposing to do me some personal damage, I would always manage to find an extra turn of speed. I discovered that it would be easier to stop playing rugby than to wait for the inevitable pain for I knew that one day someone would catch up with me and it would hurt. I did, just once, play for Ilkley Rugby Union FC and when, after only a few minutes, the opposing left-winger sidestepped me as though I weren't there, I set about after him and leapt on him in fine style. What I hadn't realised was that our own fullback, having seen the danger, had come across to deal with him also. At the same time as I was leaping on the adversary so too was our fullback – the upshot was that we stopped the winger but in so doing I landed on our fullback and broke his collarbone. I apologised profusely and decided afterwards to retire gracefully in the hope that our player would quickly forget me.

My only other ability, which appears to have very limited use and to date has been of no personal gain whatsoever, is the ability to touch my nose with my tongue, which, based on informal competition, is rare indeed.

On the basis that my character traits are largely average then the majority will understand why it was that this morning I was awake, wide awake, at five o'clock. I always find the same – when I have great anticipation of a day's activity I am awake for hours before the alarm like a little boy on Christmas morning. During the working week I could sleep all day, but by the weekend many's the time when I am sitting and planning on the doorstep with a cup of tea and cigarette in the early hours. I am a greater planner than I am a doer, and often my planning will wake me, rendering sleep impossible until I am satisfied that the next stage of a particular plan is complete.

So it was at the dawn on this second day. I made a cup of tea and rolled a cigarette, which I then smoked out of the open window while studying the map. It may have been acceptable in 1938 for the first action of the day to be to smoke a cigarette while still in bed, but in 1998 most guest houses highly disapprove of smoking in the rooms – hence my shivering position at the window, watching the very first hint of daylight on the underside of the few wispy clouds. It was cold and there had been a heavy dew left on the lawn to the rear of the house, but it would be a second fine sunny day. I had plenty of jobs with which to busy myself until breakfast at half past eight. I had to read the relevant chapter of Pennine Journey again to ensure that I knew of any particular landmarks or incidents that were visited or encountered by my predecessor on his way. I had to repack the rucksack, which was something of an art, for if the contents weren't packed in the right order there would be items left over, rather like stripping and rebuilding an engine: the rebuild is complete yet there are a few cogs and odd bits apparently spare – this was another area where I had found myself to be extremely average; I once attempted to rebuild a motorbike engine many years earlier and it never worked again.

Bags packed I was ready for a second cup of tea and cigarette at my precarious position at the window. I had a brief scan through the book Mrs Lightfoot had lent me, which outlined an alternative coast-to-coast walk. The author, David Maughan, had stayed with the Lightfoots and had sent them a courtesy copy. In the introduction to his book, David Maughan quoted Wainwright, who had said that he 'would feel [he] had succeeded better in arousing interest for the planning of long distance walks if the book induced some readers to follow their own star'. Oh dear, I thought at first. Here was I following sheepishly a walk that I knew would include vastly changed long sections of road from those quiet, car-free ones of 1938. I had already encountered nine miles of road walking and would face many more before my escapade was over. What was I doing? Wainwright would be looking down with disdain on this poor unimaginative mortal who was unable to find his own star to follow. But then I cast these negative thoughts asunder in the knowledge that I had had much detective work to do to plan this walk. His book had not been a guide but a description of his journey and I was here to follow his walk reflected against the yardstick of life sixty years ago. He would be pleased, I decided, that someone was show-ing an interest and, besides, my enjoyment would come not just from the walk but from having made the effort to re-plan it into a pleasant modern-day circular tour of history, contrasting geography and geology.

I tend to prefer to breakfast alone, however space in the dining room being somewhat at a premium meant that a communal breakfast was held with the other three guests. I had seen a pair of boots on the doormat the evening before and I now met their owner – another lone walker who was following the 'Inn Way' comprising seventy-six miles of walking with twenty-six pubs en route. The idea is that a drink is taken at each and he explained that that was not as simple as it appeared. Some of the dales pubs still operate 'old-fashioned' lunch and evening opening hours and at one he had found himself arriving at three o'clock to be refused service as the time bell had just been rung. On explaining his mission and that he only wanted a very swift half-pint, the landlord yielded but insisted that he stood outside to consume his drink and that he should leave the glass on the windowsill when he had finished. His walk today would take him in generally the same direction as me: over Stake Moss and on to Askrigg in Wensleydale. The overnight stop in Askrigg was necessary, I assumed, as there were too many pubs to allow for safe walking afterwards without a vastly increased likelihood of falling in the river. The two other guests, a pleasant enough couple, were definitely valley tourists for she especially was more than a little too plump for me to imagine her pirouetting about atop hills. A fair amount of weight would need to be shed if they were ever to be serious about walking any distance, which had been the main subject of our discussions throughout breakfast. Communal or not, breakfast was very welcome and by nine o'clock. I was paying my dues and donning my various bags and other accoutrements and thanking the Lightfoots for their hospitality.

I stepped out into a bright morning which, when a little older, promised to develop into a very warm day. During Wainwright's overnight stay in Buckden he had found accommodation with the Falshaw family and, as I was leaving, I inquired as to whether they still lived locally. It was not enough to simply re-trace the physical route of his walk; I wanted to connect with other aspects of it also, one of which was an effort to find out something of the people with whom Wainwright had stayed. Mrs Lightfoot answered immediately that the Falshaws now owned Grange Farm on the road to Hubberholme and that they provided accommodation for walkers. They had provided accommodation for bed and breakfast at the farm some years previous but now only operated on a self-catering basis in a bunkhouse barn attached to the main building. They had, apparently, a certain claim to fame in that they had provided a bed for the night to J. B. Priestley but, sadly, it was only after his death in 1984. In life he had indicated a desire for his remains to be buried at Hubberholme Church and so it was that his ashes were brought to the church only to find that all requisite paper-work was not in order and that, until it was, he could not be interred. In the light of this his remains stayed under the stairs at Grange Farm – a somewhat bizarre claim and I did wonder whether, perhaps, it was something of a rural myth.

It was a myth that I did not have the nerve to ask Mrs Falshaw to confirm or deny when I knocked at her door twenty minutes after setting out from Buck-den. After I explained the reason for my intrusion, she told me of her husband's grandmother, Ada, who had lived in the centre of the village at Prospect Farm providing refreshment and taking in guests for bed and breakfast. Ada Falshaw lived with her husband, Fred, and their seven children at the farm where the family had resided for over 300 years. Not only did the Falshaws farm the area, there had been a further five farms in the village, a sad contrast to the present when the only working farm remaining is one that was bought and is now run by the National Trust. In 1938 it would have been entirely normal in a farming community to see Prospect Farm operating from the centre of the village in its location immediately to the rear of the Buck Inn. It no longer existed as a farm but had, instead, been renovated and converted into self-catering apartments which could only serve to increase the transient nature of the village's population. All the old families have moved away from the village itself. What had no doubt been a settled but hard way of life for centuries had, in the space of sixty years, changed beyond all recognition. Like so many other villages, Buckden had boasted its own joiner and cobbler, but the services of such tradesmen had been dispensed with many years ago. This changing of the demography must add to the sense of the village having become a museum to be visited rather than a living and breathing place of domicile for anyone in particular. It is impossible for the younger generation (and I include myself) to comprehend what the spirit must have been like as the farmers would visit each other to play cards of an evening for a tanner or two. At least the Falshaw name was still linked with farming as two of the children, Gordon and Sydney, had moved to Grange Farm fifteen years after Wainwright had visited. I was told that Ada had earned a healthy reputation among the cycling fraternity with great gangs arriving on a Saturday or Sunday for her generous catering. The bed and breakfast was of simple fare with single-sex communal dormitories and an earth closet in the garden. As I had left Buckden I couldn't help but notice the plethora of signs, tasteful though they were, advertising accommodation – it seemed that almost every house offered en suite guest rooms with television and tea-making facilities. Perhaps though, these houses, all so very nicely turned out, provide for an altogether more pleasing environment and add to the village's picturesque quality. Maybe we should not mourn what has passed but should welcome and cherish the new.

I left Mrs Falshaw, thanking her for her time, and only a short walk from Grange Farm took me back to the hamlet of Hubberholme. I had returned to see the church in more detail, just as Wainwright had done, and I had quite enjoyed the walk along the valley road for it was much quieter on a Monday morning than it had been the evening before. Passing another guest house I arrived at the George Inn and crossed the quaint bridge and entered the gates of the church-yard with its mature yew trees growing to the side of the path that leads to the ancient timbered door of the equally ancient church. The church itself is proba-bly best known for two things. The first is that the pews were carved by Robert Thompson, the mouseman of Kilburn, whose trademark was to discreetly carve mice on particular sections of the pews and woodwork. The second is its association with the Bradford playwright J. B. Priestley to whom, when finally he had been allowed access after his unscheduled bed and breakfast stop, there is a plaque acknowledging his love of 'one of the pleasantest places in the world'. Priestley was a reasonable judge as he was well travelled and had, only four years before Wainwright's journey, published an account of his own wider travels in the book An English Journey. Although Wainwright never makes any reference to Priestley's book, it seems too coincidental for it not to have had a bearing on the title of A Pennine Journey.

It may well be that Wainwright would not have wanted to allude to having been influenced by anything other than his own imagination. These were days long before he had become established in his own right and although he was, in 1938, making his regular trips to the Lake District, his guidebooks were still in their embryonic stages, a mass of drawings and notes with no form. He did, however, have a hankering to be a writer and the strength of pride that lived within him would not have allowed him to admit his ideas were even remotely shaped by another writer's work. He makes a reference in his account to an earlier book of his, which was a long- and best-forgotten novel that was never published. He exhibits very much a picture of an artist who had taken a wrong turn somewhere and had, through a desire no doubt to be seen as a respected member of society, followed a career path that took him into accountancy and book-keeping. This must have been a strange environment indeed for one who preferred the loneliness of the hills and displayed talents of a more artistic nature. I never found reference to Wainwright nursing a profound and long-held dream to be a writer, but surely he must have quietly wished his life had taken a direction that would have allowed him more access to the things he loved rather than the things he had to endure; he must have stifled any dreams for the sake of respectability. I have thought often that I have an artist's mind and that I did not nurture it at the right time as to allow it to flourish, with the result being that I have, from time to time, reflected on my life's decisions – of where I have been, where I am and where it is I am going. This is a dream, but to dream is a wonderful thing for in its absence all that we have and all that we are is laid out before us with no hope or aspirations for anything better and more fulfilling.

I find that such dreaming does, though, in a sense, give us an opportunity for personal assessment to discover where we are, where we want to be and why we aren't there yet. However, I suggest that you keep your dreams to yourself for only the person who has the dream can gain any significance from it. Others are not interested in your dreams unless they share the same desire, such as the conversation that most have had from time to time about winning the lottery: what would you do if you won the jackpot? There cannot be a single person who does not buy that red-and-white ticket without seeing it as the passport to the realisation of their dreams. Without the desire to win there would not exist the motive for buying it in the first place. If the motive were solely to donate to good causes, there are far more direct ways to go about it, and without the government and the organisers diverting a sizeable percentage to swell their own coffers. Only in such very general desires will there be interest in your dreams and besides, for a dream to have genuine value it must be inwardly felt to be achievable. The desires of securing the lottery jackpot can only ever remain desires; for something to become a dream its attainment must be realistic. Perhaps then I ought more accurately to class these dreams as personal aspirations because I would not waste my time dwelling on things that could never realistically be attained for that would prove to be pure frustration.

For my own part I have questioned for too many years whether, at a certain junction in life, I took a wrong turn and by the time I first questioned my sense of direction, I felt it was too late to turn back. The problem with not turning back when a wrong turn is discovered is that at some point in the future the doubt associated with the what-might-have-been may develop into a self-absorbing desire of an effectively unachievable alternative lifestyle. Very often, by the time we recognise our earlier mistake it is too late to correct it for our lives are mortgaged to the hilt and changes of direction are impossible to implement and must forever remain only desires. So we are very similar to the goldfish that swim around in a bowl that is, clearly, too small for them; we are firmly trapped in our little environment, and we can only look out with envious eyes at the larger world around us for we know that if we smash the bowl in a bid for autonomy, it is very likely that we would not survive to reach the perceived freedom of the garden pond. I am not wishing to give the impression that I am close to severe depression; I have simply addressed my faulty navigation through life and I know where my past decisions have been found wanting. I believe that it is only a very few who have the opportunity of time to be able to pause, take stock and conclude that they are entirely at one with themselves and all that is around them. I am at one with myself because I have paused from time to time to look at myself and what lies around me. It is not dissimilar to the alcoholic – part of the battle is won when the disease is recognised and acknowledged.

I am no different to anyone else. I have a mortgage, the thought of which would be put to the back of my mind during this walk, although it would loom large immediately again upon my return to civilisation, as would the various other financial commitments with their voracious appetites. This was all part of a consumerist society that teaches us not only to spend, spend, spend, but encourages us to burden ourselves with loans that are ill afforded and that remain steadfastly holding us as a yolk to the millstone of life.

I was entertaining these thoughts as I sat on a grassy overgrown bench on the riverbank just by the church. I was sitting on this glorious day listening to the quiet tune of the river, looking at the birds playing their games on the opposite bank and smelling the pleasing aroma of Golden Virginia rolled in liquorice paper. So, I thought, why the hell was I giving time to such profound matters. In an instant I knew the answer. It was exactly because I was sitting on this glorious day listening to the quiet tune of the river, looking at the birds playing their games on the opposite bank and smelling the pleasing aroma of Golden Virginia rolled in liquorice paper. That was the answer. I was at one of those rare points on life's track from where I was able to look back and recognise and acknowledge that I had lost my way. On that Monday morning I was given the very briefest of tastes of perfection and it provided me with a harsh contrast between this moment and all the more usual moments in which my life was spent. The moral, I decided, was really quite simple: unless we are extremely lucky we all lose our way, but only the very few are given a taste of perfection, a brief taste of life as they would have loved to have lived it. This was such a taste and it was momentarily giving me the desire to want to cry over spilt milk.

This type of thinking can be rather depressing for both writer and reader, so I will venture no further. The fact is we are all trapped to a greater or lesser degree – Wainwright was clearly ensnared within his own existence and so was I. That was all there was to it. Simple. Right, then, no more grumbling about it…

I soon returned to reality as I ambled parallel to the river on the quiet road leading across the head of Wharfedale. The classic-shaped glaciated valley opened up to the right of me allowing views down toward Kilnsey Crag some eight miles away and the last strands of morning mist were being lifted off the flat grass pastures of the valley floor. The morning was now beginning to emit considerable warmth in the sun so that the shade of the trees along this stretch of the river was welcome. They were kind enough to accompany me on my way all across the wide head of the dale until I reached a fork where I turned left up the narrow and steep lane toward Cray. The road at this point is little used by traffic other than the local farmers, and the lack of cars was a blessing and made for enjoyable walking. Hedgerows either side were busy with life as birds chattered in them, bees buzzed on them and rabbits scurried under them. I knew that the pleasures of this section would be short-lived for I would soon arrive at the junction of the road from Buckden to Bishopdale where, for the next mile, there would be no escape from the dales visitors on the busy road over to Aysgarth in Wensleydale. Even had I felt that I could veer from my ordained route, there was no alternative path upon which I would be able to avoid road walking through Cray and up to the pass at Bishopdale Head.

As I slowly made my way up the hill toward the junction, I came to a corner in the lane where, resting for a few moments, a Land Rover approached coming up the hill toward me. Realising that he would not be able to see around the corner, I waved him through to indicate that all was clear ahead. As he drew alongside he acknowledged my action with a cheery wave and a smile and I raised my hand and returned his smile. Such a small action but one that pleased me and, I'm sure, gratified the driver – a little courtesy costs nothing but can give that warming sense of having earned so much. I feel sure that we both went on our separate ways a little more content than we had been just a few seconds earlier.

Wainwright had not found Cray overly endearing in 1938, sensing an air of desolation about the place. Although I had driven through it many times I had never studied it as closely on foot as I had chance to that day. As I neared the cluster of buildings, which still only comprise those that have stood from long before Wainwright was here and will remain so no doubt long after I had passed, I saw Cray was a place unchanged. The pub, the White Lion, is still there and the farm buildings are still there, but beyond these there is nothing. The pub, I was later to discover, is one of the twenty-six included on the 'Inn Way' walk and already appeared to be plying a reasonable trade, even at eleven in the morning. There was a bare-chested group of what looked like workmen sitting in the sun with their pints and cigarettes – early lunch I thought. That was all I saw at Cray and I was leaving it behind almost as quickly as if I had driven through. The pub is in a very fortunate position on a well-trodden triangular walk commencing and finishing at Buckden and taking in Cray and Hubberholme. Except for that walk, the White Lion would have long ago closed for it has not the chic style of the Buck Inn nor the charm of the George Inn, and, as all three are barely a stone's throw from one another, I fear the White Lion would have yielded the commercial battle for custom. Without the White Lion as its centrepiece there would be very little left of Cray. Even with the White Lion there was little of it now, although Wainwright was a little unfair for it does stand in a picturesque location adjacent to Cray Beck surrounded by towering fells on all sides except to the south-west down the steep-sided valley to Wharfedale.

The road up the valley follows Cray Beck as it cascades over steps in its bed at slab-like terraced waterfalls. The road twists and spirals around outcrops and spurs until it finally manages the final climb around the sharp bend at Cow Pasture and onto a more level route as it nears the gate which gives access to the green road over Stake Moss. As I climbed the stile next to the gate I looked forward to the eight miles of track walking and looked back as I said goodbye to Wharfedale – it would soon disappear from view as I continued on into my next valley, Wensleydale.

Wainwright had decided that the route of his walk would take in all the valleys to the east of the Pennines and had accurately described the topography as being like that of a single-sided ribcage, with the ribs represented by the hills separating the valleys. It is to the east of the backbone of England that these ribs lie, each running west to east. As I would be travelling north, I would have to climb each rib and descend into each valley between. On the return southern journey, down the western side of the Pennine chain, I would be walking the rib-less side of the backbone and would not encounter the same ascents and descents that I was to be confronted by for the first four days. On most of these early days I would have to traverse two dales – yesterday had been Ribblesdale and Littondale, with today's valleys being Wharfedale and Wensleydale.

It is not clear from Wainwright's account what had been the motive for his lonely expedition, especially lonely in those bygone days when cars were much fewer and walking was something that was undertaken in the main to propel the majority of people to work. Although recreational walking had become popular, the commercialism that surrounded it had not evolved. He would be astounded if he were able, in 1998, to visit a place like Ambleside in his beloved Lake District where almost every other shop, it seems, caters for walking or 'outdoor' enthusiasts. Towns like Ambleside in 1938 would certainly not have been home to such lavish shops – if a pair of boots was required, there would be a cobbler who would make them in his workshop. The cobbler would ply his trade and wouldn't be trying to impress with his window display. He existed to do a job, and that trade did not include marketing and sales – he knew the villagers would come to him and he relied upon his skill to retain their loyalty. This, and the fact he was probably the only cobbler in town, and cars were so few that most inhabitants had more than likely never been beyond the next town or village, meant his trade was guaranteed.

It is apparent from his account that Wainwright was worried about the Crisis, as the newspapers referred to it. Hitler was stomping about over parts of mainland Europe and beginning to bare his military teeth to the extent that Britain ran the risk of being backed into a corner. If the worryingly aggressive diplomacy could not alleviate the situation then it was clear that we would have to go to war with Germany. This diplomacy was at its peak when Wainwright was far away from the news stands and the only connection he had with the outside world was during evenings when his hosts might, perhaps, make reference to the Crisis during chat with their guest. Whether or not it was this concern that forced Wainwright to escape the tension for a while is never made clear. It is strange that with his great love of the Lake District he should spend nearly two weeks of his annual leave tramping up and down bleak Pennine moorland rather than the more majestic Lakeland fells. The one thing that held him spellbound though was the interest he developed for seeing Hadrian's Wall and especially in the means of transporting himself to it. To arrive at the wall on foot was to arrive in a manner the same as an arrival nearly 2,000 years earlier, and now, sixty years later I was becoming equally attached to the notion of seeing the wall after having walked for five days. By all means drive to the wall, visit the sights, buy the souvenir, watch the instructive video, but if you really want to soak in the ambience and taste the history and savour the anticipation, there could only be one way – on foot. Wainwright's objective to reach the fort at Housesteads had been set. That would be the northerly point of his walk and from there he would return to his starting point. My objective had then been established too and I could not deny that I sensed a challenge had been set for me – in 1938 Wainwright was eleven years my junior and certainly was not carrying as much baggage. I was now into my second day and, although my legs and feet had been very tired as I neared Buckden the evening before this morning, as I crested Kidstones Fell I had a new lease of life and felt as though I could walk forever.

This new-found energy was most opportune for I could not afford to fail in my venture. How could I possibly return home if I had failed, especially if I had failed so abominably early? I would never be able to show my face in public again lest I would hear the whispers of the doubters of whom I was sure there had been plenty. No one had actually said within my hearing that they considered I stood little hope of fulfilling my ambition, but I had detected that there would be knowing sighs if I did not complete the journey. As so often is the case, the doubts of others are seldom aired until after the event. It is only afterwards that retrospective wisdom provides for the 'well, I did wonder' attitude, uttered in a certain patronising tone, almost luxuriating in the admitted failure. No, I would not succumb to a few aches and pains. I was here to enjoy these days alone; I was a dog and this would be my day.

Once I had made my way beyond the Kidstones escarpment, the old green road over Stake Moss became a fine unmade track, enclosed on both sides by limestone walling with wide green verges. I wound my way over the rib between Wharfedale and Wensleydale for a peaceful six miles of silence only broken from time to time by the bleating of sheep or the call of the moorland birdlife. I was surrounded by open moor bathed in sunlight except to the east where, from Bishopdale, there crept a white ghostlike mist with its fronds reaching out toward me and its bulk apparently following me as I carried on up and up. My pace kept me ahead of the white drifting sea and when I finally reached the crest of the moor the sun was still shining strongly and I afforded myself the comfort of a quiet rest by a field gate. These gates often mark the highest point on these cross-moor tracks and, during my rest at this one, I changed into the shorts that, although I had brought them with me, I had not dared to believe the weather would be sufficiently clement to allow their wear. The changing of leg-wear proved to be a lengthy process for in and around my trousers I carried a variety of accessories that had to be transferred: my tobacco, roller and papers; a dictaphone machine; wallet and loose change; two cameras strapped to my belt; a makeshift map-holder; and not forgetting, of course, the supply of handker-chiefs that accompanied me on each day. I will make no further mention of these for I was still being a brave little soldier about the foul bug that held me in its grasp.

I was still in the throes of my undressing and redressing when the sound of approaching footsteps made me look around quickly, only to see the lone walker with whom I had talked at breakfast. He paused for a few moments, probably dazzled by the very great reflective powers of my lily-white legs, and told me of his latest difficulty in successfully completing the 'Inn Way'. His walk had, today, taken him first from Buckden to the White Lion at Cray where the first drink of the day would be consumed – that is, it would have been con-sumed had the landlord allowed him service. He had arrived at eleven o'clock to find the group of workers that I had seen sitting in the sun all partaking of a little dales hospitality. Making his way inside to the bar he asked for a half of bitter only to be refused service by the landlord who went on to explain that the workers outside were a private party and that the bar was shut to all others. The walker remonstrated with the landlord to no avail and returned back to the sunlit patio to contemplate his failure. One of the workmen inquired as to why he had no drink and, upon relating his recent misfortune, the workmen kindly offered to buy his drink for him. This proved insufficiently cunning and was not fooling the landlord who simply refused him service also. I never did find out from the lone walker exactly what reason the landlord had for taking the stance he had, but it seemed to me to be a somewhat churlish way of treating customers and lowering his own turnover at the same time. Cray, and more particularly its pub, is not so attractive as to be unmissable, and my advice to the potential author of future editions of the 'Inn Way' is to re-route the walk via Hubberholme instead. This would, presumably, please the landlord if it were indeed a lower turnover that he aspired to. I don't believe that the George Inn at Hubberholme would object too strongly.

Before I had completed the operation of reattaching all my various belongings, he was well on his way again across the flat moor. In reality it was more of an au revoir than a farewell for we were both heading for the pub at Bainbridge for a lunchtime break and we would meet again there at approximately two o'clock. He set off most purposefully for today he was not taking any chances – he had missed lunch on more than one occasion as a result of some rather draconian opening hours and was planning his arrival well before the pub might have stopped serving food.

I was not many minutes behind having finally secured all extraneous bits about my person and, checking that no odds and ends had been left strewn on the grass, I swung my rucksack onto my back. I looked around me for a second or two to see just who it was who had put half a dozen house bricks in it while I had been sitting for it seemed a great deal heavier than it had twenty minutes earlier. Satisfying myself that I was carrying only my own luggage, I set off along the track northwards towards Wensleydale and was soon walking along the stretch of flat moor where Wainwright had exclaimed that cricket pitch after cricket pitch could be laid end to end. He was only partly correct: yes, it would be possible to measure 22 yards of level ground, but the result would definitely be a bowler's pitch with batsman after batsman retiring injured due to the uneven bounce caused by the ankle-turning terrain underfoot.

As I became accustomed again to the weight of the rucksack, I was reminded of Wainwright's comments regarding his own minimalist payload carried during his walk. He had explained that all he ever took with him on his excursions were his maps, a camera, a cape and very little else. He walked each day in the same clothes – he considered their becoming wet to be an occupational hazard. He walked, on this occasion, for eleven days in the same clothes. By the end of those eleven days it must have been possible to sniff the air the following morning and proclaim 'ah, yes, Wainwright stayed in the village last night'. Throughout the account of his journey he makes reference to the girl of his dreams. She only ever appeared in his dreams and, frankly, it was highly unlikely that, in the light of his apparent ignorance of personal hygiene, she would have ever been anything more than an apparition. Perhaps, also, he secretly would not have wished her to become real for while she existed within a dream world she was perfect and without fault or vice. This is the dilemma of dreams – for all the time that they are unrealised the world is at your feet; you can imagine great happiness, great success, great acclaim. Anything can be attained while the ambition remains firmly rooted in the mind's eye. It is only when the dream steps over the threshold of reality into the cold light of day that the flaws can first be seen. Wainwright's sweet girl has bad breath or yellowing teeth or an annoying tendency to sniff. The specific nature of the flaws matter not – it is the fact that they exist at all that is the difference between imagination and reality. It is, of course, entirely possible to avoid encountering these faults, but this can only be achieved by denying reality and maintaining 'self' in a world where external influence exists only in the mind in perfect harmony with the psyche of the dreamer. For this to be achievable then a state of oneness must largely exist, without interference and without, predominantly, interaction with others. People and things can be viewed so as to fuel the imagination, but their potential effects upon the dream must mainly stem from observation – if they are allowed the opportunity of feedback then their influence takes some control of the content away from the dreamer. The whole point of such mental wanderings is that their perfection is a function of the mind of the dreamer alone. Wainwright pondered long on the benefits of walking alone, which was, without any doubt, because of his desire to be allowed to mentally wander during his days of physical wanderings. For my part I confess also to being a dreamer. I firmly believe that we are all dreamers but most have reduced the propensity to dream, through necessity no doubt, to a small rivulet whose flow is controlled by a man-made dam further up its course. Rather than allowing imagination to flow free, fresh as a cascading mountain stream whose course knows no bounds, we have become thwarted by the apparent desire for material gain and choose to forego spiritual aspirations. We look only to attaining wealth that can be measured by others in a never-ending striving to achieve our ambitions.

I have often pondered on the subject of ambition. I recall Sue once outlining that it was her aim to earn £10,000 pounds and drive a company car. It did not seem to matter greatly as to the nature of her labours that would generate this amount but, moreover, that the ends would justify the means. We talked at length over the subject because even then (it was several years ago) I was very wary of unfettered ambition. As anyone who has walked over Pennine country will know, there are many horizons that give the appearance of being the summit before fulfilment is finally achieved in reaching the top of the hill. True ambition, in the usual meaning of the word, will result in the seeker never finding the contentment of achievement because there are an infinite number of horizons with no ultimate summit – each false summit can only be a resting place in the fruitless search for the ultimate goal. Sadly, the ultimate goal is as a mirage – it does not exist and, at best, although it may lie tantalisingly close, it is still just out of reach.

True ambition relies on the seeker being able to recognise that there can be no true ambition achieved through material gain. Sue's ten thousand pounds was a finite and absolute goal. However, if the level of remuneration that signified attainment were to be indexed-linked, then I suspect she would have been so busy looking for the end of her rainbow that she would have overlooked that fact that the rainbow itself was a thing of beauty. To be able to appreciate what is around you brings its own reward; the sooner this fact is realised, the sooner the seeker of achievement is able to stand still and take stock and be thankful with whatever level has been reached thus far. Sue was very fortunate for she recognised that her love of the Lake District provided her with a sense of spiritual achievement, which is always a far greater sense of realisation of ambition than can ever hope to be felt by way of material gain. Too much in life is judged by a material code of measurement. It is somewhere along this avenue of thought that Wainwright must have mentally resided. His love of being alone was a product of his need to feed his imagination and his love of his imagination was a product of his being alone. So is created an unbroken circle with the result that he could be content with his own company. I have seriously digressed from my journey, but, then again, perhaps such digressions are an integral part of my walk for such lateral thoughts are all a part of having the time and the freedom to contemplate weighty matters.

Still deep in this reflection, and satisfied that I could see the answer, I paused, took a few moments to look around me, and was very pleased with myself. This was a time when I could revel in what existed at present, and as I progressed on toward Raydale I looked forward to experiencing new country, new hills and new valleys. Although I had visited some of the places that lay ahead, such acquaintances had always been the briefest of encounters. Now I had the opportunity to savour their delights, the first of which would be Semer Water and Raydale. Semer Water, Wainwright had been told by a Bainbridge resident, was as lovely as Windermere. Although he had never been to Semer Water, he had seriously doubted this assertion and his deep love of all that was the Lake District filled him with resentment that there may exist, in Yorkshire, a contender to Windermere's beauty. Any comparison of the two is difficult to draw because in the intervening sixty years Windermere has taken on a character that is supported almost entirely by commercial activity. Any serenity that it exuded in 1938 has largely been extinguished by the hordes of trippers who clog the approach roads. Semer Water, on the other hand, appears to have changed little, lying quietly and unassumingly in its tributary valley to Wensleydale – the only taste of commercialism being the arrival of the farmer to collect the parking fees of the few tourists that sat in their cars on the beach at the northern end of the lake. There are no steamers here plying their business in trips up and down the lake; no hotels here, vying for the best location overlooking the lake; no screaming speedboats here, with their jet-set owners; just a few people taking in the sunshine. For goodness sake, though, get out of your cars, walk around the lake, breathe the fresh air – do anything but please don't stay imprisoned in your little metal wombs. Forgetting Windermere, further comparison is not easy but if you have spied Grasmere from the summit of Helm Crag on a pleasant and quiet evening then Semer Water will not impress.

From the northern end of Semer Water the outflowing watercourse is the River Bain, England's shortest river, and the path that follows it is in a delightfully pastoral valley running two miles in a north-easterly direction to Bainbridge. Derelict barns and peace and serenity are the hallmarks of this dale. If I were to find religion, it would be here that I would open my retreat for like-minded people to discover their peace – naturally I would charge, just to cover costs you understand, and make a small commercial profit. Ahead lay Wensleydale, still shrouded in a mist that concealed its charms as though stuffed with cotton wool. Only the upper slopes of the far-northern side of the valley could be seen extending above the cloud. Over those slopes lay my goal, my ambition. Muker in Swaledale still lay nine miles away but I was content for as I walked along the well-formed path I would arrive in Bainbridge at two o'clock. and would have time to take a rest and renew my acquaintance with the lone walker. The far-northern end of Raydale is somewhat frustrating in that the easy-going path lulls the walker into a false sense of security. Without warning, the previously pacific River Bain suddenly fights ferociously for its life as it becomes trapped within a steep-sided ravine before it is victorious in joining the River Ure. At this point and the path climbs steeply to the east of the river. On such a warm day the effort of this last mile worked up a thirst that would certainly justify a well-deserved drink at the Rose & Crown in the village, first seen from a high vantage point as the path joins an unclassified road south of an old Roman fortress.

Keeping to my schedule, I arrived at the Rose & Crown at two o'clock and ordered a pint of still orange, drank it and ordered a second. Today was not a day for beer, not yet anyway – that pleasure would wait until evening. My lone walker friend was not to be found in the room in which I was sat and I assumed that perhaps I had not noticed him sat outside as I entered. But no, he arrived after me having walked a less direct route along the shore of Semer Water. He had followed the directions of his guidebook around the lake, and while that may have been the correct thing to do, it did result in him meeting, yet again, with a refusal to be served food for the kitchen had closed ten minutes earlier. No, there were no sandwiches; no, there was no soup. It was unfortunate for him that there was nothing that could be provided except a packet or two of crisps. The moral of the story is clearly if you decide to walk the seventy-six miles of the Inn Way, do so only after the most comprehensive of strategic planning if you do not wish to suffer frequent hunger.

The lone walker's remaining journey for the day was the final mile to Askrigg and, as I left him at the pub, I suspected he would spend some time chatting to, and drinking with, three other walkers who had arrived a few minutes before my departure. The three were clear in their joint hobbies of walking and drinking and they had covered fourteen brisk miles to ensure early arrival at Bainbridge where their second hobby would begin in earnest. Their route was a coast-to-coast walk and their goal for the day was also Askrigg. It was not Wainwright's coast to coast that they followed; they too were following their own star. I had addressed this earlier in the day and had satisfied myself that my agenda was different – for these eleven days I was a detective following clues as Jules Verne's characters had followed clues and the briefest of waymarks in their journey to the centre of the earth. I ventured forth from the pub into the bright sunlight and made my way for a short distance along the macadam road across the valley floor and over the River Ure. As I exited the pub I could look south up the full length of the village green and back towards the hills from which I had made my way. I did not dwell on thoughts of southward – my way was to march north until I reached Hadrian's Wall and it was north to which I then turned my attention, to look at the hills that lay ahead. The final part of this second day's walking was predominantly road walking, but there was little alternative to the crossing of the moors over the next rib into Swaledale. This side of the rib looked very steep and I decided that I would not rest again until I had reached the more gentle gradients that lay waiting for me at Askrigg Common.

Bainbridge is a spacious village with its houses not so apparently cramped as those in Buckden. Its green extends for 200 yards or so, surrounded by buildings of one sort or another, the pub being one of them. The bridge in Bainbridge is also of considerable size bearing in mind that the river it crossed only boasted a two-mile course. Bainbridge has its ghosts also: the disused mill that once contracted the locals, the disused railway that once conveyed the locals and the disused stocks that once controlled the locals. Many would argue that the passing of the mill, which I believe had been a cotton mill, was simply indicative of the change in emphasis to a more viable location for industry within urban areas where better means of communications were possible. With regards to the railway, many might consider that its closure was inevitable in the light of the growth of private car ownership. As for the stocks, perhaps we should all believe that there are better ways of ensuring that all members of society conduct themself within the confines of law than by holding the threat of such primitive punishment over them. However, regardless of such argument, consideration and belief, it is sad to note that the sense of community surrounding the closure of locally based industries eats away at the very heart of village life. It is also sad to see that the only alternative to tourism-related employment is to work away from the village hub, and with the railway link no longer in existence, this results in permanent residency within the community decreasing. Saddest of all must be the fact that it is, perhaps, our kind treatment of those who transgress that has only served to provide insufficient deterrent and that now erodes the sense of security within wider society, whether village, town or city.

It is undoubtedly too late to return our infrastructure to its more basic roots. Perhaps we should rejoice in all the improvements technological advances have contributed to our society or, then again, perhaps we could be justified in mourning the passing of a simple life as we mourn the deceased. Of one thing we can be certain: no amount of crying will bring it back. For my part there are aspects of modern lifestyle that are of extreme annoyance and extreme irrelevance. I will not, however, digress any further at present for I must press on as I still have seven miles to cover before the day's end.

Immediately after the bridge over the river I picked up the course of the defunct railway line and headed east for Askrigg. Wainwright would not have had this option for, during his walk, the railway would have been in use making its connection with the Settle–Carlisle line at Garsdale Head. Such a railway had little chance of survival once the operating ethic of the authorities was to set greater store by profit than by service. A pleasant mile brought me into Askrigg village where there was a greater general hustle and bustle of activity than I had seen anywhere else. I decided to carry straight on without pausing, which was a shame for I feel sure that Askrigg has plenty to offer the inquisitive visitor … but not for me today. I walked up the main street to find the byroad signposted Muker as being six miles.

Almost immediately the road signs indicated a steep ascent and, although I knew this from the map, the extreme severity of parts of the climb, and the length of the steeper parts, took me by surprise and I soon found myself resting regularly admiring the rearward views. I generally avoided looking ahead during these rests for that way seemed to rise forever and I knew well that what I thought appeared to be the last climb would invariably not be. When I was walking I was usually looking at the tarmacadam surface just a few feet in front of me. My shadowy companion appeared to be as tired as I for he also walked at a crooked angle and was making heavy weather of the steep terrain. Wainwright had largely written Wensleydale off as a valley that holds no surprises for the visitor – he ought to have returned, in spirit at least, with me today for as I climbed her northern slope I received the very intrusive surprise of a RAF Tornado flying low over me. When jets fly as low as this one had there is no hearing their approach – they simply arrive silently with the noise following afterwards. It is an ear-wrenching, ripping noise that is felt as much as heard. There is no chance to catch a dramatic picture for by the time the camera is to the eye, the fly-pass is over and the pilot is looking down upon another valley. He (or she, for I must be politically correct) must be able to tell apart the tourists from the locals – the tourists stare skyward while the locals go about their business undeterred for they are used to the intrusion. Besides this noisy encounter the walk to the flatter moor top was peaceful with only a handful of cars passing either one way or other.

Wensleydale as a valley is altogether less dramatic then Wharfedale – it has no level floor and it cannot boast so steeply terraced valley sides as Wharfedale. The river does meander but only because it needs to do so to navigate its passage east between the undulations throughout this stretch of the dale. Neither would the valley sides of Wharfedale allow a road to pass as straight as the road I was now on. The Wharfe valley would demand much more respect from the road builders and users and the byways would have to swing back and forth in their ascent and descent to and from the valley floor. Probably the single-most interesting vista was that looking back toward the mouth of Raydale. From my raised viewpoint across the valley it was apparent that the environment around Semer Water would have been a more closed place many years ago before the river broke through at the northern end of the valley between the hills of Addlebrough and Yorburgh. Semer Water itself would have been of much greater size and then, perhaps, would have been a serious challenger to Windermere. I do not pretend to be an expert geographer or geologist and as I looked back and pronounced my thoughts to myself I knew that someone would be waiting to correct my undoubted erroneous topographical diagnosis.

My views back into the dale became fewer and my rests became less frequent as, finally, the gradient eased and I could, at last, think about a place to pause awhile and gratefully consume my late lunch and drink the still orange that I had filled my bottle with at the pub. There were very few obvious resting places for I was seeking a location where my boots could be removed and my feet dangle – they did, after all deserve the rest the most. I finally found a drainage culvert running under the road and was able to sit by the roadside on the culvert-surround and be thankful as I removed the various bits of baggage that had weighed me down on the ascent just completed.

The road ahead of me was now much easier for I had finished all the day's ascents and now had the luxury of being able to rest for thirty minutes if I wished. I did so wish, and sat on my culvert slab very pleased with myself, enjoying the heathery vista east toward Woodhall Greets high above the valley. I was afforded a wide panorama of purple moorland topped with a sky that was clear blue save for one or two high, straggly, benign cirrus cloud formations. Trees there were none; walls there were none. The sheep in these parts are left to roam and look for what sparse shelter they can when the weather turned malevolent, which, I could imagine, it would do with a vengeance when such temperament took its fancy. Today they needed no protection for it was now one of those rare balmy September afternoons when, if three such days fall together, the fragrance of relit barbecues drifts across the neighbourhood and the question on peoples' lips is whether summer has arrived at last. This was the third day in succession of the most agreeably balmy weather and, as I sat quietly eating a piece of cake that I had found in the bottom of my waist bag, I wished that it would continue for another nine days. The cake had travelled the whole way with me and was now rather dry and somewhat flat and contorted. I doubted whether I could possibly be so lucky but was ready to take each day as it came for, unlike Wainwright, I carried with me wet-weather clothing and a change of clothes so at least whatever was thrown at me during the day I would be dry come evening.

My roadside idyll was disturbed only once by a passing car – an elderly couple heading in the direction of Wensleydale slowed as they passed where I was sat and then made their way into a lay-by a little way down the road. There they sat on such a day with windows shut and engine running. They might just as well have rented a video of the dale for in their closed metal cocoon they all but completely restricted any sensory enjoyment. They paused for less than a minute before pulling out of the lay-by and continuing on their way toward Askrigg. The only other company I encountered was the occasional flying insect and once, as though in ridiculous contrast to the low-flying jet that had so shocked me on my way up from the valley, a squadron of low-flying grouse swooped and wheeled around me. During thirty minutes of rest these were the only interruptions of my peaceful retreat.

A brief study of the map had showed that I still had something close to an hour and a half walking so, at half past four, after a splendid repast of squashed cake, melted chocolate and warm orange, I once again set off, this time on the final leg of day two. I had barely risen to my feet when a tractor approached from across the fields and made for where I was stood. I could not begin to imagine what I might have done to annoy the driver who was obviously a farmer, but I had visions of some minor altercation. I need not have been concerned for he was simply wishing to pass the time of day and inquire as to whether he could give me a lift – had I been an hour earlier he could have brought me all the way up the steep hill from Askrigg. I did not go into any detail as to how I could not possibly accept any help but I thanked him for his very kind offer and went on my way with a renewed faith in human nature. Perhaps I should have suggested to him that his kindly demeanour might be better served by becoming landlord at one of the less-than-friendly public houses. Once removed from the hard thankless slog that is farming, he could, at least, have the choice of whether or not to make a decent living – or, equally, he could choose to not serve customers and follow the example of public-house husbandry set by Cray's White Lion.

I have mentioned that the popularity of walking can lead to a feeling of being a partaker within a procession and I had rather feared that by this stage on the second day I would have come across some other wayfarer or, worse, a group of walkers following the same route. I perceived this walk very much as being my possession and I would have found it difficult not to be resentful of discovering that others were trespassing on what I saw as my territory. I decided that if there were to be others repeating this journey then I would have surely met them by now. I was, I satisfied myself, alone in the spirit of revisiting Wainwright's travels of sixty years earlier and that thought pleased me. The 'gorge road, as Mrs Lightfoot had referred to this narrow byroad, still had the guideposts at 50-yard intervals all across the uppermost portion of its extremely exposed course, only now they were no longer 10 feet tall. Concrete fence posts 5 feet high have, in the intervening years, replaced them – perhaps, I mused, the snow doesn't fall so deep anymore on these tops as a result of global warming.

The road itself had not changed in generations. It still serves as the only connection over these wild fells between Askrigg in Wensleydale and Muker in Swaledale and it still passes the spectacular gorge below Oxnop Scar, which gradually open outs into a wider tributary valley of Swaledale. The tiny Oxnop Gill leaps down the gorge into and out of a wooded valley bottom until it finally finds sanctuary in the River Swale just upstream of Gunnerside. As the Oxnop valley opened wider for me, so did the views of the Swale valley, especially east down the dale. Western views remained obscured by the shoulder of the hills that rose above me to my left and I had to near the floor of the valley before I was permitted to see my goal for the day, Muker, which lay a further mile up the main road leading up the dale. To refer to this as a main road is something of an overstatement, but with the sun shining straight into my eyes making seeing ahead almost impossible, the few cars that I did meet made for an unpleasant last half-hour to the day. I was relieved to finally cross the arched bridge into the tiny village of Muker at just before six o'clock. I had covered eighteen miles and was ready for a soak, a smoke, a drink and a meal.

Of my four wishes the first was not to be granted. Once again my plans for a long soak in a bath were thwarted and I had to make do as best I could with a shower. On the second wish I fared better for Mr Metcalfe, with whom I was staying, was sympathetic to the needs of the smoker and allowed me to smoke with my head protruding out of the Velux roof light. He would have allowed smoking in the room but as a mark of courtesy I would never want to leave a room smelling of stale smoke. Stale smells of other things are unavoidable but smoke, no. By seven o'clock I was out and about looking to satisfy my third and fourth wishes, and a walk of only a few yards took me to the Farmers Arms, the only pub in the village but one that even on a Monday night in September was bustling with both locals and tourists alike. For those following me to the Farmers Arms at Muker do not make my mistake – I noticed the sign for the pub on a building to the left of the road. On trying the door I thought that my wishes were to be dashed for it was turned seven o'clock and the door was barred. I stood for a moment looking for a sign giving details of the opening hours. Surely I was not about to encounter the same problems with pub hours as my lone walker friend on the Inn Way. I had been told that the pub would be open – it was after seven o'clock, there was the pub sign – so what was I doing wrong? What I was doing wrong, I then found out, was trying to gain access to a building that was in absolutely no way connected to the pub. The sign, had I read it properly, was simply a bit of additional, off-site, advertising. While I had been rattling at the door of the disused building, the Farmers Arms lays directly behind me with customers coming and going wondering what on earth the strange chap on the other side of the road was doing.

I walked to the door of the pub trying desperately to give the impression that I was just checking and that I knew exactly where I was going. It is always more difficult to make fools of ourselves when we are alone for there are no friends and companions with whom you can share your embarrassment. Any discomfort at my error was soon forgotten as I sank into the very affable ambience of the pub and ate and drank my fill. It would have been very easy to overindulge, but I resisted and returned back to 'Hylands' at nine o'clock to be offered coffee and biscuits in the lounge with Ron and his wife, Yvonne. We chatted generally about Muker and what I was doing here and Ron said that he would look into the questions I had asked about where Wainwright had stayed.

I said goodnight as I was tired and had notes to write up. I wanted to be up first thing in the morning for the days' mileages were getting longer and Romaldkirk lay 21 miles from Muker.

Chapter 3

Muker to Romaldkirk

As I had walked into Muker the evening before I had done so with brilliant late-afternoon sun warming my face. Until then it had been my follower or had, at best, on a few occasions, ventured around to my left cheek. All things being equal, I would finish the walk with an even tan for these first days heading north would be balanced by the second half of the journey returning south. The promise of an even browning relied on the weather remaining constant, which even in the height of summer in England cannot be guaranteed. This seemed especially true if the earlier summer weather were anything to go by. The good fortune of my first two days surely could not be repeated for the remainder of the walk.

As I awoke and drew back the blind at the roof window I discovered that I was quite correct in assuming that my good fortune could not continue; either that or the hills I had seen to the north of Muker the evening before had been stolen. No, they were there, but in the dull early-morning light it was apparent that their tops were in cloud. Perhaps, I thought, they would clear for it was only a quarter to six as I smoked my first cigarette through the open Velux. By the time that I had cleaned my boots, made a cup of tea and rolled a second cigarette it was seven o'clock and they remained hidden in the murky dawn. There was no crisp dew this morning for the clouds had kept the overnight temperature higher than the night before. All there was today was a flat quality to the light with no contrast and little relief in the features of the lower, visible parts of the hills that surrounded the village.

By half past seven I was not alone. As I peered hopefully out again from my vantage point, I was aware of a buzzing coming from just above my head and I looked up to find a drowsy wasp apparently undecided as to whether to enter the room. I gave it no option as I quickly found a new use for the map that I had been looking at. I flapped at it a few times in a state of some minor panic for I am distinctly uncomfortable in the company of these viscous creatures whose only role in life would appear to be to wander about looking for subjects to sting. Bees I am getting better with – at least bees have to think twice before inflicting pain for it is their last action. Wasps have an entirely different agenda however. They can flit hither and thither stinging merrily and have many times spoiled an enjoyable barbecue. I usually insist upon tending the food so that at least I may be armed with a spatula or fish slice with which I can fend off their evil intentions. Sue, on the other hand, will sit quietly while they fly about her and my wild thrashings have been known to quite annoy her in their futility. Yes, I tell her, I am well aware that it only makes the wasp more angry and de-termined, but when she stops dashing for cover at the first sign of a moth then I will make more of a brave fist of it with these black-and-yellow devils. As with so many irrational fears, mine stems from being stung as a very young child and the recalled discomfort is probably a lot greater than the physical pain would be if I were stung now. However, I am not prepared to take that chance and will continue to flap with whatever comes first to hand.

In the intervening years between being a young, stung child I have had one or two close calls. Without any doubt the most alarming by far was when we had, some days earlier, moved into a new house and one of my first jobs had been to erect a foldaway ladder into the loft so that we could stow all the rubbish that we would probably never want again but could not discard (you know, the present from relations that would only grace the mantelpiece when they called round, or the useful item for removing impacted nails from camels' hooves bought from a catalogue that at the time you had thought you would simply not be able to live without). I was working with great industry and very little swear-ing, which is unusual for me when undertaking DIY activities and was a sure sign that things were going well, when the telephone rang. Sue answered it for I was now trapped in the loft having dragged the ladder up behind me to facilitate its fixing and would only be able to return after I had secured the mounting screws. Although I could only hear half of the conversation, it was apparent from Sue's responses that the call had been made by the previous owner. After various half-heard niceties, Sue's part of the conversation continued along these lines:

'Oh, really, when?'

'How many?' closely followed by 'Good Heavens.'

'Do you have the telephone number?'

'Thanks very much, we'll ring them first thing in the morning.'

'Oh, hang on, I'd better go, Andy is shouting something.'

The telephone conversation was curtailed due to the fact that at the very time reference was being made to it, I was about to discover that the other half of the conversation had been held thus:

'We found a wasps' nest in the loft. I meant to leave a note to tell you but I forgot.'

'Two or three weeks ago. We called the pest controller in who sprayed through the wall into the loft and thought that there may have been about 2,000 wasps in the colony.'

'2,000!' (slight gap to allow for Sue to exclaim 'Good Heavens.')

'The pest controller couldn't get into the house because we were all out but he left a note saying he would come back to remove the nest and that we were to ring him.'

'Yes, it's 600123.'

'Well, I hope you're…'

At his point I heard a solitary droning (buzzing was too small a word) behind me and to my terror I saw the first of them. A wasp, and a mean-looking blighter at that, was on the prowl, I felt sure, for someone to give a jolly good stinging as retribution for having had his family fairly well zapped some weeks earlier. Then the second, and then the third. This was enough for me. I believe that I beckoned Sue in a controlled manner – she has long maintained that I screamed in terror. Whatever was the more accurate description of my voice, I was no longer trapped in the loft, for I leapt smartly out of the hatch and did a very fine parachute roll onto the landing below. I had not given any thought to closing the hatch, the cover for which was, rather unfortunately, in the loft with the ladder. It soon became apparent that while they were still in the loft, the wasps weren't. To my horror the first of them droned at high level around the landing and I took evasive action by retreating into the toilet – a rather fitting place I felt at the time. My instructions to Sue were clear, although possibly somewhat high-pitched I'll admit, in that she should bring a rolled-up newspaper upstairs and a can of insect spray. I would, I decided, strategically, lead the action from my toilet-bunker – it is always very important for the manager to maintain a general overview of any given situation, and this I was doing with considerable alacrity. To Sue's credit, and thanks, I felt in no small part, to my strategic management skills, the wasps were dispatched and the next day the pest controller arrived to remove the remains of the nest.

I fought alone in my battle at Muker but did finally succeed in batting the wasp through the open roof window, which I then decided to close and forego any further cigarettes until after breakfast. I had arranged an earlier breakfast at eight and was greeted on arrival at the table by Yvonne Metcalfe. Ron had already left the house to call on an elderly local resident, Margaret (I never did discover her surname), to see what light the benefit of her advancing years might cast upon the Harkers with whom Wainwright had stayed. He returned as I was part way through my bowl of cereal and imparted the news that Margaret recalled the Harkers very clearly and that both were now interred in the church cemetery and was even able to give directions as to the location of their joint gravestone. She also confirmed that their house was not more than spitting distance from the Metcalfe's guest house and was now named 'South View' and had been further modernised in the years since Wainwright's visit. It was now like so many others in the village: very tastefully presented but not so manicured as the guest houses of Buckden. In Muker the impression was not given that almost all the houses are bed and breakfast establishments. This had been more than an impression when I had been trawling through the Tourist Board accommodation register. In finding an overnight stopover, I had been spoilt for choice in Buckden but no so in Muker where the available advertised houses could be counted on the fingers of one hand of Mickey Mouse. I had been lucky with my choice, however, for the Metcalfes proved to be splendid hosts with a generous streak when it came to portion sizes at the breakfast table. They were clearly believers that a hearty breakfast sets you up for the day and I was quietly surprised that I managed to leave behind an empty plate when I finally excused myself to return to my room to complete my packing.

As an extra to the usual carefully ordered packing of the rucksack, I now had the added logistical exercise of how to find room for the gargantuan packed lunch that my hosts had prepared for me. In the event I had to hand back the fruit (an orange and one of the largest pears that I had ever seen) because it simply was not going to fit into any remaining little crevice in either my waist bag or rucksack. With what remained I was not likely to be hungry for some days to come. I made my way downstairs and looked out from the front door at the steely grey clouds. There was no break in them and no likelihood of any break for the foreseeable future, but, for all that, it was still warm and I decided that I would again be walking in shirtsleeves. Ron accompanied me to the cemetery to direct me toward where Margaret had said the grave was and while we walked we talked of Muker. Unlike Buckden it is not overrun as a tourist attraction in its own right but it has its own problems of population imbalance with many of the younger generation having moved away in search of work and careers beyond its quiet lanes. Buckden does, at least, have wider tourist-based facilities that afford some local employment opportunities.

There are some indigenous older residents whose families have flown the coup – in years gone by their offspring might have followed them onto the land, but now farming dynasties die out as agriculture employs fewer and fewer numbers of locals and seasonal itinerants alike. Some of these older folk still rarely venture out of the dale – how hard it is to imagine the speed of change where in the span of one generation the aspirations of so many have changed so dramatically. Sixty years ago the population would have been much more static with local services being available in the village. Now the younger schoolchildren have to travel to Gunnerside and the older ones all the way down the dale to Richmond. It is difficult to know whether it was a lack of school-age children that had led to the closure of the school or whether the closure of the school led to the lack of school-age children. Whichever it was, the result is that that village is now home to only three under school-age and six between seventeen and twenty-one. There are none between these two ranges and no doubt the majority of the six in the older group would look to move away as soon as possible.

It is sad because while indigenous village life in Buckden was being unwittingly strangulated by the heaving tourists and the place fast becoming a picturesque museum, Muker might be looking at a future where it quietly dies, at least as a vibrant community. For a community to thrive and buzz it should have a cross section of all age groups and have sufficient locally based employment to stay alive during the day and not just come to life in an evening when all the commuters return. I do hope I am wrong, but I cannot help but feel that unless there is a shift in the population structure I fear for this delightful little village's future. In 1938 Buckden and Muker must have been quite similar – perched near the head of their dales – but since then Buckden has been allowed to grow. Muker has not, and it is only on walking through the streets that any lack of new development is noticed. Wainwright's account tells of how Mr Harker had told him that there had been no new buildings erected in his lifetime. Now, sixty years on, the same comment could be made: there have been one or two barn conversions but no new dwellings.

Perhaps I should not be so melodramatic about Muker's future for in only two days I would be visiting Blanchland, which is a place that has not been allowed to change for many more generations than Muker and survives very nicely, thank you very much. Perhaps Muker's population will simply adapt to being bereft of youngsters and perhaps the day-trippers will provide a transient community ambience, at least through the summer months. We entered the churchyard and found our way to the gravestone of David and Margaret Harker, he dying in 1962 aged eighty and she six years later aged eighty-two. There was something rather trainspotter-ish about looking down at the simple stone with its rather overgrown bed, almost as though I could now tick it off in my Observer Book of Wainwright memorabilia. For all that, though, I was glad to have walked this way and I thanked Ron for all his help and asked him to express my gratitude to Margaret. I also thanked him for his and Yvonne's hospitality and the packed lunch provided me, and I especially thanked him for his Savlon, for I had developed something of a personal problem in the chaffing department which need not be expanded upon. I bade him goodbye and made my way toward the signpost and between the houses, onto the open fields to the north of the village. It was turning nine o'clock as I left the village behind and wondered what in another sixty years the lonely walker would find. I suspected that I would have to leave the return visit to someone else, as I would be 102 and therefore realistically somewhat unlikely to be able to make the pilgrimage.

I have learnt to accept that I am approaching that time of life where men decide that they are staring at middle age. The fact that this point in life is reached is not of itself something that should hold any fear, except for the concern that instead of subconsciously counting up the days spent since birth, the question begins to be posed whether it might be of greater pertinence to count down the days left. Of far greater concern, though, is that it is also at about this time that we question the level of personal achievement in life and often fail to comprehend the point of it all. The vast majority of life can seem to be a chore to be endured, very occasionally interspersed with short-lived pleasurable activities (most of which are undoubtedly bad for your health and should not be entertained!). Corporate management consultants will spout about the importance of having goals, targets by which actual performance can be adjudged against. This is fine insofar as it goes, but in life proper the goals are more dynamic and three dimensional and it is very unlikely that the possibility will exist to assess results against clearly and separately defined targets. There is also the matter that there are no rules about when comparison against targets should be undertaken. In the absence of guidance about when to look at performance, it seems reasonable to suppose that most people will start to look at their own lives when it begins to dawn on them that, statistically, they are likely to be halfway through life and the countdown is beginning. The problem with looking at life's achievements is that the yardsticks or targets against which to compare were never actually set but more evolved through upbringing and the sociological environment during the formative years. In other words, outsiders (be they parents or peer groups) had a hand in establishing the parameters by which we then later measure our own achievement. This result is that we judge our own level of success not against a set of personal targets, because they don't exist, but substitute these for comparison against how others have performed. This is very dangerous because unless the view is genuinely held that there is always someone worse off than you, the tendency is to look at those who appear to have achieved things that we have not. This would be more realistic if we judged ourselves against another person holistically but generally we don't, tending to take one or two aspects of their apparent success in isolation, leaving despairing questions as to our own failings against those limited parameters. We ignore the fact that they have no social life, have to work fourteen hours a day, have stress-related problems, couldn't hold down a conversation with anything but a mirror, are grossly overweight through lack of exercise or a whole variety of other faults that we choose to overlook. Measure yourself against your own aspirations by all means, but leave others out of the equation for their perceived successes will surely frustrate.

I could rest easy in the knowledge that for now at least I was luxuriating in one of those interspersed times of enjoyment and while I could I would revel in it. I could look forward also to reliving it upon returning home when I would write my own account of my eleven-day liberation, revisiting all the places again as I brought them back to mind. I concluded that Muker would be one such place that I would recall fondly as I slowly ambled along beside the River Swale as it makes its way between the steep flanks of Kisdon and Black Hill. The first section of the walking was no longer through wet and muddy fields for a fine path of Yorkstone flags had been laid running between gated stiles in the field boundaries, and as I headed yet again northerly, I was soon folding and stowing my first map. I would return to it again on day ten, but for now I was looking at my second Ordnance Survey map, which would see me as far north as Weardale. I would have to walk the full south to north extent of this second map in little over a day and I already knew that by the time I arrived at Blanchland I would be well aware that I had done some work.

The path around the eastern side of Kisdon follows the valley floor and only when Keld is neared does it rise well above the river and give spectacular views over a young River Swale as it writhes through an ill-fitting bed in a series of tumultuous rapids and falls. It was as the path rose away from the river that I passed through a gated stile to be confronted by a small but inquisitive herd of cattle. The adult animals were all cows but there were also a number of calves and I would have no alternative other than to pass by them at altogether too close a proximity for my liking. Before I had set out on my journey it had been my mother who had indicated her unease at the fact that I was walking alone. She had wished for me to be a part of a group and would not understand my assertion that walking is something best done unaccompanied. By way of an appeasement I promised I would take with me my monopod, which is, primarily, a piece of photographic equipment but would also serve very nicely, I assured her, as a weirdo-hitting implement. She appeared to be convinced that I was almost sure to be set upon by hoards of moor-wandering lunatics whose sole aim was to assault lone walkers. She seemed relieved when I showed her the stick-like gadget and she felt the weight of its pan-and-tilt head. Happy that I would be able to bludgeon my assailants, her fears appeared to ebb away. As I approached the cows with their calves I was glad to feel as though I had with me a tool that would also double as a cattle prod. As it turned out, I need have had no concern for they all paid me little or no attention as I passed through their ranks and out of the field at the other side.

I was enjoying the views from high above the river when I approached a gate, beyond which was a clear pathway with post and barbed wire fencing to both sides. To the left of the path it provided field boundary fencing and the to the right it acted as a safety fence above the ravine with the ground sloping steeply away, providing a home for undergrowth and scrub and small gravity-defying trees. As I was about to open the gate I noticed a sheep and its lamb grazing some few yards along the path. They saw my approach and in a panic the lamb squirmed through the fencing above the ravine and proceeded to stand a few feet below the level of the path, leaving the ewe pondering what to do next. If I made progress along the narrow path then the sheep would only run in front of me, further separating itself from its offspring for the ravine became steeper farther along the path. Initially I stood with the gate propped open with my monopod (I had found another use for it) for if they would only walk toward me then they would be reunited. This was, of course, to no avail and however much I tried to conceal myself in the undergrowth they knew I was there and had no intention of making any move in my direction. There was only one way around the problem and that was for me to climb over the fence into the field and bypass the ewe and then hope that I could return to the path over the fence at some point further on. This would leave the sheep to work out for themselves how best to regroup. I had found a lower point in the fencing where I could gain access to the field, but when it came to egress I walked some distance without finding an easy way back onto the path. In effecting my escape I finally had to settle for a part where an old broken-down wall had been supplemented with posts and strands of barbed wire as a makeshift repair. The operation involved straddling the painfully sharp barbs while manoeuvring on loose, damp and potentially slippery walling stones. With one leg on either side of the topmost strand I was only too aware that one small slip would be very likely to do more damage than my newly acquired Savlon could hope to repair. After some delicate footwork I did manage to swing my trailing leg over the wire and return safely to the path having successfully circumvented the sheep.

Some little way before the last outpost of the dale, Keld was reached where the path is joined from the left by the Pennine Way, and I followed its route for half a mile before it swung down, at a second junction, into the valley to cross the river and on up the other side to Tan Hill. My way proceeded as Wainwright's had done, into Keld and along the road. Sixty years ago Wainwright was probably not aware of the right of way on the northern bank of the river and as I was following his route then my way also was to forego the more pleasant, but boggy, path that was now a part of the Pennine Way. Keld still appears barren and inhospitable in its harsh surroundings and even though it nestles on the routes of both the Pennine Way and the Coast-to-Coast Path, it has attracted neither quaint guest houses nor the commercialism of a pub or hostelry or shop of any sort. There had been a pub in the village many years earlier but now all that exists for the traveller is a youth hostel and one or two stark dwellings offering bed and breakfast. I enjoy solitude but, as I wandered through the village, I questioned whether this was just a mite too lonely for full-time residence. Perhaps on a warm, bright summer's day my view might have been different.

I left Keld without undue delay and made my way up to the road that heads over the bleak moors to Kirkby Stephen. Following it for half a mile I could look up to my right to see the valley of the Stonesdale Beck rising and disappearing into the low cloud and, on the right-hand slope of the valley I could make out the Pennine Way path. This was another of those times when the purist in me was leading my expedition, for while I had four miles of road walking ahead, just across the valley lay a perfectly good path to follow, both having the common goal of the Tan Hill Inn. My stall, though, was clearly set out – I had chosen to follow as closely as I could Wainwright's route and would do so if it killed me. With the amount of road walking that was demanded of me, all my concentration would be required to avoid that prospect becoming a distant possibility; not so on this particular stretch however, because the road up the western side of the Stonesdale valley is just as it was sixty years ago, with wide springy verges once the hamlet of West Stonesdale is reached. Nothing had changed from when Wainwright had come this way including, sadly, the weather which, as I gained height, closed in all around me so that visibility was reduced to little more than a couple of hundred yards. He had said that walking in a mist is to be enjoyed, and so he was correct, but only in a proper mist that sets a challenge for the walker's navigation skills. The low cloud of this day hung like a characterless veil which gave an impression of viewing life as though through a muslin cloth where all about was reduced to a featureless barrenness. While I had been at a lower height I had been as a spectator in the valley looking up at the clouds. Now I was in its damp and clammy domain where the spectacle wearer is at an extra disadvantage, for although it was not actually raining, my glasses were no sooner wiped than a new fine film of moisture would again restrict visibility.

The road ahead twisted and undulated its way up the valley and looked for all the world as if it had been laid as a monolithic layer, simply dropped on the earth as though from some magic road-making machine. Cuttings or embankments to aid its passage were non-existent – it had simply been laid to curve and bend with the topography. Perhaps the local authority had been approached by a contractor who had some macadam and chippings left over; they'd laid a few drives and just had enough left to pave the way up to Tan Hill – no VAT, no bill, no questions, know what I mean. To either side of the monolithic strip the loose gravel chippings that had spewed out of the machine lay as a pebbly verge, which sounded just like an arrival at some frightfully posh residence with the scrunch of gravel underfoot. Beyond this noisy verge lay the soft silent grass cut short by the wandering sheep, and I alternated between walking on the road, the gravel or the grass verge depending upon whichever took my fancy. I was walking today with a zeal that was of great relief, for I had been very tired during the first two days and had become increasingly concerned about my ability to succeed. Now, as I flew up the four miles from Keld, I felt there was no question as to whether I would achieve my overall aim. My confidence was high, as were my spirits, and when we attain such self-belief nothing is beyond our grasp.

It is only when we are knocked by others that we begin to question our own ability to achieve our aims. It is only when we do not have control over the setting of our goals that we question the entire validity of our objectives. It is only when we do not have belief in our goals that we fail to be committed to seeing them succeed. My journey was an opportunity to set myself a clearly defined goal and although it would test me to the extreme, I would succeed because I believed in it. I would succeed because I alone had set my target, save for the fact that arguably Wainwright himself had set the ultimate challenge. I would succeed because now that I was here alone there were no doubting Thomases to cause me to question my goal or its validity. Moreover, I would succeed because in failure I would have let myself down. With these positive thoughts coursing through my veins supplying power to my muscles, it mattered not whether I was to walk twenty-one miles per day or thirty miles. I would surmount all obstacles that might be placed before me because I believed that I could overcome them. It had been very similar during my very short spell playing rugby – it was always the player making a half-hearted tackle who would suffer the injury. If the same player went into a tackle with self-confidence and belief in his ability then he would have his man and would get up to make the next tackle. I would like to point out that my credentials for making these comments as far as rugby is concerned are mostly based on my observation of others. I watched good players hurling themselves headlong with little or no apparent regard for their own safety with, at worst, only minor consequences. Any attempt on my part to emulate their majestic actions nearly always led to my staying on the ground with my body hurting in one place or another. I was most relieved when I found my vocation was to run up and down on the wing, nicely out of the thick of things and well away from imminent danger provided, of course, that I continued to move fairly smartly.

I pressed on of with some purpose, with the aim of being at the Tan Hill Inn for a brief respite and in sufficient time for a swift half and a dry cigarette. I covered the ground with such rapidity that I arrived within sight of the highest pub in England at half past eleven and was sitting down not many minutes later in the large stone-flagged bar area. It came as something of a surprise that I was not the only patron – there were already a number of walkers and cyclists sat around the large wooden tables or surrounding the great warming fireplace. I talked with a group of three young cyclists, who, I learned, were making their way from coast to coast on bikes. As we discussed their plans and their various destinations, I noticed that I was concealing a slight resentment of them not asking me of my journey and this was added to when a couple stood at the bar also showed great interest in the cyclists' endeavours. What about me, I thought. Does no one want to know what I'm doing here, all on my own, sitting at the table with my book and map on my lap? Apparently not, I discovered, for the conversation continued to centre solely on the progress of the cyclists. I eased myself out of the discussion upon noticing two framed pages of Wainwright's Pennine Way Companion hanging close to where I was sitting and I spent my last two minutes in the Tan Hill Inn admiring his neat handwritten work and fine drawings. Noon arrived and if I were to be in Bowes by three o'clock I knew it was time to reacquaint myself with the mist and the clouds outside.

The route of the Pennine Way immediately before and after the inn was the subject of the mounted extracts I had admired, and I was not surprised by Wainwright's reference to it being a rather unpleasant traverse of a wet and boggy moor plateau. He was not a great fan of the Pennine Way for the nature of the geology en route has a tendency to demand of the walker the utmost of patience as crushingly slow progress is made through bog after bog. The geological idiosyncrasies are added to by the nature of the topography, which has an inclination to result in the Way spending an unreasonable proportion of the time in clinging mist. The only time the cloud is not down is when there's a good wind to clear the tops. The nett effect of these adversities is that for much of the time the way is a most unwelcoming place offering only wet feet and little shelter. I turned from the framed extract, smiling as I did so as if in a silent greeting of the man in whose footsteps I was following, and finished my drink in readiness for the next three hours of walking. I have to confess to making a very deliberate show of donning all my various bits of baggage so as to provide one last chance for any of the gathered throng to show an interest in my enterprise. Alas, no one did and I left the inn leaving behind me the general conversation of cycling, distances and destinations.

There had been no particular reason why I should wish for an interest to be expressed in what I was doing other than we all crave some attention from time to time. The attention that I had sought at the inn was largely to prove to myself that my own grand tour was of public interest. I had not been along its route for even quarter of the distance yet, but I already felt that with some replanning I could earn the kudos as being the initiator of a new long-distance walk. Not just any long-distance route but a walk that had its inspirational roots planted in the mind of the man whose name was synonymous with such courses. Wainwright had been instrumental in establishing the generally accepted itinerary for the Coast-to-Coast path, yet here lay the course of a walk that linked so much variation along its way but one that he had never pieced together. My hope would be to assemble it for him and present it to an eager public; hence, if no one inquired as to my motives, I could not measure the depth of his or her interest in my venture.

There was an impression from Wainwright's narrative that during his rest at the Tan Hill Inn he had been the only patron. It was a foul day and travellers and tourists were then few and far between. Not so today, for as I passed out of the front door I did so leaving fifteen or so customers behind. The increased patronage and prosperity of the inn is witnessed by the extent of additional buildings that have appeared over the years. The inn walls are littered with old prints of how it had been at various times in the past, showing an initially modest hill inn extending, firstly, with a single-storey annex and later being rebuilt to house two storeys. The Tan Hill Inn will continue to go from strength to strength for our thirst for escaping from towns will not diminish. It is something of a wonder that a large hotel chain has not stepped in with an irresistible offer and produced a themed establishment with hotel and conference facilities. I could only hope that the present owner relished his role as a provider of sanctuary and would resist all such commercial incomers and that the spirit of true hospitality would survive for another sixty years.

Leaving the front door of the inn at just after noon, my schedule was to arrive at Bowes at three o'clock, rest for thirty minutes, then saunter over the last few miles to arrive at Romaldkirk at six o'clock. The Pennine Way signpost indicated that the path spurred off at an angle to the road in a north-easterly direction. The waymarked path runs dead straight over the moor toward Sleightholme, but here I left the Pennine Way to follow the macadam road in the direction of Richmond. My route was to follow the road for two miles before finding a byroad to Bowes that would again join the Pennine Way some two miles before Sleightholme. Even if I were not so keen to follow the Wainwright route, I might well have decided to follow the road in any case. The waymarked path looked to me to be either worryingly indistinct or, where it was more clearly trodden, like a quagmire with no obvious deviation.

As I veritably marched along the edge of the road I was looking forward to the sun making an appearance and ridding the landscape of its two-dimensional character. Afternoon sun had been forecast, I had been told at the inn, and I was ready for it anytime that it liked. Just anytime at all. Although I wasn't cold, my ascents were largely finished for the day and a little warming sun would do no harm at all. The previous two days' walking had comprised two very distinct halves with a climb and descent before lunch and a second climb and descent before the final goal was achieved. Today was different. Once I emerged out of Swaledale via the Stonesdale valley I had arrived on a wide plateau-like landscape and from here it was a gradual north-east descent toward Bowes. Beyond Bowes the map indicated a fairly gentle route to Romaldkirk with contours that were well spaced over the intervening Cotherstone Moor. It was only tomorrow that the valleys and hills would seek their revenge for this easier day.

Although the mist had noticeably lessened in its opacity, the sun was still proving bashful and did not, apparently, wish to be seen. Even had it been a fine and clear day, I suspect that the views north over the plateau-like Bog Moss would have been as equally uninspiring as today. There was little to divert the eye from the immediate surroundings of heather and bog with its backdrop of … well … heather and bog, actually. As I marched I calculated that Bowes represented a minor milestone – arrival there would signify that approximately quarter-distance had been attained. I would hopefully find a tearoom where I might privately celebrate my achievement over a pot of tea and sticky bun.

Between Tan Hill and Bowes there were two further significant moments. The first was that for the first time I was not walking in the Yorkshire Dales National Park – the entire route until just passed the inn had been within the park's boundaries. The second was not many minutes later when I finally left Yorkshire behind and crossed the border into County Durham. Border changes over the years have shifted county boundaries with alarming regularity, so much so that if there were to be a physical border the fencing company would have been permanently employed in taking down and re-erecting huge stretches. No sooner would they have finished one section than a mandarin at Whitehall would provide them with the latest flavour-of-the-month, vis-à-vis county boundary changes.

When Wainwright had walked this way his stay in Yorkshire had extended to reaching the River Tees at Middleton, a fact that had, indeed, formed a part of the discussion at the Tan Hill Inn. It has never been adequately explained to me why we seem to have developed a desperate need to see change. It is a need that runs deep in society and extends to many areas that appear to be functioning perfectly well. I can only assume that boundary changes are set in motion as a conspiracy by officers of local authorities who are fearful that if they aren't seen to be doing something then perhaps someone might question whether they are needed at all. I was brought up on the old adage that 'if something isn't broke, don't fix it'. There is a whole raft of other aspects of modern society that has seen change seemingly just for the sake of change. At best these generally cause confusion and at worst they eat away at the very heart of the heritage of our country. I will undoubtedly return to this subject so, for the time being, I will continue my progress toward Sleightholme Moor

For my part I crossed the border into County Durham just after turning left onto the byroad signposted as seven miles to Bowes. At least a river provides a clear and distinct boundary – it hails to you that you are about to make your exit from one county and enter another. There can be no doubt, not like wandering, as I was, where all I knew was that somewhere underfoot I had stepped from God's own county of Yorkshire into County Durham. I was not too far along the byroad when I heard the sound of distant gunshots behind me. This was, no doubt, the shooting party I had passed some minutes after leaving the inn. The hunters were an awfully well-heeled group of well-to-do ladies and gents dressed to the nines having just enjoyed their al fresco luncheon before setting out onto the moors. The beaters were lunching too, but discreetly out of sight of the hunters in order that their dubious table manners would not cause any distress or offence. Counting seven personalised number-plated executive four-wheeled drive vehicles, I paused for a moment or two and watched as they all made their way toward the butts.

I had, years earlier, been employed as a beater, but only for one day. My personal contribution to the demise of the grouse did not sit easily with my conscience and I was relieved when the long day was over and I was able to count my ill-gotten gains. My principles were not so affronted that I refused recompense, but I could not help but feel for the grouse. I am not a grouse expert, but I assume they get up of a morning, look out of their nest and think how pleasant it is to live in such a place: 'I think I'll have a fly around', they perhaps consider. Then the distant cracks of gunshot sound and before you know it your arse is full of shot and someone will be later picking out the bits over dinner. Or if, as a grouse, you have become wise and avoid flying when you have noticed a gathering of dark green Range Rovers, you lay low only to be half beaten to death by a stick-yielding youth if you don't fly off. I'm sorry, grouse but it's heads we win and tails you lose.

My reaching the track signified, also, an end to the road walking – for the time being at least. I had walked the last six miles on, or adjacent to, tarmac roads and it was now a pleasure to be walking alone along a gravel-surfaced byway that could be seen stretching ahead as a winding grey serpent. If I stopped and looked from whence I had come the same serpent twisted behind me with a green and purple sea to either side. Progressing along the track I could forget all about the map and was able to simply enjoy the subtly changing scenery. The most noticeable change was in the increased visibility and the first hint of a break in the cloud. There was only a hint, a suggestion of the cloud base thinning – almost as soon as a brighter patch appeared then a second cloud would quietly drift across it to obscure any immediate hope of improvement. For three miles the track winds and twists among heathland covered with tussocks of reed and heather, heading generally in a north-east direction, making for the junction where my route would once again be joined by the Pennine Way. For a short distance the path swung north before returning to its north-east direction when, soon after, I came upon the signpost indicating that I had been joined once more by the Pennine Way; its route and mine then proceeded to follow one another for the next two miles.

During my passage across the moor path toward Sleightholme I had come upon an old railway freight wagon presumably now used for feed storage by the local farmer. There was something altogether incongruous about seeing the wagon up here on the moor, but I suppose I should have been pleased that in the death of one aspect of industry new life had been breathed into another. It would have been all too easy to discard the old without a thought for whether it may have a use in the new order of things. Perhaps the freight wagon was redundant if a different attitude were taken, but with lateral, multidirectional thinking there are undoubtedly many things that could be reused or recycled. So it is with people also; the scrap heap can come early for many. So early for some that barely has there been time to formulate the dream when their hierarchical superiors, judging them superfluous to requirements, shatter any grand plans or aspirations. Life is, for so many, like a magic carpet: in the beginning there is a belief that we have our own which will carry us through life. So often, though, by the time the operating instructions have been digested, not only do we realise that ours is the model that isn't capable of flight but also that it has been pulled out from under us in any case. Despairingly life's plan is quickly redrawn, but this time the pencil is blunted and the sharp, self-confident edge has gone. The blurred redraw is begrudgingly accepted but, from that point on, the focus is difficult to maintain and the cynicism of life's futility makes its first appearance. Unless the inevitability of this recurring cycle is recognised and acknowledged it will appear over and over, gradually crushing any last vestiges of optimism from the plan's architect. Only when the certainty that these disruptions will thwart are we then able to positively react to them and, when they happen, remove our blinkers and apply the mind laterally to the problems that beset us. It is when we think in this multidirectional way that we think at our best, for nothing is taken for granted, nothing is assumed and we open our minds to new ideas and new ways of achieving our goals. We are all capable of these multidirectional thought processes, for if we were not then we would succumb very quickly to the 'slings and arrows of outrageous fortune' as Shakespeare once wrote. If you fail to comprehend this analogy of life you are very lucky, for your magic carpet is clearly one of the flying models. Or, beware, for if you are still reading the instructions look out for those who would surely steal your would-be steed.

So it was with the freight wagon, for it at least a new use had been found in this splendid isolation. Seeing that wagon reminded me that before I had begun my journey there had been worrying headlines in the press that we were on a collision course with recession. If the forecasted downturn were to happen there would be plenty of other areas of the economy that would see such outrageous fortune piled onto man and machine alike. The survivors would be those who could most readily adapt to their changing environment and accept, perhaps, their more limited aspirations. There is, however, always a positive side if some effort is made to seek it out, and the positive aspects are that very often these upheavals provide the means through which an escape can be made from a narrow rut that has held us trapped without our realising.

I passed the wagon and decided that I would reduce the weight in my waist bag noticeably if I could find a suitably sheltered place to stop awhile for lunch. The Metcalfes' sandwich of corned beef salad with onion (they had prepared this to my request had felt by its weight upon packing it as if most of the tin of corned beef had been stuffed between the two thick slices of bread. Also included was a carton of orange juice, piece of cake and one or two biscuits. At a point about half a mile short of Sleightholme Farm, the track dipped to cross a stream valley and I was able to find a reasonably protected dry spot where I could relax for half an hour or so over a leisurely lunch.

Where I had paused for lunch was also where my route returned to a macadam surface underfoot and would remain so for the rest of the day – a further ten miles. I was not greatly looking forward to the afternoon's walking because I suspected that the six miles from Bowes to Romaldkirk would see a return to unpleasant progress among traffic similar to my first six miles from Settle to Horton. I was, however, looking forward to finding a tearoom in Bowes (although having eaten lunch the idea of a sticky bun was much less appealing), so much so that I got back to my feet after only fifteen minutes rest. My decision was also influenced by the fact that the breeze had a chilly edge to it and also because my legs were seizing up – they were becoming used to the interminable left, right, left, right and when the repetitive action stopped they quickly protested.

Very soon after restarting along the track, now fast becoming a roadway with walls to both sides, I was aware of a watery, hazy sunshine giving a greater luminosity to the surrounding fields. Then, shortly after, the first shafts of sunlight would illuminate circles of the landscape as though by some heavenly spotlight. In this type of light, when the majority of the sky is still overcast and grey, the green of the fields always looks all the more verdant. The shade of green, if presented in a painting, would give the impression of having been mixed by a strictly amateur artist who couldn't quite obtain the correct colour. Yet here it was; the true colour of the land with sheep and cattle the spotlighted stars of the show. Finally, at quarter to two, I greeted my shadow, to my left, for the first time and I looked north over an increasingly brilliant landscape toward Bowes and its castle. With the sun came the warmth and as I continued my easy progress I was glad of some relief, for during the stop for lunch I had become chilled and was only now beginning to warm through.

The Sleightholme road follows, more or less, the contours around Gilmonby Moor and parts company from the Pennine Way, which lay below me in the valley of Sleightholme Beck. The beck itself makes a direct route for the River Greta and on into Bowes, which all in all was a more preferable route to the one I took. When Wainwright had been in these parts he had done so without a map because Bowes then lay just beyond the edge of the 1-inch map that he had with him. He had found his way into the village (for it is hardly a town) by asking directions of a farmer who had also told him, initially, that the large building to the west of the cluster of roofs was a new air-raid shelter. In his narrative Wainwright admits for a moment or two to having been taken in by the farmer before the local admitted to his little wheeze. It is hard to imagine in 1998 that I might have fallen for such a prank and we can't now appreciate the scurry of pre-war activity that had been taking place even during 1938. Declaration of war was still nearly a year away as Wainwright strode over the north Pennine countryside, yet there is barely a chapter of his account in which the threat posed by Hitler does not weigh heavy on his heart.

In 1938 gas masks were issued to the populace. One million people were sought for air-raid wardens and instructions were included in the press on how to dig a trench. The Territorial Army was reorganised to gear up for the eventuality of war. Indeed, only two weeks before Wainwright had commenced his journey England had formally advised Hitler that she would not stand aside if Germany were to press ahead with invasion plans. We are used to hearing such rhetorical statements nowadays from politicians aimed at some dictator or other – it has become almost every-day international tittle tattle to threaten to blow so-and-so from here to kingdom come. With a thoroughly more sinister undertone, the Nazis and the Jews were making the headlines in 1938 in a way that seven years later would have the world reeling in shock at one person's treatment of another.

It is a mystery to me how we would prepare for war now, but the type of modern warfare that would be waged would not be the sort that would rely so heavily on comradeship as the Second World War had and, to an even greater extent, the First World War. If all-out war was to be declared, and in all-out I include use of nuclear capabilities, then there would be little point in erecting a modern-day version of the Anderson Shelter or nipping down to the nearest tube station to seek protection. The ability for unerringly accurate military strikes has been exhibited well enough in minor skirmishes to know that the most pragmatic solution might well be to telephone the Ministry of Defence. Upon getting through to them, and patience may be required for the lines could well be busy with others having similar ideas, inquire of them as to where their most top-secret installation is sited. Having established its location, proceed exactly to that spot. One thing you can rely on will be that the country's aggressor will already know of the installation and will already have his missiles targeted. This is a dead certainty, which, thankfully, is what you will be also in something close to four minutes. I accept that the downside to this plan is that you do not survive to live out your days in the subsequent peacetime that will, more than likely, return, but, let's face it, would you really want to? In peacetime we have already managed, quite nicely, to damage the planet, in part beyond repair, and frankly, I have no desire to see the destruction reaped by our latest warring capabilities. All this and no one has had to even get out of their chair – all that will have happened will be that a small number of men (or women will have been charged with the authority for pressing the buttons. Just like typing really, only more people are affected by your words. No trenches, no flying of dangerous sorties over enemy territory, no naval blockade to starve the opponent, no marching armies, no real unpleasantness at all, in fact; just a few buttons and there will be no soldiers, no pilots, no seamen. There will be nothing. No, the answer will be to find the nearest likely epicentre of the holocaust and stay there. You'll find me there, quietly rolling a cigarette and possibly studying a map of the area.

Unlike back in 1938, there would seem to be very little point in undertaking any form of preparation for such war where there would be nowhere to hide, nowhere to seek effective shelter. There would seem little point in mass evacuations of cities and little point in establishing civil defence forces other than as some form of puerile morale boost. There would be very little point to most things other than maintaining your patience while the ministry finally answer the tele-phone.

I have digressed into a most unseemly amphitheatre. Here was I on this fine afternoon, with the weather warming as the day progressed and the shadows darkening; how could I entertain such black thoughts? I would not be taken in as Wainwright was, but I discovered as he did that the road into Bowes has been laid to frustrate. Instead of accepting its ultimate fate of being the way across the valley of the Greta and, accordingly, making a course directly to the village, it loops round to the south-east before finally turning north. Once heading north it soon arrives at the hamlet of Gilmonby and, immediately after, the bridge over the Greta and on and up the hill into Bowes itself. I was fast approaching quarter-distance and was also nearing my long-awaited pot of tea – four miles of walking since lunch had also seen to it that I regained sufficient appetite to entertain the prospect of that sticky bun.

I momentarily returned to the subject of devastation when, as I had approached the bridge over the Greta, I moved to the side of the road to make way for the same four-wheel-drive vehicles that I had seen earlier on the moor shortly after Tan Hill. Surely, I thought, they can't have killed all the grouse and now moved on for greater glory elsewhere. Or maybe there weren't any grouse to be had; could they have possibly devised new strategic arse-buckshot-avoidance tactics. I doubted it – it was far more likely that the beaters had scared the poor buggers half to death so that the vast majority had flown off and the pickings had become so lean that it was time to move on.

Of Bowes itself, the first thing to say is that the Unicorn Inn is still there, on the right as I made my way up the quiet main street. The second thing to say about the place is that the castle is very well kept and cared for with mown lawns and wooden benches. Bowes was a pleasant enough village lacking in only one major facility – a tearoom. Whether there ever was is another matter, but I had formed a picture in my mind of a haven with linen tablecloths and net curtaining and an elderly waitress engaging me in conversation while I decided which cake to have with my tea. I would have rested for thirty minutes with my silver teapot and hot-water jug and the choice of cakes having been presented to me on a three-tier silver cake stand. I would, instead, have to make do with the last drink of plastic-flavoured water from my bottle, the final piece of cake that I had carried with me for nearly three days and by now was little more than a collection of crumbs, and of course the customary cigarette.

The A66 is one of the wild roads that crosses the Pennines and, until the mid-1980s, Bowes used to suffer it passing through the village's heart on its way from Darlington to Appleby. I had seen the traffic from the south side of the Greta valley as I had been forced to prevaricate by the meanderings of the road around Gilmonby Moor. There were a great many articulated trailered lorries thundering along it and in Bowes itself it must have become a nightmare to negotiate its crossing before the bypass was completed. I had also noticed from the map that Dr Beeching had plied his trade here also for winding its way up the valley serving Barnard Castle to Kirkby Stephen was the course of a yet another dismantled railway. It would ultimately have made a connection with the Settle–Carlisle railway at a point that I would come very close to on my southerly return in a few days. The road-improvement scheme for bypassing Bowes had had the cheek to rub salt into the wound and use the course of the defunct railway line for part of its route to the north of the village. All that existed now of Bowes' past active life was a main street that was too wide for its status and a petrol station long since closed down, presumably through lack of business. The only reminders of the site's former use was the sign 'Sadler' petrol and the raised kerbing which had acted as bases for the petrol pumps – these had simply been left as sad remnants of busier times. The only commercial outlet was the village shop, which doubled as the post office and was a hive of activity when I had reason to call in as I left the village. There are some towns that thrive on the good fortune of a bypass where the lifeblood returns to the centre and the sense of community is restored by the removal of the sheer weight of unwelcome traffic. There are other places, though, where an impression is gained of the settlement either having died or dying through commercial starvation with the reduction in passing trade, but it is too late when the bypass is in place. Whether Bowes is dying or is already dead I cannot say, for this was my first encounter, but I couldn't help feel sadness for a place that seemed to have enjoyed happier times even though they would undoubtedly have been busier. It had lost its railway and the road now skirting around its northern edge had left it isolated and almost frozen still in time. I decided that it was the ghosts left behind by the old A66 that gave this impression – perhaps if the road were narrowed or part pedestrianized then its impact on an outsider's view like myself would be lessened. The old petrol station should be removed and, on a personal note, a nice little tearoom would make a splendid addition…

My impromptu picnic was taken on one of the pristine wooden benches on the south wall of the castle. Sheltered from the breeze, where I had sat proved to be a most obliging suntrap that left me in no hurry to move on again. I was joined by another lone walker who, during our ensuing conversation, told me that he was part way through the Pennine Way and was camping just along the road from Bowes. He had started out with a companion who had retired after three days because the walk had proved more arduous than he had bargained for. The remaining walker had now to carry an oversized tent and all the provisions that he needed, many of which are of the same size regardless of whether there were one or two in the party. His was a salutary tale that illustrated the vagaries of walking with others – they can let you down. To cap all this, he also mentioned that he was sixty-odd, but was making the trip very slowly. I was suitably, quietly impressed and wondered whether in another twenty years I might be able to entertain attempting the two hundred and seventy miles of Pennine Way, however slowly. I looked at my cigarette thoughtfully.

I had sat down at three o'clock, and after resting and chatting and calling at the post office I was heading back down Bowes' main street at quarter to four. There was a further six miles to cover until I reached my destination and the break had done nothing for my feet or legs which had begun to seize up and were crying out for a bath. As I walked down the main street I was confronted by a decidedly mangy looking dog of undoubtedly questionable temperament, which, as I neared it, began reversing while holding its steady gaze on me. Whether it was the sight of a dog reversing or whether it was the mean look in its eye I'm not sure, but I thought it best to cross over as casually as possible and hope that it was guarding only one side of the road. I glanced sidelong as I passed and was relieved to see the animal sidle off in the other direction. Perhaps it was the rare sight of passing trade that had alarmed the creature.

Retracing my hobbling steps back to the road island at the east end of Bowes, I turned left and found my way through the maze of the new road layout to the unclassified road to Cotherstone.

Refreshed, warm and on schedule, I did not need to hurry these last few miles. My accommodation was all booked ahead and I had warned my hosts that I might not arrive until early evening. The planning for my journey had extended to ensuring that I had lodgings for each night and I could not imagine setting off on such a trek without first having made provision for overnight stops. It is apparent from Wainwright's commentary that, for all his liking for planning, he had not the first idea where he would bed down for the night. He had set himself loose goals for each day and for the third day his aim was to reach Middleton-in-Teesdale, a walk of twenty-five miles in the day, but he fell short of his target and reached only Romaldkirk. Upon arrival in a village at dusk the impression is given that he would knock almost at the first door he came to and ask for lodgings for the night and was admitted by more than one host. Equally he would, if he desired a cup of tea or a meal, knock at a door and inquire as to the possibility of food and drink. I suspected that his reference to having had tea in a cold parlour of a house by the castle at Bowes probably was as a result of simply asking a private homeowner for refreshment. I could not imagine invading the privacy of a complete stranger and making such a request and then trying to agree some form of reimbursement for their trouble. Has society changed so much or are Wainwright's references to these occurrences prone to artistic license and, in truth, omit to include the fact that there were plenty of signs advertising teas and sticky buns.

The road from Bowes to Cotherstone provides a relatively direct course laid to a gentle arc as it first ascends and then descends the slopes of Cotherstone Moor toward the village itself. The four miles that lie between Bowes and my destination, which Wainwright had so quickly decided was rather pleased with itself and bore the hallmark of prosperity, was mildly frustrating inasmuch as the immediate scenery had little to commend it. I was in an unexciting undulating countryside of grazing cattle and arable crops with no particular points of interest. The saving grace was, at least, that any residue of the earlier haze had now completely cleared and I was able to see behind me the dark moors that had been my companions as I had passed from Swaledale and over Tan Hill and on into this new country. It was altogether gentler, although even here there were a number of short, sharp descents and ascents in traversing the valleys of two or three streams that tested already tired legs and feet and made these four miles seem much longer than their actual distance. Looking to the north I could begin to see the outline of much higher lands and I knew that I would be invited to make their acquaintance tomorrow when I would return to having to climb out of two dales – Teesdale and Weardale.

For now I talked quietly to my shadow who, for the most part, walked along the wall to my right. Where there was no wall and only fencing he proceeded in the fields. From his crooked gait he appeared rather tired and would be glad for the chance to immerse his exhausted body in a relaxing bath. I hardly dared break the news that if my memory served me correctly this night's billet was yet another that had only a shower room. Deciding that conversation with this lengthening companion was unreasonably one-sided, I looked down and inquired of my feet as to how they were coping. I had some sympathy for their plight for I had been forced into having to buy a new pair of boots not many weeks earlier. Not enough weeks really to have allowed them to become comfortable and reliable, but I had been given no option as my previous pair had, without warning, taken to rubbing my heels raw and had generated the largest blood blister that I had ever seen. Notwithstanding the fact that they were now grumbling, they were getting used to one another and I was confident of their compatibility.

It was probably a reflection of the scenery that I had taken to mental wandering rather than being fully engaged with my environment. I do not mean to belittle Cotherstone Moor, and perhaps my senses had been dulled by my exertions, but I was looking forward to leaving this short stretch behind and arriving at Cotherstone to see the place for myself. There were two principal reasons for my eager anticipation. The first was to be able to consider Wainwright's views, and the second was that I had somewhere in a box (yet to be put on those shelves that are still not built) an old lantern slide of the village. It was a view from the turn of the century and I always find it fascinating to compare these old scenes with the present day to see the marks that have been left by the intervening years. It is a personal opinion that it is rare indeed to compare old and new and consider the changes to be an improvement. Whether it be over-development, litter, huge numbers of cars or the ugly intrusion of street furniture, there is always something more aesthetically pleasing about the past's simple life depicted in the old image.

There are a few times when the modern morphology of a village or town manages to retain a timeless quality, yet is clearly a living community without the feel of being museum-like. As I passed the church at Cotherstone and came to the green that I recognised from my old slide, so I knew that this delightful village had succeeded in juxtaposing modern life with its rural village roots. I could live here, I thought immediately, as I strolled slowly down the green to the little bridge over the beck. I could live here, but I suspected the desire for residence was also felt by many executive types, which could only result in spiralling property prices. I don't recall seeing an estate agent within the village, but had there been one I would not have dared look. I suspected that to live in this idyll would not extend to those who, like me, found it imperative to look at the price tag while shopping. Nevertheless I could imagine, for looking is still free. It is also plain to see why Wainwright had made his somewhat disparaging remarks about the place and the same basis for his views still exist today. It may be a fact that its church could grace the finest avenue of a city; it may be a fact that there are few guest houses; it might even be true that there is a curtain-twitching mentality (now usually more positively referred to as neighbourhood watch. It is however perfectly justifiable that the village should be pleased with itself and it is a fact that there is a sense of prosperity and that the houses are of good appearance. It is also a fact that is as plain as a pikestaff to see that Wainwright was as jealous as hell of the village. The heaviest piece of luggage being carried by my predecessor as he looked at Cotherstone was the bloody great chip on his shoulder.

The Wainwright family lived in terraced housing with severely limited facilities in the urban streets of Blackburn. The streets of the Lancashire town were worlds away from the serene setting that he had now found himself in. His childhood home had long since been demolished to make way for modern development, but it is a fair bet that it would have been a thoroughly more lowly abode when compared with the fine residences with which he was confronted in this quiet suburbia. In his narrative he had made no reference to these stark contrasts and his scathing attack suggests that something peculiar to Cotherstone jaundiced his view of the village. He would surely not have expected the doors of this sleepy community to be flung open in welcome – they had not been at any of the other settlements that he visited on his Pennine journey. His jaunts to the Lake District had already been frequent by 1938, so it must be assumed that he was well familiar with idyllic hamlets and I could well imagine that the local residents there would keep themselves to themselves.

In coming to his defence, it may be that he had been looking forward to finding accommodation but, denied, had to press on a further two miles to try his luck at the next village up the dale, Romaldkirk. That may have partially coloured his attitude, but does not explain why his apparent view of Teesdale as a whole was one generally of disdain. I was to find that his bemoaning of the dale had not been forgotten and I did not succeed in finding many with a half-decent word to say about him, apart from, that is, an elderly gentleman who I happened upon as I walked through Cotherstone, for as we passed the time of day, I explained my mission, and he said that he knew of Wainwright and spoke kindly of him having seen him on television. He was the only one that I encountered in Teesdale who did not pour scorn upon the words written by the man who had come here sixty years before me. It is rather likely, I now think, that my elderly friend had not read the Wainwright account. Either that or perhaps he too was a visitor.

Leaving Cotherstone at five o'clock I would also have to carry on the further two miles to Romaldkirk, and these two miles seemed longer than the four I had just completed. I was forced to walk at the edge of an uncomfortably busy road that snaked and dipped for the full two miles. I was forced to cross over and back interminably to keep to the side where the traffic risk would be least and, although there was a verge, it was of long grass with hidden ankle-twisting pits and hollows. These two miles must have been nearer to three with the necessary serpentine route that inhibited my progress. After an eternity I spied habitation and, as luck would have it, the first dwelling was 'Millriggs' and my temporary home sweet home as far I was concerned. Mrs Wickham welcomed me graciously and showed me to my own private annex with small living room, television and separate bedroom with twin beds and, I noted glumly, a shower room. My memory of my booking had been correct and for the third night my hopes for a bath were dashed.

Mrs Wickham hurried away to make a pot of tea while I dumped my bags unceremoniously about the bedroom and checked the directions for the operation of the shower. I always make sure that I can operate the shower before I get in – spectacle wearers will understand my reasoning. When you are part-showered and lathered with soap the last thing you are able to do in the event of the water suddenly becoming either freezing or scalding is read the dials. After retiring from the cubicle in extreme haste, you are left standing on the bathroom floor dripping soap, probably slipping on the tiles and swearing while desperately trying to find your glasses. Having digested the dial details I looked around the door into my living room and there was my teapot, hot-water jug and piece of cake with cheese. The only item missing from my earlier absent tearoom was the three-tier cake stand. I fairly swilled the tea and ravaged the cake and was showering only a brief few minutes later for every time my legs ceased their movement their complaining became more pronounced when asked to start working again.

Showered and refreshed, I was dressed to hit the bright lights of town by seven o'clock. My planning for evenings had also been more thoroughly thought out than Wainwright's. I had no intention of wearing the same clothes for the evening that I had worn for the day's exertions – I had brought a light-weight pair of walking trousers and deck shoes that could be packed in very little space. Sartorial elegance it was not, but at least other customers would not be able to smell me even before I entered the pub.

Romaldkirk, by the way, has no bright lights. In fact, it has no lights at all and, as I walked the half-mile to its centre, I knew I would be glad of the torch that I had taken with me for it would be dark when I made my way back to Millriggs. My destination was the Kirk Inn where Wainwright had stayed having decided that he would not be able to afford the Rose & Crown. It was a fair bet: looking at the Rose & Crown, they would not have wanted him. Of the two pubs the Kirk Inn still looked as though it were the poor relation of the other, but the fact that it was still there at all would probably have been of surprise to Wainwright. He had found lodging at the pub and was the only customer all evening in the deathly quiet of the bar, with the only activity interrupting the silence being the ticking of a large clock. I had been told that Denis was now the owner of the Kirk Inn, so when I entered to find a young girl was serving I kept half an eye on the small gathering at the bar in the hope that I would glean which of these was Denis. It was not long before another customer entered to be greeted by a man who was clearly the Denis I was looking for from the far end of the group. I felt strangely odd conducting my investigative questioning about former owners along the full length of the bar, but it was Denis' night off and he was not about to engage in conversation with a complete stranger about some issue that was sixty years old. He was generally affable enough and I enjoyed a second pint before discovering that not only was he the owner but he was also the chef, which meant that on a Tuesday night there was to be no food. During our brief discussion he outlined the history of the pub and how it was very likely the oldest building in Romaldkirk, so it was unfair of Wainwright to say that it averted its shy face from the gaze of other village buildings. The church and Kirk Inn overlooked the lower of the two village greens and, presumably, the village subsequently developed up the hill away from these two earliest of sanctuaries.

Little light was cast both on me and my inquiries as I left the pub at half past seven to move a hundred yards up the road to the Rose & Crown where I had been told I would find an excellent but expensive repast. Both proved correct as I revisited a cuisine that was rather too rich for my common pallet. I did manage to find on the menu omelette with chips, which, when it arrived, was a splendidly generous offering that served to leave me replete to the point where even the usual attractiveness of apple pie was insufficient for me to be tempted. The only shadow on this otherwise enjoyable evening was the company: I had had no choice where to sit and had landed next to Mr Crushingly Boring Old Fart who loved nothing better than the sound of his own voice save, perhaps, for yet another gin and tonic. He was entertaining a group of four terribly good friends who were all rather like him, only not quite so old, not quite so loud and not quite so drunk. Time would, I suspected, change all that, some elements quicker than others so that in another half-hour the only difference would be the age between them. They were very obviously huntin', shootin', fishin' types who, by instances I have witnessed from time to time, appear to have a great propensity for liking nothing better than the sound of their own voices.

I did not tarry at the Rose & Crown. I would not have been able to stay long in any case, but the presence of these men for whom coarse fishing had a whole different meaning did curtail my desire to have another drink. I would have a cup of tea instead, I decided, while poring over my maps, my notes and my route of twenty-three miles for the following day. The next day's walk was to be the longest of the eleven and I would feel if I could achieve my goal of Blanchland then the remainder of my excursion would be child's play. I could not pretend however, as I lay on the bed, that I was finding the distances easy and my last conscious thought of the day was that I had walked for three days and still had over a week to walk with no rest day. I could not simply assume that I was going to attain my goal, regardless of however clear and definable it may be. The fact remained that if Wainwright was a fitter man than I then I might well have to accept failure and I was not at all sure how I would cope with that for I would have failed in what I had seen as destiny.

Chapter 4

Romaldkirk to Blanchland

My first action of this new day was to find out whether I was to be fortunate in seeing a continuation of the most agreeable weather that I had been blessed with for the majority of the previous three days. Although yesterday had started overcast, it had ended with an orange ball sinking slowly into a clear western sky. Inspection of how the elements were likely to treat me was not an entirely straightforward exercise principally because I had again woken early and I could see through the crack in the curtains that any true hint of daylight was yet to be heralded. It was also made all the more problematic by the fact that while my brain wanted to get out of bed and cross to the window, my legs most certainly did not. This was the first time that these limbs had been rebellious before the day had even begun and gave me not a little cause for concern. I did finally manage to swing them out from under the duvet, bend them and then slowly sit upright on the side of the bed. All that remained now was to see if I could stand on them, which was hastened by some vigorous massaging of the calf and thigh muscles. They were going to have to be coaxed into their pivotal role of carrying me to my destination 23 miles away in Northumberland. During my wait for them to become more amenable to movement, I rolled a cigarette which I would use as reinforcement of my desire to get to the window. Now not only did my brain want to see the new day but so did my lungs; the legs, outnumbered, acceded to my insistence that they transport me the 3 yards across the room to draw back the floral curtains, giving a fine vista over the valley toward Eggleston.

The kettle boiled for my morning cup of tea as I looked out of the window at a sky that showed cloud cover but with a promise of improvement. The first signs of the rising sun softly illuminated the undersides of the clouds so that they glowed a gentle shade of magnolia tinged with a pink hue. The forecast I had seen the evening before was optimistic that a fine day would follow a cloudy start, and I hoped that I might be able to complete the stiff climb to Swinhope Head and get the first eleven miles under my belt ahead of any increase in temperature. A mug of tea with a cigarette out of an open window was becoming par for the course, but at least here, unlike either Buckden or Muker, I was marginally more comfortable for I could sit at the sliding sash window observing the day's dawning.

As I sat I completed my study of the way that lay ahead of me and I read again the relevant chapter of Wainwright's account of his fourth day. So far on my travels fortune had smiled on me for I had only donned any form of jumper to venture out in the evenings. He, on the other hand, had been drenched on his third day and had left Romaldkirk in clothes that were still damp from their previous day's soaking. I have mentioned his penchant for travelling light and how, on his journeys, he carried as little as was absolutely possible. On this Pennine trek he only had the clothes he walked in, five maps covering the route, a variety of pills and potions for the relief of his ailment, drawing equipment and one or two items for maintaining some sort of semblance of personal hygiene. Perhaps even now he would be looking down on me laughing loudly as I thought about packing the rucksack again with the great variety of things that he might well have considered trivial. I had no wish to burden myself with unnecessary weight and carried with me only those items that I believed would be essential for my comfort and safety.

Although my journey was largely within earshot of civilisation throughout its length, it was no excuse to omit equipment that catered for a worst case scenario. I include in this list a whistle, a torch, a bivouac bag, a compass and a Swiss army knife. I had given Sue precise details of where I should be each day and where I would be staying each evening. I carried sun cream, lip protector, micropore tape and blister patches. I have already referred to the GPS and in addition I carried a dictaphone, two cameras and films and spare batteries for all. I had with me a whole plethora of resealable plastic bags, some toilet roll, a bag to keep wet laundry separate from dry clothes, and a drinks bottle. These were in addition to toothbrush, razor and sachets of soap and shampoo. These items all added some weight to my pack but they all played their part in helping to make each day as safe and as comfortable as possible. If a modern-day fell rescue team were to be called out to a walker prepared as poorly as Wainwright admitted to having been, then as well as being remembered for his total lack of preparation, he would also be seriously reprimanded by the emergency services. The mountains of the Lake District command respect from those who enter their domain and to enter without a change of clothes may have been acceptable to Wainwright in 1938 but in 1998 it is considered lunacy to venture among them with such scant regard for safety. It is selfish in the extreme for it diminishes the ability of the walker to fend for himself in the event of an emergency. Sue and I had once walked on a snow-covered winter's day to Sergeant Man above the Langdales when, without warning, Sue fell through a drift and into a stream below. We had with us extra clothing and she was able to keep warm and we returned back down to the valley floor without incident. Had we been so ill prepared the consequences might, with luck, have been restricted to only a severe chill or equally she may have suffered exposure. As much as I respect Wainwright for his spirit and his character, it is only a fool that fools about in the high places, especially when walking alone. If he were to be looking down and laughing I like to think he would have agreed that it was I who was having the last laugh.

Among my items of clothes I included sunglasses and sun hat, both of which had been of extreme use on the first two days as I had walked in the baking sun. We might joke about sunburn or blisters but they can both stop a walker dead in his tracks if either is sufficiently severe. I admit that the spare bootlaces may have been slightly overdoing things but, nevertheless, when distances such as those demanded on this journey are involved, and shops few and far between, details like these are ignored at a walker's peril. My other belongings extended to a waterproof jacket and overtrousers, thermal underwear and clothes for the evenings. I was ready for any and all eventualities and I would have it no other way. In some ways I was hoping to make use of all that I had with me with the natural exception of the waterproofs, the whistle and the bivouac bag. The final thing that I carried was spare tobacco and rolling papers – these being ensconced deep in the driest place I could find.

Mrs Wickham had been very accommodating in my request for an early breakfast at half past seven in order that I might be on my way by half past eight, the prompt start being necessary due to the length of the day's walk. The majority of the twenty-three miles would be either on macadam or on roadside verges and I knew that my natural pace would cover three miles an hour over such surfaces on level. This approximated to eight hours of actual walking which, when added to a slower speed when proceeding uphill and allowing for rest stops, would stretch considerably. There were three ascents to be made during the day totalling about six miles of relatively steep climbing that would add an hour to my journey time. In addition to this, stops for breaks and lunch might increase the time by a further hour, so I had to allow ten hours, therefore setting my mental schedule for arrival at half past six at Blanchland.

Before I could entertain any thoughts of breakfast, I had concluded that a morning shower might help to ease the leg muscles. I walked to the shower as though I were a cross between Kenneth Moore as Douglas Bader and a cowboy who had just spent all day in the saddle and stepped awkwardly over the 3-inch-high sill into the shower cubicle. What I really needed was a relaxing bath and, upon looking at my accommodation confirmation details (yes, I'd brought these with me as well), I noticed that my lodgings at Blanchland included a bath. Oh, what joy for I could at least look forward in gleeful anticipation to sliding my tired body into a deep, hot bath. But that was ten hours hence and for now the shower would have to work a miracle. Partly through having the shower and mainly, I expect, through straightforward use, my legs began to move more freely and I walked easily into the nicely appointed dining room with its Welsh dresser and cottage furnishings that were very in keeping with the house. On the table lay a fine choice of cereals and that silver teapot again which had been so appreciated the previous evening. I sat down and looked out from the window onto a scene of quiet pastoral serenity and thought it difficult to imagine that such a valley had once been a hive of activity in the lead mining industry

Romaldkirk, I discovered, was one of the few places in the dale that had its roots in agriculture rather than the dark and dirty industry that had still blighted the valley when Wainwright had visited. I was looking forward to seeing how the intervening sixty years had treated Teesdale for its industrial heart had been removed and I wondered whether the remnants of this bygone era were still evident as bodies on a battlefield. I wondered also whether the fantastic shapes fashioned by industry, to which Wainwright had referred, would still be present, albeit perhaps now below a recently laid superficial veneer. I wondered whether anything about the valley might retrospectively change Wainwright's view of the ruination of this dale. More immediately than these I wondered whether Mrs Wickham might notice if I helped myself to another bowl of crunchy nut corn-flakes.

Over a good and hearty breakfast we talked of the dale and of Wainwright's earlier visit. My heart sank a little as Mrs Wickham told me of two walkers who had visited her while following what she described as Wainwright's route. I felt as though someone had got here before me, that my virgin was no longer pure and I feared that my growing desire to convert my journey into a long-distance walk would be thwarted by someone else's earlier endeavour. I knew that it must be too good to be true that I was to be the first and only one who had re-traced his steps and I could sense my grand plan was being dashed upon the rocks. Mrs Wickham went on to explain that the two gentlemen had, she re-called, stayed with her some years earlier and had appeared, by her description, to be only very loosely following the route. I settled myself with the thought that any fruits of their labours would surely have been forthcoming by now and that, in any case, their mission had clearly not been as mine was. I was becoming really rather obsessive about this journey and saw it more and more as a posses-sion that was mine and that I alone had the authority to do with it as I pleased. Otherwise I could not comprehend my quiet resentment at the Tan Hill Inn and my feeling of my way having been besmirched by the two earlier walkers to whom Mrs Wickham had referred.

I told my host of my profitless inquiries as to the previous owners of the Kirk Inn. I had been intrigued from first reading his account of his evening at the inn by the woman who ran the pub when Wainwright had stayed. He had been filled with a feeling of desperation and that the woman and her two daughters had found themselves clearly in deep poverty and that with their wealth their cheer had evaporated too. He may have been correct as to the lack of cheer in the household for the landlady, Mrs Walker, who lived with her two daughters, Beryl and Jean, had been widowed just prior to Wainwright's visit. I was reliably informed that she was popular in the village and had something of a sharp wit, for when she was once asked by a rather brash holidaymaker as to whether there were any village idiots, her reply was 'Only those that come in the summer.' I rather think that if she were alive today she might have regretted not saying something equally cutting to Wainwright as retaliation for his remarks. Springing to his defence again I can only assume that he did not appreciate how recent Mrs Walker's loss had been. As to poverty, he was again incorrect for the Walkers had moved to Romaldkirk after his retirement from the police force in Derbyshire and his widow would have received a good pension. My trusty information extended as far as the knowledge that the younger daughter Jean, as a girl, had been the proud owner of a bicycle, which was more than many families could afford at the time.

Much of Wainwright's commentary while within the hills of Teesdale was derogatory, and in the case of the Kirk Inn was perhaps more than a little unsympathetic. His conclusion for the apparent shunning of the pub was that it must have been as a result of some village scandal and this conclusion appears to have been drawn with no evidence other than the inn was quiet the night he was there. It was probably fortunate that his comments were not made public for nearly fifty years for I'm sure that he would have been on the wrong end of a libel action. The Kirk Inn on my visit had been an entirely different place with a fine choice of real ales and the unmistakable noisy atmosphere of a serious drinkers' pub where the conversation is of beer and brewing and brewers. By serious drinkers I do not mean drinkers who consume serious quantities, but that the quantities that they do consume are done so very seriously and reverently and then only after careful inspection of the head and clarity of the brew. I had left the inn at half past seven just as Wainwright would have been arriving, and as I did so I left a fair number of men at the bar inspecting heads and clarity. It was only afterwards that I pondered as to why it is that a great percentage of these serious drinkers wear long, straggly beards with anoraks and corduroy trousers, looking as though they belong to an earlier decade. A fair number of them also smoke pipes, although I assume this to be a safety measure to avoid setting fire to the long, straggly beard while lighting a cigarette. Please don't misunderstand me; I enjoy a beer, particularly after a day's walking, but I would have difficulty getting into heated discussion as to whether it was 'hoppy' or too bright – it is there to be drunk and not talked about. Enough of the Kirk Inn except to say that I was pleased it was still there. Long may Denis hold station at the bar and thank you for the decent pint of beer. I thought that the head was especially creamy and adhered to the side of the glass and the clarity … well, nothing could be improved, but perhaps the body was just a little yeasty with the…

I passed by the few dwellings on the main road through the village only a few minutes after setting out at half past eight as planned and I looked down the green to the Kirk Inn and the church opposite. Apart from these, and the Rose & Crown, Romaldkirk could boast little else by way of amenities. In the bygone days of Wainwright's stay there had been a shop and post office with black-smith, policeman and district nurse but these are all now but memories for the older folk in the village as they are in so many other places. The trains used to draw up at the railway station but the line was long since dismantled and the station converted to a dwelling house. The only traffic using the line now was pedestrian, as it had been renovated to form the Teesdale Railway Walk. All these services had gone with the remaining inhabitants undoubtedly having to rely on private car ownership to get them anywhere at all. Nearer to my course was the Rose & Crown from where, as I passed, exited the same people that I had seen yesterday in the four-wheelers with the personalised plates. It had also been some of their number that had caused my curtailment of the evening in the bar with their loud 'hooray bloody Henry' attitude and their silver-spoon up-bringing being so crudely evident as they guffawed their rude way through the evening. This is usually done with little or no consideration for others and is always associated with an expectancy that preferential service will be lavished upon them with a total disregard to the niceties of informal gentlemanly waiting one's turn at the bar. I would not wish to give an impression that I do not care for such people – believe me I want it to be abundantly clear that I loathe and detest the ill-mannered oafs, never mind giving impressions. So as not to casti-gate myself from a whole sector of society, I am sure that it is, as ever, the minority that tarnish the reputation of the majority and that there are some aw-fully nice upper-class Johnnies – it's just that I await making their acquaintance.

It is so often the case that our perceptions are formed from views of the mi-nority and usually a false image is established. It is the views of others that form our own perceptions of the vast majority – we are not able to experience all things at first hand and a reliance is placed on third parties to advise us. Ideally we would be so advised impartially, but in most instances we are not and our own views are based only on the activity of the few with the silent majority be-ing considered responsible for their actions. There are many examples of this, but one of the more obvious is that a considerable percentage of football fans are seen as half-crazed delinquents who should have been drowned at birth. This belief is quite simply a response to the bombardment from the press who, each week, will find seek out crowd trouble to create dramatic headlines for they know well that such headlines will boost sales. Or there may be a per-ceived belief that the majority of Germans have returned to neo-Nazi indoctrination. The belief is engendered by the press for they know that their readers like nothing better than to sit in judgment over this type of international reportage, where they can pass sentence to quell their own indignant disquiet; in other words 'if they did that I'd', and so on. Or there have been the unnerving reports creating the sensation that if an English person were to visit Scotland it would be quite likely that he or she would be the subject of discrimination or racial abuse. In reality, while there may have been instances where this has happened, the perception is vastly inflated by the press in the name of so-called 'public interest' stories to sell more newspapers. The fact is that in all cases it is the minuscule minorities who have tarred others with the same brush. If we believed all we read and heard we would all be too nervous to venture out of our front doors. I was reminded of my mother's sense of contentment when she knew that I was, at least, armed with my monopod for the battle that would surely follow as I encountered a Scottish neo-Nazi football fan on some lonely moor.

I could not imagine being confronted by such a fellow as I left Romaldkirk behind and followed the road for the four miles to Middleton-in-Teesdale and then the further three miles to Newbiggin. A total of seven miles of road walking were required of me before I would be able to escape to the unclassified gated byway over Swinhope Head and down to Westgate in Weardale. For these first seven miles it was once more the purist in me that led the way and I could not recommend that others follow for the road is busy with cars and lorries. It is the principal road from Teesdale over to Cumbria, it provides the tourists with their route to High Force and it serves the remaining quarrying activity further up the dale with large and dusty lorries thundering past at all too frequent intervals. I came to realise that these lorries transporting the quarried material were the only physical link with the past that was still active for all other major industry within the dale had died out when the railway finally closed in 1964 after ninety-six years' service. I was barely a mile out of Romaldkirk when I first noticed below me, to the right of the road, large earth mounds that were too uniform in shape to be anything other than spoil heaps. Near them lay the evidence of derelict long-forgotten buildings and I was disappointed that a greater effort had not been made to rid the landscape of these blemishes. Removal of the skeletal remains would not take long and would surely reduce the visual impact of their reminder of a heritage that is probably best forgotten for this residual dross is of no beauty or aesthetic quality. To the left of the road, and running more or less parallel to it, lay the course of the railway that now provided what must be a pleasant track from Romaldkirk to just short of Middleton. The road and rail links followed a similar line on the lower slopes of the south side of the valley and it seemed hard to imagine the comings and goings of locomotives as they busied themselves with their cargoes of ore for smelting.

The next settlement that I came upon was Mickleton, a long strip-like village that must have measured a full mile in length but felt as though its depth on either side only extended to one house, as if it were some type of façade for a film location of a wild west town. For all its unusual morphology, Mickleton was not uninviting and, to my surprise, did not show any unsightly evidence of an industrial past. I think I was expecting to see disused and rotting buildings scattered among grubby rows of terraced workers' cottages, but if they were there they remained well hidden and the houses lined either side of the main street (really the only street) to watch me as I passed. They and their occupants would more than likely have been suspicious of incomers like me and would eye me very carefully for there was a time when one came much earlier then went away and made severe criticism of their home. I had not walked far but my impression of the dale was that any evidence of an association with a dark and dirty past had been erased so effectively that, had I not known of my predecessor's comments, I would have seen a largely agrarian historical development.

My pace had quickened very nicely from the stumbling buffoon who had had difficulty coping with negotiating the shower tray sill a couple of hours earlier and Mickleton was soon lying in my wake. Once back in the rhythm my legs were happy to propel me along with good speed, which suited me for there was little to be gained by dallying where my route was so predominantly macadam road surface. The sooner I journeyed these first seven miles the better and the more time I would have to savour the landscape beyond when I would be back in the more wild places. Only a little way outside the village and I came to a five-arched viaduct across the River Lune, a tributary that would soon enter the Tees on the opposite side of the valley floor. How strange it was that when

Wainwright had passed this way he would have viewed this structure as an intruder into the dale, detracting from its beauty and helping corroborate his general criticisms. Now these railway remains are viewed as monuments to our past and as majestic reminders of our heritage as a leading industrial nation. Britain had led the way in so many things for so many years and by the 1940s Teesdale was a pioneer town of damage caused to its environment through pollution. I knew from reading the evening before that in 1867, a year before the railway opened, salmon caught in the Tees numbered 100,000 but by the mid-1940s they had all left the river due to pollutants. It is only more recent environmental that works have succeeded in seeing the return of some stocks.

Some little way beyond the viaduct, still having seen little sign of permanent environmental damage, I was beginning to think that Wainwright's belittlement of the dale must have been influenced by the fact that he had still been damp from the previous day – this and the fact that as he approached Middleton the rain was falling again had presumably soured his mood. Then about half a mile before Middleton my admiration for the dale and its accomplishments in repairing man's earlier damage dissipated as I came upon the small but ugly 'Lindon' industrial estate, which had a distinct air of not having been quite finished. It was as if some tenants had taken up occupation but the remainder of the site had been left on a Friday night and the workers had never returned. By way of rubbing salt into this visual wound, directly adjacent to this eyesore was the household tip with its skips and overflowing rubbish. Across the road from these was the decimation left by an old disused quarry. Here were the fantastic shapes in the land to which Wainwright had referred and here were the remnants of a tainted landscape that even time could not ameliorate. If the valley bore any resemblance to this sixty years ago, it was easy to see why he had passed out of Teesdale a sadder man than when he had entered it. Incredibly, in amongst this squalor and demonstration of and monument to man's powers to destroy beauty was a caravan site with a selection of both static and mobile homes. I wondered whether the mobile vans were simply over-wintered here for surely no one would choose to holiday here, sandwiched between the household tip and the somewhat rundown industrial estate.

Having concurred with Wainwright's more general views, it is only fair to state that, by and large, Teesdale has tried very hard to make amends for its previous ruinous life. Its reincarnation has been almost wholly successful and if he were to walk this way again, I am sure Wainwright would feel that the time was right to compose that poem to High Force which, he had feared, could never be written. The mineral railway above Middleton has now been ripped up, the quarries closed, the scum disappeared from the river and the sense of countryside has returned after having spent so many years in the industrial wilderness. As I rounded the corner by the old station, joining the Pennine Way again for a few hundred yards, ahead of me across the valley lay Middleton-in-Teesdale. My reacquaintance with the Pennine Way was short and sweet for while it turns left just before the bridge to follow the south bank of the river, my way would take me on and up into the town.

Like Wainwright this was my first visit and, as I stood on the bridge across the river, I tried to imagine this place as he would have seen it but could not for I had seen views mainly of tranquillity and of man being largely in harmony with nature. In this I excuse the hiccup that is Lindon estate and the tip, but at least their visual misdemeanours were concentrated in one area. Apart from that the dale should be proud of its shrugging off of the past and welcoming the dawn of a more beautiful day. My reading about the dale had also informed me that its pollution was at its worst in the 1930s and '40s. Wainwright's visit coincided with a time when he would have seen it at its height with the mineral railway, the quarries, the scum on the river and the countryside being raped by mankind's demonic endeavours. I looked over the steel balustrading of the bridge and decided that, whatever else I did, I must pay testimony to Teesdale's beauty, albeit its beauty must be judged in contrast against its former state. I could not do this as a means of correcting Wainwright's earlier assassination of the dale for I am sure that he was right to be disappointed with the upshot of man's labours. It will never have the beauty, in my eyes, that Upper Wharfedale has, but it certainly merited closer inspection. Another time though, for I had to maintain progress on this occasion as it was a quarter to ten when I climbed the road into town from the bridge. It seemed rather inversely appropriate that in the town there is a permanent reminder of the mineral days – the employees of the London Lead Company erected a testimonial fountain in 1877 in appreciation of their employment. Perhaps the people of the valley ought now to erect one in recognition of all the efforts to return the dale to a place of beauty.

While in the town I met with yet another example of the contempt in which Wainwright is held hereabouts when I called in at a shop which I had noticed selling leaflets giving details for the area. The assistant recommended this walk and that walk and so on, and I advised her that I would have to walk up the road to Newbiggin before turning off on the Swinhope Head road. She, not unreasonably I suppose, seemed surprised at my choice of route so I explained my reasons and that I was following in the footsteps of Alfred Wainwright. Her only words in response were 'Oh, him'. With that the conversation ceased and I was left with the clearest of impressions that this lady knew of him and would certainly not be looking for a lifetime membership in the Wainwright Supporters' Club were there to be such a thing. I liked Middleton. It was an agreeable little town although when I call again I will do so without ever referring to my erstwhile walking companion, for even in death the very mention of his name appears to taint the locals' desire for continued conversation.

The road to Newbiggin comprised another three miles of walking and sharing of the way with larger dusty lorries, the majority of which seemed to be travelling laden down the dale. I saw very few returning empty to the quarry somewhere further up Teesdale. I had gradually ascended the northern side of the valley so that I was able to look between the trees at the river below calmly winding its snake-like route to and fro across the valley floor. Every so often I could make out the course of the abandoned railway that would have served the quarry below Crossthwaite Common. I could see also the paths to either side of the river and I wished, each time one of the large dusty lorries thundered by, that I had been on one of those more amenable routes. All I could do was to stride out and be relieved when, sooner or later, I would spy the small cluster of houses of Newbiggin. It seemed like an age that I had been walking when I finally arrived at the hamlet and looked for the road to the right which would lift me out of Teesdale and up to Swinhope Moor and then down into another dale that I not previously visited, Weardale.

Although Wainwright had not been a great lover of Teesdale, his opinion of Weardale had been even more damning, judging it to be a dreary and ugly place. I would try to avoid allowing his comments to influence my own impression for I had already borne witness to a valley that had much improved over the gap in time that had separated our visits. My preconception of the dale that I was now leaving behind had been formed by his description. I had been expecting a dour and sad valley with dour and sad people (although I exclude Cotherstone from this generalisation for at Cotherstone I had been not at all sure what to expect). What I had found was quite to the contrary, where the congenial dale folk resided proud of their valley and contemptuous of those who would pen a scathing critique as to its attractiveness. I had fallen into the trap of reading a report and forming an opinion based solely on its estimation. As with the newspaper coverage of the actions of the minorities influencing our perceived notions of the majorities, I had found that when given the opportunity of first-hand investigation, we very often find reality to be quite different. We discover that the majority of football fans really are quite sociable and don't roam the streets looking for the next fight. We discover, too, that the majority of Germans are indeed convivial and that they do not all hunt down their immigrant brethren. And, we discover that the majority of Scottish people are companionable folk who do not want to see the total alienation of all us from south of the border. The press will exaggerate any aspect of society that will enable them to run a headline to grab the reader's attention, closely followed by the reader's money. To the press good news is bad news and bad news is good news, and so we see these minority stories that arrest our attention, arouse our consternation and potentially assist in the development of rifts between differing sectors and cultures within society. I was hoping that my assessment was correct for I was about to venture into wild and lonely moorland – if I was to meet that Scottish neo-Nazi football fan, it would be in such a place.

Having found the road junction I proceeded to ascend steeply, and as I did, I was afforded a number of long-distance views from time to time back over Teesdale as I climbed the narrow gated byroad. With fine panoramas opening out behind me as I headed north, I concluded that Wainwright's High Force poem could most definitely be written. This quiet road progressed steadily over the moor and I was chased up the black strip of macadam by intermittent shafts of sunlight that spread across the valley below me as though they were a lady's fan. Their advance, although in my direction, was slow and they showed little serious effort in catching me. They would appear, disappear and then reappear, illuminating another part of the landscape. They were always behind; never did they light the way before me and their presence gave a strange luminescent and ethereal quality to the scenery.

Above Newbiggin as the road had begun to pull up the gradient on its four-mile winding journey to the watershed at a little over 600 metres above sea level, there had been yet more evidence that further testified to the area's industrial history. Decrepit shacks, tumbled-down buildings and scars in the face of the slopes of Hardberry Hill bore witness to earlier human activity that cared little for long-term consequences. These wounds were very old and had been inflicted at a time when man's capacity for injuring his environment was limited by the technology at his disposal. They were more the cuts and bruises of primitive mineral extraction as opposed to the full-blown major invasive surgery that had been allowed in the years following. Cuts and bruises will mend of their own volition given time and the skin will return to normal leaving only the slightest of scars that the ensuing inhabitants become accustomed to. Surgery, though, requires more than just time; it demands stitches to rejoin the open wound and expert and continued attention to ensure that the reparation process is progressing well. In and around the valley the wounds left by major surgery, which had been accelerated by the opening of the railway, had been attended by a plastic surgeon and the evidence of his work would diminish. The quarries

were different; they were as an amputee. Where the surgery had involved am-
putation the wounds of the stumps that remained would improve in time as they
weathered and perhaps their impact upon the patients would be lessened as they
became used to the restricted use of their limbs. At least here on the hillside the
slightly unreal contours produced by the more rudimentary implements left a
more genuine testament to the hard physical work undertaken by man's own
hand rather than of some monstrous machine.

My narrow way amongst the heather-clad and rounded hills soon had me
approaching the abandoned Flushiemere House that lay up a rough track off to
the right. As I neared the building it appeared to be in a reasonable state of repair
with the exception that the last owners had taken more with them than was
usual when moving house. Plentiful are the tales of sellers who have removed
light bulbs or garden plants. Indeed I had at one time heard of a case where all
electric fittings had been unscrewed and taken, but never had I seen anything to
match the removal from this lonely and isolated dwelling. With the masonry
and roof in an apparently fair condition, the only items missing (in addition to
any sort of boundary fencing or delineated garden) were every door and window. Following the road meant that I viewed the house from about 300 yards
but I could see that the masonry apertures had been left as neat as if the windows and doors had never been fitted. Ripe, I thought, for the do-it-yourself
enthusiast but getting the refuse collected might prove problematic. Flushiemere
House would be the last remnant of civilisation that Teesdale had to show me
and every now and then I would stop and look back and admire the rearward
view for on the way ahead lay just heather and reed and road. I would also
watch the increasing numbers of fan-like formations of sunlight playing over
the hills and valley and getting tantalisingly near to me now but still not quite
reaching me.

I had left Middleton at just after ten o'clock and had agreed with myself (I
have long since given up arguing for I find it as futile as arguing with a woman
– even if the argument is won you still feel as if you lost) that I would rest only
when I reached the top. In his account Wainwright wrote of entering Middleton

at half past ten so I had been content that my progress was satisfactory. I was watching the time for I had no desire to arrive at Blanchland as late in the evening as he had done, but I had made good progress as far as Newbiggin and was continuing in fine style along the four miles up to Swinhope Head. Nearing the crest I glanced at Wainwright's account as I walked and was surprised to read that he had rested at the watershed between Teesdale and Weardale at twenty minutes to one. He had caught me up as though I had been standing still for it was after half past twelve when I opened the gate at the very top of the shallow col and could look at the wide vistas both to the north and south. The way south still showed the playful sunbeams dancing over the dale, but the way north was altogether more threatening with darker overcast skies and a chilly breeze that had sprung from nowhere. I was lucky in that as I sat down, having not found that rock that Wainwright had rested upon, I did so in the dry while rolling a cigarette, which, eerily, I smoked at exactly the same time as he had done so many years before.

As I rested I became aware of that breeze; it seemed to be emanating from Weardale and for the first time in three and a half days, having walked 66 miles (one-third distance), I was forced into seeking the shelter of my jacket. I chose to rest for only as long as it took to smoke my cigarette, take a quick drink and eat one of the biscuits from my lunch ration as it was a cold wind of change that blew at me from this new valley. It appeared to blow from the north, although this may have been a localised affect caused by the topography of the surrounding hills and, if so, its influence should reduce, I thought, as I descended the north aspect of the next valley. The jacket that I had donned was no simple cape, as Wainwright described the article to be that he had worn – in 1998 there exists great technology in the artistry of jacket making and no longer do we just throw on some old cycling cape. There are specialist shops dedicated to nothing else other than supplying jackets and other waterproof clothing to walkers and climbers. There are still more specialist shops dedicated to only selling boots and footwear to walkers and climbers. The walking and climbing fraternity represents a huge market and if Wainwright were able to enter and inquire as to the price of their capes, he would receive two surprises. The first would be the choice offered, with double- or triple-layer protection taking into account its breathability and durability. The second would come as such a shock that a chair would be required whilst his ashen face regained its colour. It would be of such magnitude that it might well cause him to consider whether it might not be better to just get wet – the price. I had gone through a similarly steep learning curve when I purchased the jacket that I was now wearing, and I treated it with the extreme reverence its price tag demanded. If I was at an inn for a lunchtime break and a call of nature was required, the jacket would come with me for there was no way that I would leave it alone in a house full of strangers.

It was of some slight concern to me that my progress appeared to have slowed and that my feet were showing the first signs of aching, which would, undoubtedly, provoke them into becoming mutinous. I had walked eleven miles and still had a further 12 remaining as I set off down into the valley of the Swinhope Burn. I had assumed that I would have the stamina to attain my goal, but now that I could see across to the far hills, I felt tired and the hills looked a very long way off. Looking north at Swinhope Burn I could see the road stretched out before me, laid to long straight lines separated by very deliberate corners as it gradually descended into Weardale some four miles distant. The valley formed a long indentation into the southern flank of the dale with a very regular and steep-sided profile – so steep sided that the road had to twist and turn to negotiate the first half-mile. It was here that Wainwright had noticed there was a more direct route, which he struggled to find and when he did regretted it bitterly for it proved to be a boggy morass that clogged on his boots. His advice was to pass it by and follow the road, which I gratefully did.

I have already referred a great deal to the extensive road walking that was involved in retracing Wainwright's steps. In 1938 the Ordnance Survey had not introduced within their maps many of the paths and bridleways that we now take for granted. Local walkers would know of their existence, but there was no guidance for those unfamiliar with the area, so he would have no indication as to where it was possible to seek an alternative route to the metalled roads. It is also apparent from the story of his journey that in those pre-war days he came upon very few other road users, so the inability to avoid the roads would not be as consequential as now. Sixty years ago the minimal traffic levels would have resulted in the roads and byways being a joy to walk on, if a trifle hard on the feet. In 1998 they provide a very different means of progress for the walker – the sheer weight of vehicles renders them very frustrating with endless stepping aside and maintaining of a keen vigil to reduce the risk of the walk ending in the back of an ambulance. When Wainwright found his soggy and clinging shortcut the particular path was marked on the map as a black track. It still exists as a black dotted track rather than a public right of way. Apart from similar tracks he would have found nothing to keep him off the roads for public rights of way had not been brought into being and so, although in 1938 pedestrian routes existed, their inclusion on his maps was something for which he would have to wait. It was only after the Second World War that a commission was set up to ratify certain routes as rights of way for the public. So it was that the purist in me had a desire to retrace his precise route where I could establish it, but I knew that to do so would entail some periods of bothersome walking.

For all that though, the way up and over Swinhope Head was something entirely agreeable for I had seen but one car, which had been when I sat at the top and I had opened and closed the gate for him to pass, for which labour I had received a cheery wave and a hailed 'thank you' by way of acknowledgment. It is always most gratifying and payment enough to do a small service and to be rewarded in such a manner. The opposite is also true however: where a minor act of courtesy does not generate some polite reaction it creates extreme annoyance at the rudeness of the recipient of such civility. Something I had observed during my recent extensive road walking was that there existed widely different levels of response from the variety of road users I had encountered. On many occasions I was aware that to avoid a vehicle having to slow down it was necessary that I took steps to place myself, possibly in some discomfort, at the roadside in order that it might pass unhindered. If the roles were reversed in this scenario, I would indicate my thanks to the pedestrian for their gallant stepping aside; they would give a small wave back and both would be content that they had respected the other's right to use the road. I had been slightly saddened, although it had not been completely unexpected, that on the whole it is the younger driver, regardless of gender, who is far less disposed to indicate any form of appreciation. The older the driver seemingly the more generous the acknowledgment and, generally, the greater was the effort on their part to give a wide berth to my relatively precarious position half-buried in the hedgerow. There is, without any doubt, an increased propensity for aggression that is inversely proportionate to the age of the driver, and the meeting with the older driver is an unavoidable encounter whereas with the younger it is more of an avoidable confrontation. I wondered whether this had always been the case or was it that just that I was getting older and becoming less tolerant of the younger generation and therefore was more ready to face them and their selfishness. Or was it that it had been simply that the greater percentage of road users I had met had been young and therefore my recollection of these discourtesies was biased toward them for there had been more instances involving younger drivers. I had been aware of these balancing factors as I had walked, so I believed that I was sound in my conclusion that they share the road willingly with no one. They grow up in a world that increasingly recognises only success, and that for success there has to be victory and that for victory there has to be the vanquished. The dog-eat-dog survival of the fittest is stronger in the young for they have learned only how to win and have ignored any lessons of humility. The acceptance of market forces and profit being the motivation driving modern existence generates the unpleasant side effect of 'win at all costs' where there is no honour in being second. There is an expectancy rather than a hope of victory. The result is an increased lack of consideration for others and a decrease in the common courtesies of communal living. I spent some time struggling to remember whether I had ever viewed the world in such a way and I concluded that I had not for I had been taught, rather than expected to learn, that there was a code by which we should abide. The code was usually enforced by parents or teachers but its unwritten conduct appeared to have become faint and forgotten as I stepped out from yet another hawthorn bush at the roadside.

I am ready to accept that my thoughts were of sweeping generality and were based on only a small sample so that any firm conclusions might statistically be brought into question. Please be assured that I still live by the Bible teaching of doing unto others as they would do unto me, but more and more I seemed to be having to do it first. Faith must be placed in those who live by the unwritten code continuing to do so, for if they ignored its edicts society would surely accept behaviour at the basest of levels and would sink into the abyss where anarchy looms just around the next corner. I was left with the hope that perhaps, again, I had only witnessed the acts of the minority and that my judgment was flawed.

As I made my way down the valley north toward Weardale I came across the same vehicle on a number of occasions. It seemed to pause in every lay-by and would pass a few brief words with the driver as I walked by. With the exception of this and two other cars, I saw no traffic on my descent until I reached Westgate. I was pleased to be descending, although I knew that for every metre I dropped now I would have to make it up again on the other side of the valley ahead of me. For the time being though, I was using different sets of muscles and giving those that would carry me uphill a deserved rest. The only part of me that did not share the relief was my feet; they, if anything were having a harder time of it as I clomped down the slopes on the hard surface or, where I could, on the adjacent softer verge. Covering the ground quickly, I soon came to Swin-hope Head House where Wainwright had observed the laundry hanging to dry in the rain. There was no washing line as I passed and the house had a deathly quiet air about it – a feeling there had been no recent signs of life and a look as though it had remained empty since he had been this way. This was the house at where he had looked enviously at the simple life in such splendid isolation and had remarked that, with the right companion, the lonely vigil could be Arcadia. This desire for a companion was, on the face of it, a strange comment from a man who gave the impression of wishing to live a solitary life with just his hills, his drawings and his quirky commentary. Indeed he might perhaps have happily led an entirely solitary existence except for the fact that he had never once prepared a meal and had never once ventured into the scullery to launder clothes. His reclusive life would soon be cut short by hunger and shortage of things to wear.

The road from the head of the valley was largely of little interest as there was not a great deal to see or admire around me. I was fast approaching the dale that Wainwright had had so little praise for and I was beginning to see why. As I came to the widening mouth of this tributary valley at about 400 metres above sea level, I was able to see both up and down the dale and I did not like what I saw away to the east. At three miles down the dale was the settlement of Eastgate, a village that detracts from any aesthetic qualities the valley may hold, not of itself but as a result of it being the site of a huge cement works. This massive grey monstrosity lies sprawled along the valley with its enormous chimney reaching high into the sky, overpowering all that lay around it. There is no escape for the eyes from this abomination short of closing them.

During the descent I had been looking out for a suitable place to pause awhile for lunch. It was at half past one, just less than a mile south of Westgate and sheltered from the breeze, that I found a raised through-stone in the wall that provided a most suitable seat. The wind, which although less strong, had not dropped enough for me to remove my jacket and I was glad to be sitting in the lee of the roadside wall as I lunched. As I ate and drank I could look down into the village of Westgate and above it to a torturous narrow winding road that followed a contorted route up the steep opposing valley side. Once or twice I saw a car slowly and carefully proceeding around hairpin bends that were a feature of it as it made its exit from Weardale. Perhaps the road took such a direct route to get out of the dreary and drab dale as quickly as possible and to move north in search of better fortune. Whatever the reason, it would not be long before I would have to mount that way and make my escape too. I studied my map over lunch and noted with some pleasure that not far beyond Westgate I would be putting away OS map Landranger 92 and following the route on a new map, number 87. Landranger 87 was my third map and was the most northerly that I had required for it accommodated the remaining walk to the north and major part of the westerly route along Hadrian's Wall. It also covered from where I would finally turn south from the wall and would take me all the way to Haltwhistle. Although I had, out of necessity, followed a meandering route up the map that I studied, my points of entry onto it and exit from it were, within a few yards, on the same easting. There was a certain adrenalin rush from a map change for it meant that I was progressing. I was achieving and it meant that there were fewer miles ahead and more behind. It felt as though the event ought to be marked by a formal ceremony – to thank the old and welcome the new. Then again, I was just pleased to be able to stuff one back into the rucksack and replace it with another.

Westgate is a fairly nondescript place with nothing especially memorable to draw upon except perhaps for the fact that at it appeared to centre not around a village hall or a church, or a village green or a duck pond, but a caravan park. While this may be a different approach to town planning, it was rather less attractive and did not do anything to endear me to the dale. I had entered the village passing by yet another dismantled railway, which now terminates down the valley at the cement works at Eastgate. All that remained here were the buttresses of what had once supported the bridge under which Wainwright had trudged in the rain sixty years before. Unlike him I did not explore Westgate's full length and I met no one as I found my way to the junction that would lead to the steep ascent I had seen not many minutes earlier.

Very soon the incline, and that fact that the weather was at last showing signs of improvement, rendered me uncomfortably warm and the jacket was removed and fixed back under the straps of my rucksack. The rays of sun that had thus far followed my progress were at last beginning to touch me from time to time and, when they did, the effect of the chill breeze was nullified. Such a rapid ascent gave me a grandstand view of Westgate and I could see that it comprised a long and narrow settlement with its dwellings straggled untidily along the floor of the valley with the caravan park unfortunately prominent. The saving grace as I looked down upon it was that the sunlight now gave the same elegant quality of illumination that I had seen over Teesdale earlier in the day.

I noticed little else about Weardale and found it difficult to be positive about a place where the ugly intrusion of industry was so obvious. My liaison with the dale had been very brief for I had come straight down into it and was now proceeding equally straight up out of it, and maybe I was missing some part where I might have gaped in awe at its beauty. Somehow I doubted it and the final assault on the eyes was left until I was all but out of the valley and above its steep lower flanks. To either side of the road lay industrial devastation so crude that it deserved criminal status. The long-disused quarry workings had ripped the land open and simply left it. The surgeon had made his incision very deep here but seemingly had had no intention of any subsequent stitching, with the result that these wounds lay open to infection. I was astounded that Wainwright had made no mention of these septic gashes and could only assume that he was unable to see their full extent because of the mist that blighted his journey. This parting shot of Weardale did nothing to review my initial expression of displeasure at its apparent lax attitude to its own appearance. Weardale was like the weather ahead: drab and dreary and still more threatening than from whence I had travelled.

I paused only to photograph the evidence as a coroner would photograph the body and I carried on up the lessening gradient. My next summit was Scarsike Head, the cresting of which would open up the next dale. Swinhope Head was to be the greatest altitude that I would reach on the northern leg of my travels, but Scarsike Head was no pushover for my legs were continually complaining. If they could have spoken they would have been asking for formal confirmation of whether my journey constituted a holiday or whether they had done something to upset me and that this was my idea of just retribution. It would not have soothed them to hear that there was still eight miles remaining. The only consolation I could have provided was that the dale that lay ahead comprised more of an elongated and shallower dished indentation in the surrounding plateau-like moorland and, accordingly, its form was not so U-shaped with such severe sides, thus the climb back out of it would be at a lesser incline. The dale that I was approaching was Rookhope Dale, the scene of ancient workings much older than any I had previously happened upon. Nearing Scarsike Head my looking back to Weardale provided views of a patchwork of fields laid to a limited variety of crops and grazing. Turning to the north as I reached the brow the valley of the Rookhope Burn was devoid of any field systems other than a very few for grazing near the valley bottom around Lintzgarth. For the greater part of the dale all I could see was wild and desolate moor. This was a very stunted dale for its overall length stood at no more than eight miles from its source at Rookhope Head to its demise at Eastgate in Weardale, and as a dale it did little more than rise, turn a quick corner and disappear. The only population centre was the village of Rookhope sited where the dale turns and heads south for its confluence with the River Wear. It is a young valley where I traversed it, a mile upstream from Rookhope and only about four miles from its source, and the burn is only a minor watercourse with not a great deal to commend it, save, that is, for the tremendous sensation of detachment – once on the byroad heading north-east across Lintzgarth Common, passing the moonscape of old mineral workings, the loneliness pervades all else, and all that can be seen are very occasional isolated farms. I could not imagine many being able to attract the holidaymakers to this place as Foxup had done three days earlier. Littondale's attraction had been its peace and quiet, but here the same silence was not an attraction but a reminder of death and the eerie feeling that I was being watched was never far from my mind. For all that, this valley oozed character because of its remoteness.

At the very base of the valley there lay further abandoned indication of man's earlier industry with the centrepiece of the display being the remnants of some old structure that looked for all the world like the central span of a bridge. Any evidence of access roads to either side of the structure was no more, leaving the remaining mass as some abstract reminder of the extent of the industry that had existed in an earlier century.

The other testament to this valley's industrial heritage was the number of signs that read 'The Mining Trial' pointing down various tracks and paths that led indistinctly across the surrounding moorland. Following these tracks I could see the occasional shattered residue of the early lead miners' harsh lives in this remote and bleak place where their mining activity had left its indelible mark.

When he had been here Wainwright had been similarly struck by the presence of the valley's past miners and the debris that had been left. In 1938 he referred to crossing the abandoned railway at the side of the disused mill. The railway is now gone, as is the mill, and there is little to serve as evidence of their existence except, perhaps, a narrow and level terrace where the tracks might once have been laid to transport the spoils. His map had suggested the way out of the valley northwards toward Blanchland would be no more than a rough path, but he discovered that it had been recently metalled with a finish of multi-coloured chippings. As I prepared to make my way along it I could see only one thing: its first stretch from the valley floor was unmercifully steep and it was laid in a zigzag to facilitate egress from the valley road near to the Rookhope Burn. I had one last mile of climbing to negotiate before I could reasonably anticipate a long steady five-mile descent from Hunstanworth Moor.

Very often distant appearances can be misleading and in the case of the road up to Rimey Law I had hoped that the fearful incline looked worse when viewed from afar. Sadly this was one of those times when the appearance was borne out by the reality and I struggled up the slope for what seemed like an eternity. I felt to be getting nowhere and my progress was slow in the extreme. Views back were plentiful as I rested often, breathing heavily and wiping the sweat off my brow. My lungs were thankful for these stops but my legs were finding it increasingly difficult, on setting off again, to re-establish a walking rhythm and they would have wished me to carry on uninterrupted. As if to emphasise my plight, I was no longer being cooled by any breeze and the sun, which had earlier only visited as infrequent shafts on far hills, was now breaking through the thin cloud cover becoming unsympathetically warm. By the time I had passed the worst of the incline all trace of any wind had dropped and the sun was shining more strongly than at any previous time during the day, throwing a more amiable light onto this otherwise malevolent landscape. This new light gave the acres of purple heather that carpeted the rolling moors surrounding me on all sides a vivid luxuriance and it revealed all the details of the hills. They had earlier seemed as a featureless plain but now they stood out in bold relief as the shade and light played upon their discreet nooks and crannies.

All around lay more distant memories of the area's history and away to the north-east there were two huge chimneys that, although they remained standing proud above all else, were impotent now. Their powerful presence was but a sham for they are now only follies and stood as a monument to times past. Their existence as monuments would, no doubt, be short-lived because there would be no one taking care to maintain them and they would, in time, crumble away to nothing and suffer the same fate as had befallen the rest of the area's industry. More than once I paused to take in the full panorama in which I was enveloped and more than once I recommenced walking with a lumbering gait and aching muscles. So severe was the pain upon restarting that I soon concluded that the most expedient solution was not to stop at all, which also meant foregoing any further cigarettes until I reached Blanchland as I am not capable of rolling one while moving. Even pausing to take a photograph was decidedly unwise and so, for the last five miles, I never broke my left-right, left-right stride.

After an age I came to the point where I was looking ahead at a very gradual and almost constant descent and my way was clear across Hunstanworth Moor for the last few miles. The bleak harshness of this wilderness was only too apparent and during the worst of winter's excesses the moor would be a despicable companion if traversing it were to be necessary. Steel guideposts 10-foot-tall at the side of the road would be the only item that would give any bearing for a snowbound traveller. As I passed the lay-by at the top of the moor I was disgusted to stumble across (almost literally and most fittingly in the light of my hobbling) far more recent evidence of man's presence. A pile of cigarette stubs marked the place where some mindless and thoughtless moron had simply opened his car window and tipped out the contents of the ashtray. This would no doubt be the same type who, when driving, would throw the empty cigarette packet from the car rather than take it home. At least man's tarnishing of the landscape had arguably been out of necessity in the name of industry, but this degradation was entirely avoidable.

My last few miles were marked by very little other than an increasing desire to witness civilisation, for when I came to the first signs of habitation I knew that I was nearing my goal. With the exception of a number of individual dwellings on the moor road, and a small cluster at Townfield, I knew that Hunstanworth was the first hamlet that lay en route and that less than two miles further would be Blanchland itself. It was at one of these remote dwellings that I noted there was a fearsome-looking hound carrying out is duties efficiently – looking and sounding distinctly terrifying. The only thing that lay between it and me was a rickety fence and gate. If the animal were to break out onto the road, there could be no running – my feet would have steadfastly refused. The dog would just have to eat me. It made no effort to look for a means of escape and I passed unmolested as it continued its low husky bark until I was out of sight. Like a desert mirage or a will-o-the-wisp, Hunstanworth seemed to get no nearer and I hiked on and on forever north-east with the redundant chimneys still in view to my right. They had been in view for hours and still were not falling behind me. The reservoir that I could see ahead had lain ahead of me also for hours and still it seemed no closer. However the trees, which I knew lay south-west of Townfield, were, almost imperceptibly, becoming larger. This meant one of two things: either I was stood still and they were growing or I was getting nearer to them. I was delighted when I finally reached them, passed through them on my tree-lined avenue and at last saw the houses of Townfield with Hunstanworth only a few hundred yards further down the hill.

Hunstanworth is a quiet hamlet comprising of a small group of houses centred around a quaint church remarkable for its roof tiling, as is the old chapel that has now been converted into a very fine private dwelling. The tiling had been laid with two colours to create an inlaid pattern of repeating rhombuses. It was remarkable that the tiler should have gone to these lengths but now provides a lasting credit to his workmanship. Beyond Hunstanworth the road drops at a steeper rate as it begins to find its way to the river crossing at Baybridge, and as it does so I was afforded the views over the River Derwent that had so charmed Wainwright. He had enthused about this beautiful location and it was easy to see why. The road runs parallel to the river but high above it picking a way down where it can through the tree-lined valley sides until they ultimately meet at the ancient bridge across the River Derwent at Baybridge. My arrival here was of some note for I was crossing another county boundary as I had left County Durham and entered Northumberland. I would remain in Northumberland for the longest of any of the counties that I was to visit, being within its borders for the next three days, only passing into Cumbria for the final approach to Alston. Alston was an age away. Alston was many miles away. I would have seen the wall when I was at Alston. My aching legs would hopefully be nothing but a distant memory when I was at Alston. I had no desire to dwell on thoughts that would draw my mind to times that were nearer to the end of my liberation so I thought only of Blanchland as I crossed the bridge and turned right for, relatively, the last few steps.

I had walked twenty-three miles, all of it on or at the edge of hard-surfaced roads. The only disappointment had been the first miles in Teesdale where I had been forced to walk with raging traffic. After that I had been treated to wonderfully quiet byways where instances of encountering cars had been few and far between. Nevertheless, twenty-three miles had taken its toll and as I arrived at a quarter to six at the arch enclosing the northern end of the square at Blanchland, my first priority was to get to my night's lodging and remove my boots. Thankfully, Blanchland's size meant that the guest house could not be more than a few yards from where I stood and, as I received directions from a friendly local, the 'Surgery' was no more than fifty yards away. This was just as well for I didn't believe that the local, as friendly as he was, would have taken too kindly to my asking for a piggy-back, which I was sorely close to having to do. Mrs Richardson showed me in and up to my room where I gratefully removed my bags and boots. She inquired as to whether I would like a pot of tea and did I want a bath running. A bath running? A bath running! That magic word: bath. I could have kissed her. Yes, I most certainly did want a bath. In fact, I would have had my pot of tea and evening meal in there with me if I could have done.

Invigorated after my long bathe, I found my way across to the Lord Crewe Arms for my usual beer aperitif and asked to look at their bill of fare. I tried to act nonchalantly as I searched for something on the menu that I could afford – once again, I had discovered a hostelry with a rich taste in food and an assumption of a rich taste in clientele. I settled for a plate of pasta that was intended as a starter but was served to me as a main course. This was very clearly another huntin', shootin', fishin' establishment so I hoped that those too close to whom I had sat the night before were not also working their way north. I was thankful that they were not and the only person I spoke to during the evening was the barmaid who was very helpful and told me something of this strange, unchanged village where time had stood still. I had barely eaten my food when my tiredness began to hit me. One more beer, I thought, and then to bed. We talked of the few changes there had been in the village and how none of the houses were owned freehold but were all rented from the Trustees of Lord Crewe's Estate. I was tiring fast. One more beer, I thought, and then to bed, I was tiring even faster. One more beer, I thought, and then to bed. After telling her about my trek I asked whether she knew of a family by the name of Elliott with whom Wainwright had stayed, but she was new to Blanchland and suggested that my host might know. I was absolutely dog-tired by this time. One more beer, I thought, and then to bed. I have to admit to being slightly pleased when a couple arrived and engaged her in conversation. I was able to break the cycle of ordering more beer and bade her good evening. I returned to the Surgery to have a similar discussion with Mrs Richardson as to whether she might know something of the Elliotts. She wasn't entirely sure but would ask her husband upon his return from working as chef at the Lord Crewe Arms. It was a shame I had not known that earlier – perhaps I might have secured some small discount.

Bed followed very shortly after our discussion and tonight there was no long note-making session. I decided that all my usual nocturnal activities could quite easily be completed the following morning. I would not be in a hurry for tomorrow was my day of rest in as much as I only had ten miles to walk with no severe hills or dales, just a gentle slope to Slaley Forest and then fairly level walking to the largest town that I would visit on my travels, Hexham. That was tomorrow and in the meantime I had some serious sleeping to savour. I guessed that my dreams would be sweet for I had reached this far on schedule and felt that as I managed up until now, then the remainder was largely a formality. I had no reason to question my abilities now.

Chapter 5

Blanchland to Hexham

My morning in Blanchland did not begin as early as had the previous days. Today was not a day for waking at five o'clock. In fact, if it had not been for the alarm clock I believe I would have continued in a land of slumber until sometime in mid-October. I would have been tired this morning in any case but, as it was, after any hopes for an early night had been thwarted by the antics of some noisy village youths, I was shattered. My room was directly opposite the entrance to the church grounds and overlooked an area of courtyard adjacent to the arch that seemed to be the gathering point for the local adolescents. On the night of my stay they appeared to be hosting Blanchland's answer to the Bike Show, where the exhibits were restricted to one or two small but loud mopeds. It was also apparent that one or two of the youths must have been inspecting the mechanics of the machines, otherwise I could not understand why they would want the engines running and revving permanently. The engines would run regardless of whether any member of the group was actually proposing to travel anywhere. From time to time the noise would diminish only to return some minutes later, and I concluded that these peaceful interludes must have been potential customers taking test rides. While this disturbance continued I had decided that rather than lie wide awake, I would complete the diary of my day's events on the walk to Blanchland.

The small group had finally sidled off to their homes at some time between half past ten and quarter to three in the morning. I knew this because I had looked at the clock at half past ten and the next thing I was aware of was lying on the bed at quarter to three with the light and my glasses still on having fallen asleep while making my entries. There is no better way to guarantee a bad night's sleep than to interrupt it by waking up fully clothed and then to have to start the nightly repose all over again. The first four hours of disturbed sleep were devoid of any sort of dreams, sweet or otherwise, and during the second four hours I was more unconscious than asleep, so any dreams I had looked forward to would have to be put on hold for another night.

Although I had needed the alarm to wake me, it was still early and I was standing at the open up-sliding sash window having my first smoke of the day at seven o'clock. I had laid in bed for some minutes before I dared move for I was not keen to find out whether my legs would be willing assistants or whether they may require some gentle coaxing. When I had first stirred I was relieved and surprised that they did so with a gusto that had been so absent yesterday. Either I had gone through the pain barrier and had walked them into submission, or last night's bath had worked wonders. Whatever the reason, I would be able to take it easy today and have another long soak upon reaching Hexham for I was planning to arrive there mid-afternoon. I would have the luxury of a look around the town and had it in mind to send some postcards to let people know that if they had had any lingering doubts as to my success, they may now dispel them.

Looking out at a dull and damp scene, I was bleary-eyed and this must have been influencing my mood for I ought to have been joyous that I had reached this far. But I seemed not as full of anticipation for the day ahead as I should have been. I looked at my belongings and thought of the daily packing of it all as a chore. Today was an odd day; it was not a great walk in its own right; I would not arrive at anywhere that was of particular import; I would not visit anywhere that was especially interesting. It was, moreover, a day that only provided a means to an end. It provided me with the means of reaching the ideal launch pad from which to visit my primary goal, Hadrian's Wall. It provided me with the means by which I could recuperate and leave me ready to be able to enjoy the site. There was no urgency about any part of today, including breakfast, and I had time aplenty to visit the post office to see if I could buy a new battery for my dictaphone for I had discovered that I had not, even after all my planning, brought all required spares with me. I was out of luck, not able to finish transcribing my notes from yesterday's walk. I had left the tape playing as I had fallen asleep and the battery was totally exhausted – I knew well the feeling.

Breakfast was a leisurely affair and instead of swilling my tea in a rush to be away, I was able to linger and enjoy what had been put before me. During my scrambled eggs on toast I chatted with Mrs Richardson about this charming and hidden little village. It transpired that it was, perhaps, a little too hidden for she explained that I was to be her last bed and breakfast guest. Trade had been poor over the preceding weeks, so she had decided that she would seek full-time employment, had secured a post at the Slaley Hall Hotel and would be commencing the very day after my stay with her. She also told me that she had not any further news as to the Elliott family except to say that over the years there had been a number of residents by that name. The ones that I was in search of were, according to Wainwright's description, elderly at the time of his visit – a fact that did not appear to tally with the only grave I had found on my earlier quiet wander around the cemetery. The one grave that bore the name Elliott would have placed those interred only in their mid-thirties in 1938. The only light that she was able to cast was that the caller to the Elliott's house, to tell of the radio broadcast, may well have been a local lady, Vera, who had often called on her elderly neighbours. The generally agreed view as to which house he had stayed at was No. 9, an end-of-terrace house in the courtyard. I thanked Mrs Richardson for her help, made the last entry in her visitors' book, paid my bill and prepared to leave.

Suitably more inspired after my repast, I set about packing my bags, fastening my boots, and set off to follow her recommendation that I should inquire further at the local shop. They, in turn, recommended that I try two doors down, which I did. A kindly lady there recommended that I try across the square, but from that door there was no answer. Slightly despondent, I called a halt to any further investigations and spent a few moments just ambling, rather aimlessly, about the cobbled courtyard.

Blanchland is a picturesque village with a quality that is ageless save only for the roadworks sign and barriers and a small number of modern cars parked randomly around the court where I was standing. Its timeless air has been secured by the nature of its occupation and the rules that govern its development. The residents hold only tenants' rights to their properties, the freehold being held by the Lord Crewe Trustees. Any development applications in the village, from the erection of a garden shed to the conversion of an existing barn, are required first to be put before the Lord Crewe Trustees for their deliberation. Lord Crewe was clearly a big name in these parts and much of my conversation with the barmaid the evening before had revolved around Lord Crewe and his influence locally. To understand Lord Crewe's effect upon the village, it is necessary to know something of its unique history.

I have no desire to transform my story into a history lesson for there are, without doubt, erudite historians who would be more adept at relating Blanchland's full chronological story, and I can only paraphrase the information that I gleaned. Essentially some guy named Norbert was riding his horse in Germany at the beginning of the twelfth century. Norbert's own life plan had been to make a go of it with the church and, by all accounts, he was doing just fine, having refused a bishopric – it being too lowly, and he now riding around in silk clothes and with an attendant. Not everything went his way though, for while he was riding there was a violent thunderstorm and, his horse startled, he was thrown to the ground and knocked senseless. As he regained consciousness he heard voices urging him to undertake good deeds rather than continue his pursuit of wealth and recognition. This "road to Damascus" experience sent Norbert into a penitent self-denial-type of mood and, after two or three years of prayer, he became a wandering preacher teaching the good word in what is now Belgium making him the third famous Belgian after Hercule Poirot and Georges Simenon. In 1120, while in the forest of Coucy, at a place called Prémontré, he dreamt of a band of white-robed monks and took this as a sign to locate his headquarters in the forest. The abbey was built and the order of monks that he founded became the Premonstratensian Order. In cutting a long

story short, the monks wore white robes and lived a life of strict religious following and extreme personal hardship and self-denial. (Apart from the strict
religion I consider that I would make a fine Premonstratensian monk with much
self-denial and hardship.) The more accurate name for the monks was that of
white cannons and the order of which they were part became very popular,
quickly spreading across to England and arriving at the Blanchland site in 1159.
It seems reasonable that the abbey they built at Blanchland, or White Land,
would have taken its name from these white canons. The canons would have
been left very much to their own devices in this out-of-the-way location, and so
remote was it that it figures very little in formalised history, only really being
noticed twice, and sadly both times by people who were distinctly up to no
good. On the first occasion, in 1327, Edward III called round to make ready to
do battle with a Scottish army who were rather partial to good raiding parties
south of the border. They had already wreaked havoc on the abbey earlier during the campaign and no doubt the canons were pleased when the Scots thought
better of doing battle and scampered back home without a sword being drawn.
The second spell where Blanchland was noticed followed Henry VIII's dis-
agreement with the Pope on the matter as to who was to be the great chief over
the English branch of the church. Henry took his bat home, divorced whichever
wife it was at the time, and took over the control of the church in England including abbeys such as Blanchland which promptly faced dissolution. This
particular abbey was given a reprieve however, largely because of its location
being the only hostelry for miles around that could provide accommodation for
travellers, although this stay of execution only lasted three years, at which time
the canons were all pensioned off. Blanchland might have remained forever
hidden, but on the occasion of the King's Commissioners seeking them out,
they became lost in a hill fog and the canons thought they had been passed by.
Joyfully triumphant, they rang the abbey bells only to find that the noise attracted the Commissioners' unwelcome attentions and the canons suffered from
going off half-cocked.

129

After this, what was left of the estate, it having fallen into disrepair, passed into the ownership of the Forsters, one of who married the Bishop of Durham, Lord Crewe, in 1699. The estate was bought by Lord Crewe in 1704 and so began his association with the village that remains very evident today. When he died his will stated that Blanchland should be administered by trustees and it was they who, from Lord Crewe's considerable bequeathed wealth, built the village, now so little changed from 200 years earlier. The houses are built from the walling stone that once formed the walls of the abbey and its associated buildings. This generous benefactor has a permanent memorial to his name in the Lord Crewe Arms and, in some small way, my one-beer-too-many of the night before had helped to swell the coffers of his trustees. Actually, at two pounds a pint, it hadn't been in such a small way – I discovered over breakfast that most locals go to the Sports Club where the beer is much cheaper and the food would, by the sound of it, have been more to my liking.

Under the jurisdiction of the trustees, the only development allowed is that which is approved by them and there is only minor evidence of new building except for the barn conversion that had been granted approval directly to the rear of Mrs Richardson's house. This will provide three houses and I only hope they are for local folk and not to be let as holiday homes to wealthy incomers. I suspected there might be objecting voices at some of the trustees' rules for it was only as recent as 1995 that the first greenhouse had been allowed. As to satellite dishes, the trustees' policy was firm: there were to be none – a decision that I hold with entirely for we are already subjected to far too much dross that is churned out in the name of entertainment. I passed the new buildings and did not look to discover further about them as I detected some ill feeling that they were being built at all and I had no desire to prod any tender wounds.

Instead, I slowly sidled up by the north gate and headed for the track that would lead me, ultimately, on to the moor on my trek north again, toward Slaley Forest. I very quickly came to the north end of the village and looked back at this sleepy place. I was struck by the sense of retirement that it exudes – the majority of the residents had been here for many years and I imagine membership of this lucky band is only available through stepping into dead men's shoes. I passed the old school, which had closed in the 1980s and had become home to an artist and gallery. It was now closed again and the hotel was considering taking it over for conference facilities. Even here the smell of commercialism wafts among the otherwise perfumed air.

My forward planning was paying dividends for today was cooler but dry and I stowed my jacket but wore the fleece that I had brought with me (another item worn). Dry in the valleys, I gained height on the rough track north-west to Pennypie House. I did so increasingly in a clinging hill mist that wet you without you realising. The path had begun in a sheltered and wooded ravine, slowly climbing away from Blanchland and the inclemency of the weather was only gauged when the protection that the gully had provided was no longer present. Very soon I was swapping fleece for jacket and accepting that today was not to be a day for long-distance views or, indeed, any views at all for that matter. The mist and the drizzle reduced the visibility to nothing more than a hundred yards or so.

After Pennypie House, the track which thus far had been passable by car turned north and changed to a moorland trail cut neatly through heather uplands which, on another day, would have been a riot of purples and reds. The two miles from Pennypie House to Slaley Forest were damp and dismal along a well-formed and smooth unmade road, with the only company being a plethora of grouse. Every few yards there would be a startled fluttering of wings from the undergrowth from one side or the other and I would start as a bird lumbered up from the heather with all the aerodynamic qualities of a winged medicine ball. Although we had talked the evening before of the poor state of the grouse season due to disease and many young birds drowning in their nests during the wet summer, on Blanchland Moor they abounded and their individual call was with me throughout. The huntin', shootin', fishin' brigade would have had rich pickings up here all right.

With the exception of the grouse, I was entirely alone in this featureless landscape and could see nothing beyond my immediate surroundings. Wainwright's appointment with Blanchland Moor had been altogether more pleasant and on a day of brilliant sunshine he had loitered, lying back in the heather and contemplating the few clouds that passed high above him. I was not able to lie back and look at a distance at the clouds for I was a part of them. He had lingered long among the black-faced sheep, but today the sheep must have sought shelter from the clammy elements for I saw none. He had heard of beekeepers who would place their hives on the moor so as to sweeten the honey. If such a tradition were still to continue, I saw no sign of it, although, in fairness, no self-respecting bee would want to be out on a day such as this. Unlike him I carried on my way, undeterred and, having set out at ten o'clock, was planning to arrive at Hexham at two. I had several tasks that I would have time to fulfil and Hexham would provide my only opportunity.

I had not brought changes of clothes sufficient for all eleven days, so at Hexham I would find a launderette. I had my postcards to write. I would have to write to let mother know that up to press I had not been accosted or kidnapped by heathen northern moor-dwellers as she had feared. I would have to find a second notebook for my diary entries had proved to be of such length that my first book was all but full. Having had no repeat of my camera juggling of the first day, I had taken many photographs and would need more film. I would find a tourist booklet about Hadrian's Wall for I knew next to nothing about it and wanted to learn more of it before our meeting tomorrow. I also wanted to find the Abbey Tearooms that had provided Wainwright's icy accommodation for the night. I had my doubts as to whether, in a larger town, I would find any trace of my earlier companion. Villages and villagers are different: they have long memories and a care for what has been said of them – a fact that had been made abundantly clear in Teesdale and especially Romaldkirk. The village had rallied to protect its own good name and its past residents. Town dwellers have a different demeanour however, which has been moulded by a diminished sense of community and there is a more perfunctory attitude where the visitor is simply lost in the crowd. The hustle and bustle provides for an all-consuming anonymity to the extent that although there may be much going on, barely any of it is noticed by anybody. The larger the town, the greater is the sense of being alone within the crowd. The ultimate is to be found within the city where the only encounter will be with people who are all entirely alone in the melee. Few care about the business of others for they are only concerned with their own affairs, so the itinerant's words and deeds are soon lost from memory. Although Hexham was, by no means, a city, it seemed on my map to be sufficiently large as to create this sense of anonymity and I had severe doubts about finding any evidence of Wainwright's stay.

Although I have complained of my misfortune regarding the weather, I would not wish to make statements that appear to detract from the enjoyment that was gleaned as I strolled quietly across the open moor between Blanchland and Slaley Forest. Like Wainwright, I find there is something quite revealing about walking while enveloped in mist. It is not revelation as it would normally be comprehended for the eyes can see little. It is more that the absence of physical vision allows self-revelation – more of your own thoughts surface at such times and the best thinking is done when there is a lack of interruption, be it oral or visual. It is, of course, for this reason, why the ritual of meditation is performed in silence, where the mind can be better cleared of all external interference. It is also a similar reasoning as to why operations that require total darkness will often be carried out with the eyes shut. It is also why we are taught to pray with our eyes closed. So it was today as I made my way over this plateau-like land with my thoughts ranging far and wide on a variety of subjects. They could run free for they were not fenced in by having to share them with anybody or anything.

A recurring topic throughout this voyage of deliverance revolved around my own life plan, where I was along its course and whether I would still retain any control over my destiny when ensconced once more into a normal existence. Once I was away from my dream world I would return to an entirely new future from that which I had left. Having worked in the textile industry for the previous two years, I had received the dire news four weeks earlier that my services were no longer required and I had listened to the 'we're having to let you go Andy' speech. Why do employers say that they are 'having to let you go' as though they are acceding to a request from the employee? The inescapable fact of the matter in my case was that the flower of profit would bear more fruit if the dead wood were to be removed. It is not my intention to carp, but it had very quickly become apparent that if I wasn't actually dead wood then I was perched on a branch that was. Like so many others in modern society, our lifestyles are geared around an earning level that required two salaries and the consequence of one of those being removed from the equation is dire. One other aspect of modern society is that at the ripe old age of forty-two, there is only marginal hope that can be attached to securing alternative employment. Two years earlier, when I had changed direction at yet another crossroads, I had done so erroneously. I had switched from a role in construction and the intervening two years had seen too many days pass for me to switch back – I draw this conclusion from the consistently polite refusals I had received in the weeks prior to my escape. I would return to take up the honourable and respectable role of postman (more correctly termed post-person). Honourable and respectable it may be, but it is also poorly paid and would surely sentence Sue to working forever more as the major breadwinner, a prospect that grated very severely at my male pride. This was not part of any plan that I had drawn up, but then again any pretensions that I had to being in control of any semblance of a plan had long been destroyed many times over. I had seen this as altogether different; this I viewed as effectively the end of any serious earning capacity on my part. There were, I comforted myself, the various things that I was able to do from which I might be able to develop an income, but if I were to be brutally honest, I doubted it. When we doubt our abilities it is very likely that our expectation of failure will all too soon become a reality, and it is only when we, and those upon who we look for support, believe that success is possible that there exists any real prospect of victory.

Where doubt exists there also exists the potential for the emergence of the destructive danger of seeing life as a futile and meaningless exercise where hope cannot live for room has not been left for it. Doubt and its ever-present cousin, failure, live hand in glove and one will follow quickly on the heels of the other, producing a self-prophesying catalogue of one disappointment after another. Success will only come to those who have the foresight to believe in their own abilities and the courage to see them through regardless of adversity and in spite of whatever obstacles that may block their way. We have all visited the land of futility from time to time and I had ventured close to its borders in more recent days. I had come close to viewing life through the eyes of a pessimist. There are three basic ways of looking at life – pessimistically, optimistically and realistically – and, of these my usual attitude is that of optimism. The pessimist will tell you that if you start out with an expectation of your labours being frustrated, you'll never be disappointed when they are. The flaw in this approach is that the inevitability of one's plan being thwarted already exists in the mind and this expectation will invariably become a reality where the prospect of failure is a probability rather than a possibility. It will come as little surprise to the pessimist when obstacles are placed in their way, after all, these obstructions have occupied much of their thinking, so much so in fact, that their anticipation has obscured any likelihood of their plan bearing fruit. The optimist on the other hand believes all that glitters might be gold and that perhaps the street ahead is paved with gold too, and that their scheme, whatever it may be, has substance and is within their power to be realised. Admittedly, in the event of the same impediments, the barriers will seem all the greater for not so much thought was given to their appearance, but at least energy has not been expended considering something that may not happen. If a belief dwells within from the outset that failure is a possibility, the greater is its likelihood. No, believe in your plans and your ability to carry them through for only when you do, in their deliberation and execution, will your manner be positive and will there be a meaning to life. Realism is far more difficult to comment upon because everybody believes that they are realists. The pessimist will assert as to they're 'only being realistic' in considering the possibility of failure and the optimist will maintain the view that fulfilment of their plan is entirely possible and represents, therefore, a realistic goal. I am somewhat partisan in this particular philosophy for I can conceive no benefit whatsoever in entering into something other than with verve and a belief that my performance would be nothing short of utterly convincing and of total mastery.

Up on Blanchland Moor, in that silent contemplative arena, all earlier negative reflections were an age away. They were the thoughts of a loser; the thoughts of someone with no imagination; thoughts so shallow that while trapped in their presence there could be nothing but defeat. I would return and, when I did, I would proudly wear two uniforms: the first would be physical and comprise blue with red piping; the second would be spiritual and of far greater authority for it would be worn at all times. It would be the uniform that would be recognised for its ability to overcome doubts, whether self-expressed or otherwise, and it would be the uniform in which I would find accomplishment and a measure of pride in my own ability to provide.

The moor had been a cauldron for meditation and it was only upon seeing the vague dark outline of something ahead that took me away from my train of thought. I took out my map and decided that this ghostly horizon could be the first glimpse of the trees of Slaley Forest. As I neared the plantation I could begin to see colour within the grey bulk that lay ahead and spread the entire width of my visible horizon. No longer were the trees just a few feet high as when Wainwright had passed this way. At the point where the path entered the forest, the conifers to the east now stood 50 and 60 feet tall. They had been saplings when he came off Blanchland Moor but now, sixty years on, they dominated the scene and very soon I was surrounded by their grandeur, sheltered from above by great branches that stretched across the forest track. The trees at either side of the gravelly track would spread their branches to form a covered avenue for the mile-and-a-half trek to its northern boundary. Woodland walking can feel almost restrictive in places for there is nothing to see other than the immediate arboreal environment, but today I was pleased for it gave shelter from the drifting moorland mizzle.

The other aspect of following woodland trails is that the only bearing the walker has is the compass as there are no landmarks that enable an accurate location to be established. I was fortunate in that the route through the forest was almost totally north and that after some distance the track would change to a macadamed surface – all, of course, on the proviso that I had entered the trees at the correct point. I had no reason to doubt that I had lost the trail but was, nevertheless, relieved when, some hundred yards ahead, I could see that the surface became a more formal roadway. The way to the northern extremity of the forest comprised a gentle descent until I again reached signs of civilisation on the narrow byways leading to the busier second-class road from Blanchland to Hexham. Once I came to the road, I was destined, again, to have hard made-up road surface underfoot and it would also herald a return to traffic-dodging with steep and overgrown verges that lent to exaggeration of the hazard.

The last four miles would, I knew, be beset with unpleasantly heavy traffic for as I drew closer and closer to my rendezvous with the road, I had watched the cars charging back and forth. I decided very swiftly to take a break from my discomfort and sought refuge in the aptly named 'Traveller's Rest'. Looking at my map it was all too apparent that there were far more favourable routes that I could have chosen to proceed to Hexham, but, regardless of my puritanical desire to follow Wainwright, I particularly wanted to visit Linnels Bridge. He had incorrectly noted the place in his narrative as Linnetts Bridge, but the location to which he was referring was clear and his romantic enthusing over it meant that I, too, had to pay my respects. The description of his emotions on chancing upon the house adjacent to the bridge was sufficiently compelling for me not to be able to undertake this walk without also witnessing its beauty first hand.

I allowed my respite to extend for rather longer than I had planned, for my desire to set out once more into the traffic was very readily cast asunder by my wish to remain seated at the bar stool and continue my conversation with the barmaid. Our discussion was of a somewhat staccato nature for she was required intermittently to break off and serve the various other travellers who had found their way into the pub since my arrival. Its content was largely of the usual niceties, but it provided a friendly interlude in an otherwise fairly drab sort of day. The weather was drab, the road walking was drab; even the trees had been slightly drab for one conifer looks very much like the next and my spirits had been tending toward drab on this day that was really just a means to an end. During one of our conversational intervals I cheered myself with the prospect firstly of viewing Linnels Bridge and secondly that I was now less than twenty-four hours from my true goal, Hadrian's Wall. Closing in on it Wainwright had become absorbed in its attraction and I was also beginning to anticipate excitedly the assignation that awaited me. I had walked over eighty miles and now only a further ten would satiate my growing enthusiasm for its acquaintance.

I bade farewell to the barmaid and left the Travellers Rest at half past twelve and even though I had tarried there, my earlier pace would, I calculated, still allow arrival at my destination by two o'clock. Two miles would take me to Linnels Bridge followed by a further two into Hexham itself. The road became even more hazardous than it had been previously and I cannot recommend it to anyone who may care to tread this way. Whatever Linnels Bridge held in store, it would have to be of some magnificence to mitigate the eternal criss-crossing that was required to facilitate a safe passage to it. The endless twisting that allowed the road to negotiate the sharp descent into the valley of the stream, suitably named Devil's Water, resulted in my having to cross from one side of the road to the other in order to reduce my exposure to the traffic. Strict adherence to the usual advice for walkers to face the oncoming vehicles would have been decidedly unwise at a sharp right-hand bend where instead of a verge there is only a near-vertical shrub bank. An oncoming car would have been upon me (more than likely literally) before I was able to take evasive action. The only solution was to cross the road to its left side until visibility around the crown of the bend was possible, followed by a rapid dash back across. On the occasions where there was a double bend, I found that open-eyed praying helped marginally, as did an ability to be very fleet of foot. More than once it was only some nimble and fancy footwork that made good an escape from incidents that might well have curtailed any further progress. When I finally arrived at a road junction where a sign demanded that all larger vehicles were required to take a lengthy detour to avoid the narrow and weight-restricted bridge, I knew that I was near. Not many yards further I came upon the narrow bridge to which the sign had referred and which had provided Wainwright with the view of the house of his dreams. As he had done so many years before, I admired its location from my position perched on the low parapet wall of the ancient stone structure. It was indeed a fine residence and very much beyond the price bracket that I might ever be able to entertain even in my fantasies, for ownership of this house would stretch the realms of achievable dreams to well beyond the point of credulity.

It was plain to see why he had ogled it with envious eyes with its stream that still tumbled to its demise in the deep waters below and the paths that toyed with the steep contours as they traversed the slope above the water. They were not so meticulous now though, and the gardens looked in some need of tender loving care. Still, the potential existed for this to be an idyll hidden amid trees on all sides with the one exposure to prying eyes being the bridge from which I jealously regarded it. It was also easy to understand his romantic notion of living a perfect life in the arms of his fantasy girl as he fondly imagined her walking among the flowers that bedecked the terraced garden. As I read his account I naturally assumed this young man of thirty-one to be a flighty young thing with a healthy libido and, perhaps, an over-active imagination. Certainly the assumption was of a bachelor and his search for Mrs Right – someone who would make a fine and faithful wife with no imperfections worthy of serious criticism. Someone who would keep house, raise his children, look after him and prepare meals. Someone who would never say a word out of place, who would remain at his side if asked or would sink into the background if circumstances so required. Someone who would obey him, cherish him, never chastise him, hand him his slippers and newspaper upon his return and generally wait on him hand and foot. His part of the bargain would be to fulfil the role of hunter-gatherer, providing the daily bread and acting as general protector to the family unit. His woman would very clearly be his chattel over whom he had total power. For all that, she would never be called upon to work for any commercial return and neither would she ever need to be concerned about anything unpleasantly financial. That would be Wainwright's part of the marital arrangement as it was in many households in pre-war England. The man would take to the role of provider while the woman provided him with the domestic bliss in which he could carry out his role in comfort. She would ensure that dinner was on the table upon his return from work and he would interact with the children in a fatherly way for twenty minutes before their mother took them upstairs to bed. He might choose to call at the pub or visit his club in the evening and if he decided to stay there until rather late, the only consequence would be a slightly bleary head the following morning as he awoke in his bedroom. Naturally his first action of the day would be to enjoy the tea delivered by the lady of the house. The exception to this way of life might have been at the weekend when he would prepare the early morning tray of tea. Any discord was muted and, to all intents and purposes, the family tie was strong, for people understood the roles that were largely preordained as a product of their sex.

It was to this life of acknowledged roles that Wainwright subscribed in his wanderings and he displayed great displeasure at women who held aspirations that were contrary to it. He berated the woman who, unless through necessity, showed any desire to trespass into the male domain of working once married and he equally loathed the woman who, when married, spurned the opportunity of the union to produce children for her man. It was, quite simply, the destiny of the female to have children and to look after all that was related to the family's domesticity. How things have changed in the intervening years is almost beyond belief. As the war dragged on women took on an increasing share of the workload on the home front and perhaps it was this that, after the war, led to their demands for what they perceived as equality. Slowly they entered what had been exclusively within man's boundaries and slowly they demanded a greater influence in all aspects of life. No longer were they to be treated as second-class citizens. No longer did they request any courtesy being afforded them – many's the time that doors would be held open only to be met with a stony silence. No longer were they excused the rigours that life had previously been dished out exclusively for the male of the species. Equality in all things was the only watchword and a combative attitude began to develop which set the sexes apart in a manner where the harder the competitive edge could be engendered the better. This had become a battle of wills, a battle to the death.

Wainwright would certainly not have lasted long in this new world before he fell foul of his outdated beliefs and there can be no doubt that he would have been set upon with a voracity that would have left him tattered and torn due to his opinions. Many heated discussions about very many things have centred on the relationship that exists in the workplace between men and women. One of my own more memorable incursions into the dangerous territory of women's liberation heralding the introduction of equal opportunities occurred when I was set upon verbally by the female members of our table while enjoying a Friday evening drink several years earlier. One of the party had, for some reason, set out a scenario and I arrived at what I believed to be the only honest and practical solution which went along the following lines: a small quantity surveying practice with one partner and a secretary required a qualified staff member to assist the partner and receptionist, bringing the total staff to three. The two applicants shortlisted were of identical qualifications and experience, both had just become separately married, were of the same age, had requested the same salary level and were identical in every way, save the fact that one was male and the other female. To which applicant would the post be offered? I had only one logical solution, especially bearing in mind the size of the practice. I would employ the male using the simple and, I felt, justifiable reasoning that there might be the possibility in the not-too-distant future of the female exercising her rights for maternity leave and pay, which could leave the practice with serious problems. Well, by 'eck, you'd have thought I'd just committed some capital crime by the way the ladies among the group turned at one into a metaphorical lynch mob. There was to be no quieting their disdain and baying calls for employment of the female, and certainly no understanding of the fact that to do so might be seen as not giving an equal opportunity for the male applicant. It very quickly became apparent that in the eyes of a female perhaps life can only be truly equal when it favours women. (I have a sneaking suspicion that the justification of this viewpoint stems from years of vacuuming and ironing.) To all those who are now gainfully employed, searching high and low for a rope and tasteful gas lamp or similar, please be assured that I am joking about the vacuuming and ironing and that my stance in respect of equal opportunities is that of most modern men. I will do most things that provide an even chance of a stress-free existence, for too much stress leads to premature hair loss, premature aging and one or two other problems related to more personal things being a mite premature.

I smiled as I recalled the story and wondered what Wainwright would have made of our modern ways. He probably would not have allowed them to touch him – he would, I suspected, have carried on in his own curmudgeonly way in blithe ignorance as to whether he was breaking any law or not. The extraordinary aspect of his tale as he leant against the parapet and yearned for a harmonious life was the fact that as he stood he had been married for seven years and had a young son of his own. No mention is made in his commentary of his wife and it was only on further investigation that a side of Wainwright's character comes to light. He had married Ruth in 1931 and when, very soon after, his mother died, he appeared to take against her and lose any respect that he might have ever held for her. He led his own life and she hers where she could. Marital bliss was in short supply but they remained together for, in those days, divorce would be the death knell for any professional aspirations that Wainwright may have held. His wife, of course, had no hope of liberation with little choice other than to remain true to the commitment they had both sworn. That commitment endured until the mid-1960s when they did finally separate, but even then only because he probably felt that his impending retirement would enable his career not to be damaged by the scandal. Wainwright later remarried when he finally did manage to find his Mrs Right – dreamt of thirty years earlier while adrift on his romantic magic carpet overlooking the house next to Linnels Bridge.

I was unable to indulge in any great sensual thoughts as I stood on the bridge because every few seconds a car would approach and the driver would delicately peek around the sharp bends that led onto the bridge at both sides. It was so narrow that only one car could pass and the driver would try to see whether there was oncoming traffic, rendering it necessary to wait until clear. Only someone standing on the bridge was able to see both ways. Being the kindly soul that I am, on the first occasion I waved to the driver scrunched over his steering wheel to indicate to him that the bridge was clear to cross. It soon became apparent that I would have to undertake this task for all approaching vehicles and most of my few minutes spent at Linnels Bridge were done so acting as traffic warden, waving first one hand then the other to guide cars safely across. My pause at the bridge would have been longer had it not been for these continual interruptions. I passed to the northern side of the river. I was afforded a view of the main entrance to the house by the bridge and I noticed builders' vans parked on the driveway. The house and its garden had looked dishevelled and I could now see why: it was empty, undergoing extensive renovation works of a type that seemed to suggest that its final use would be a nursing home. Rather apt, I thought, that if he had still been alive then perhaps Wainwright might have been able to affect his wish to live here. However, I doubted whether he would have wanted to see out his days surrounded by elderly folk languishing in easy chairs with only rare stimulus to separate them from what would otherwise have seemed like a living death. Maybe one day I would end up there, or somewhere like it, but I rather hoped not for I would pray to die as though a candle had been snuffed out and not allowed to silently burn away to nothing. I had no wish for my stature to diminish to be inexorably replaced by an ever-growing sea of melted wax slowly filling the saucer in which I had previously thrived.

I left Linnels Bridge and Wainwright's house and began the sharp ascent of the valley north of the river in changed weather that by now gave a suggestion of imminent sun to brighten this thus far dull day. I had not proceeded very far when the effort of making the climb saw the first of several stops to catch my breath and to mop my sweating brow with the back of my hand. The fleece, which I had worn all day, had to be packed for I was rapidly over-heating and my legs were fast becoming sticky (with perspiration, for goodness' sake). I could not bear the prospect of the rigmarole of changing into shorts with only two miles remaining before reaching Hexham so I would have to bear any associated discomfort. My feet and legs were beginning to ache intolerably and my lungs appeared to have dropped out some way back down the road. My stomach was, by this time, complaining that nothing except a pint of beer had been sent its way since breakfast and my shoulders did not appreciate the additional weight of the fleece having been repacked, slight though it was. My nose was running, my lips were chapped and I had difficulty finding any part of my body that did not have something to complain about. Less than an hour to go now, I told them all. In an hour's time, I promised them, we would all be booking into the Beaumont Hotel. My feet and legs would be able to bathe, my thirst and appetite would be quenched and satisfied, my shoulders would be rested, my nose blown and my lips eased with the lip gel that I had not been able to find while en route. Mutiny in the ranks was never far away and insurrection was only averted when the slope levelled and the road began a very gradual descent. I had assumed that I had grown accustomed to the aches and pains of yesterday and that today, my day of rest, would allow a well-deserved reprieve from previous days' sufferings, but I was wrong and would be relieved to see my goal. There, at least, I would be able to muster fresh and more energetic troops for the morrow when we would jointly storm the Roman wall.

Strolling uneasily along, I was pleased when I at last came to a formal pavement at the side of the road and knew that this signalled the beginning of civilisation. The first signs of approaching urbanisation were further confirmed with the appearance of buildings on both sides of the road, one of the first of which was a Jehovah's Witness Kingdom Hall. The hall was of single-storey stone construction and had, I guessed, been built within the last ten years. This struck me at the time as being slightly bizarre as I recalled that it was the Witnesses who held the view that the world would come to a sticky end in the not-too-distant future. The committee that ratified its construction must have found the decision very difficult. 'Yes, Mr Chairman, I know that the world is going to end but the Development Subcommittee feel that the expenditure ought to be approved just in case our estimate of the climactic end may have been slightly premature.' It seemed rather similar to a man sentenced to the gallows deciding to buy a timeshare or take out a long-term pension – short of a miraculous pardon for previous wrongdoings it would prove to be a little rash and a dire waste of expense.

Not very far beyond the hall the road turned and commenced a sharp descent into Hexham. From my elevated position I could see the town nestling below with the squat form of the abbey centre stage. Huddled around it were a variety of grey rooftops of old Hexham and, over these roofs I could see the faint outline of hills beyond. There was little detail in their form because the clarity of the day, although much improved from earlier, did not permit views of any great extent. I knew that somewhere not too far over those gentle hills I would find Hadrian's Wall. I studied my map and knew that if I cared I would only have to walk another mile or so north of them to witness its existence. Not today, though; I would save that pleasure for tomorrow. As Wainwright had approached Hexham he reflected on the solitude of his journey thus far. He had seen very few passers-by and was able to count his encounters on the fingers of one hand. Although he made no reference as to whether the roads and lanes had been so quiet, it was safe to assume he would not have had to brave as many confrontations with cars, lorries, vans and motorcycles as I had. The ways that he had travelled were, in many cases, now off limits to the walker if it were solitude that was sought. Nonetheless, with some planning to accommodate the present levels of road traffic, his walk could be developed into a fine pilgrimage for a modern-day long-distance walk. In the formulation of my adventure I had only ever considered my wish to follow in his footsteps and had given no thought to the viability of re-plotting the route for others to follow. But now, as I tramped with heavy legs down the final hill, I was suddenly taken by the notion of not only recording an account to compare and contrast with Wainwright's, but also to devise a route that would bypass the parts that were no longer of any merit. There was much of its length to be commended unchanged and where change was required, sufficient paths and tracks are shown on the maps to provide more pleasurable alternatives to the parts that had been best forgotten.

In 1938 Hexham had been expanding with a profusion of new houses being built. Its sprawl has continued unabashed and new estates have crawled up the hill that I was descending. These new houses do not detract from the visitor's appreciation of the town for they are modest and, on the whole, in keeping with their environment. What came as more of a surprise was the building that the planning authority had allowed to be built quite close to the town centre which comprised bright-blue tubular framework with light-coloured infill panelling. No more than a quarter of a mile from the abbey this vivid aberration stood out like a sore thumb from the brown and grey forms that stood all about it. Perhaps I am out of step and might stand to be accused of not wanting to see change. I have no objection to change but fail to see why it needs to make its mark in such a brash and ugly manner, paying no respect whatsoever to its more demure and well-bred surroundings. It was as much sacrilege as is the one red-brick terraced house out of the terrace of twenty that has been defaced by the use of stick-on artificial stone panels. In the right circumstances standing out from the crowd is to be admired, but beware as there is a fine line between making a statement of style and demonstrating a total lack of taste and breeding. There are certain things that will endure and there are others that will wax and wane as their arrival in the form of a fad is quickly followed by their departure from our minds. This strategy has been well used by fashion designers and has deluded us into believing that the clothes we wear have a limited 'shelf life' with magazine articles and advertisements tempting us with the latest fashion items and accessories. As a marketing exercise their success had been exemplary with the gullible customer buying one thing one minute and another thing the next. There was a time when this blanket advertising had more readily fooled the female of the species, but in recent years men have been sucked into a cyclical purchase/discard mentality where the only winners are the designers and retail outlets. It is rapidly becoming inbred in us that our credibility is directly proportionate to our appearance and that we must be seen to be wearing the right clothes. This generates an apparent disregard for any inspection closer than purely superficial, obviates character assessment and establishes a subliminal class system that successive governments have been at pains to say no longer exists. Of course the class system exists and it will always remain so long as we continue to be influenced and indoctrinated by the display philosophy that is forced upon us through the power of the advertising billboard. It is for this reason that I have always believed in the compulsory wearing of uniforms for all schoolchildren, regardless of age. A uniform creates a sense of evenness and precludes the fashion disease from biting too early in life. It is not a large step from being nurtured in an educational atmosphere where believing that what we appear to be matters more than who we are, to developing into a society of the haves and the have-nots. We are not allowed to smoke or drink below a certain age, presumably because they are adjudged dangerous and that we should know our own minds and be capable of making our own decisions before being led into such temptation. I maintain that fashion should be seen as being no different.

Surely there must be more to our perceptions of others than the skin-deep scrutiny of their outer layer. I am confident that there must be, for if there were not then I am sure Sue would not have chosen me. I have never considered myself to be the greatest of catches and, whatever else it might have been that attracted her to me, it certainly wasn't dashing looks, full head of hair, family wealth or sports car. I did once have some aspirations in the direction of my professional executive prospects, but these had long ago disintegrated as I had reeled from one career mistake to another

These various tangential deliberations were still floating around as I finally entered the trading heart of Hexham. Like many other towns of its size, it seemed to provide a haven for banks and building societies, although it is likely that in the surrounding hinterland it is the only location for their respective outlets. No longer, sadly, do they put their service to the public above all else and the majority of the small-town branches have been closed as a result of their modern modus operandi of profit-driven performance. Like all other large organisations, they will spend many thousands of pounds on measuring their patrons' levels of satisfaction but then seem to do very little about it when they receive answers they would rather not hear. The financial institutions are no different to many other high-street retailers and there is a growing expectancy that their customers will all have the use of a car. The gargantuan out-of-town developments seem to be predominantly based upon an assumption of a vast patronage by car users and a visit any day of the week to any of the more popular ones will prompt the conclusion that their assumptions are correct. It had hardly been of startling proportions to have read a few days earlier that many town centres are dying commercially in the face of such competition. This change to the very nature of the activity of shopping will, ultimately, leave towns devoid of custom. Drastic reductions in available services had already occurred in many of the villages I had visited en route and perhaps in another sixty years residents of Hexham and other similar-sized towns will only have vague and distant memories of their trading past. For now though there were still a great many shops around which I could browse, but first I had promised myself to be rid of weighty baggage and boots so I sought out the Beaumont Hotel without further ado.

I had entered the plush foyer feeling rather out of place and I am sure that my appearance secured me speedy service to clear me from the reception. I was politely shown to my room and was told of the hotel's laundering service after I had inquired as to whether there was a launderette in the town. By the time we reached my room at the far end of the first-floor corridor I had agreed that I would leave my various damp, dirty, smelly (delete whichever not applicable) items for them to deal with. This would save some time, allowing me to spend longer doing other tasks, all far more interesting than sitting watching my clothes slowly turning in the washing machine. At first the maid waited for me to give her my laundry, but when I advised that it would include all the clothes that I was standing up in she retired fairly smartly and I delivered the offending articles to the receptionist some minutes later. All the parts of my body that had been rebelling an hour before felt infinitely better once their variety of ailments were attended to and I ventured out into the town to acquire the numerous items that I needed. I found my postcards and stamps, some more films, a new note-book, a booklet about Hadrian's Wall and a fresh supply of tobacco and adjourned to the nearest pub for I was relishing the prospect of a pint or two while writing the cards. Prior to finding a pub I am ashamed to admit that I wandered the streets greedily tucking into the two sausage rolls that I had bought from the first delicatessen I had come upon. The four postcards all broadcast very much the same news: that I had arrived on schedule and that I was thoroughly enjoying my exploits. After that I ran out of things to say of any import for I doubted whether anyone would be able to share in the full extent of my emotions, so I mentioned the weather and one or two other mundane and entirely forgettable bits of information. I could not honestly wish that anyone was here and I suspected that no one really wished they were in any case. I wrote them slowly to ensure that I had time for a second drink, after which I made my exit to seek out the Abbey Tearooms. My suspicions regarding the town's anonymity proved correct in that there was no obvious trace of the café and its letting rooms. I did, of course, find a number of buildings that might have fitted Wainwright's description, but none that was so apparent as to have been the definite article. The only letting rooms that now remained so close to the abbey were those in posh hotels – business rates would have seen to it that more lowly accommodation would be restricted to residences outside the im-mediate town centre. Slightly disgruntled at my lack of success, I decided that I was tired enough to have a lie down and read all I could about Hadrian's Wall. I returned to the hotel, made a cup of tea and, without delay, fell hard and fast asleep.

I awoke with a start at six o'clock when some disturbance or other outside jolted me from my slumber. Not immediately aware that I had been asleep, I took a drink from my untouched cup of tea, which by this time was icy. It was then that I looked at my watch and realised the tea was two hours old. Making another brew I settled at the dressing table for half an hour to learn about the wall and to half listen to the news on the television. With the exception of the first evening, this was the first time I had heard any news at all of the outside world. None of it held the interest in the same way that the news must have done when Wainwright made his journey and it had indeed been at Hexham during his stay that peace was delivered to the nation by Mr Chamberlain on a piece of paper signed by Herr Hitler. Of course, twelve months later that piece of paper found its way into history for the wrong reasons, but when Wainwright had awoken at Hexham he, like the rest of the country, breathed a sigh of relief at the great diplomacy of Mr Chamberlain and his policy of appeasement. All the news could boast in 1998 was that Bill Clinton had continued to be asked some serious and searching questions on the matter of his sexual urges and hour after interminable hour of news had already been broadcast relating to the subject. Just exactly who the bloody hell was bothered in the least was entirely beyond my comprehension. Other subjects of newsworthiness revolved around Mr Blair's latest foreign visit – when will he stop smiling that inane grin, I wondered as I caught a glimpse of his polished teeth out of the corner of my eye. The queen and royal family were mentioned in a bad light as ever, about what I cannot remember – there seemed to be a permanency about attacking them I recalled as I pondered on the relevance of them as an institution. The world's sad little bickerings were distracting me from my from reading, so I turned the television off, finished my tea and switched the shower on so as to take the chill off the shower room.

I had been told of the good-value food a hungry traveller might find at a pub named 'Heart of all England'. I never did discover why, at this outpost of England not too many miles from Scotland, a pub should be so named but then I was not overly concerned. I was, however, overly hungry and fairly marched passed the abbey following the directions I had been given. I found the place without difficulty and asked to see the menu. The straightforward options were a joy to behold and provided such simple and extensive choice that I did not know for which to opt. On three of the previous four evenings I had had to eat food that was not really to my liking and a meal had been chosen on the basis of disliking it least of all the things on the menu. Here I was struggling and took the menu to a table to consider the options while rolling a cigarette with my renewed tobacco supply. My stomach had thoughts only for the fare listed, but it relied on my eyes to do the looking and their attention was temporarily diverted by the sight of the barmaid who, a few moments earlier, had walked in reporting for duty. She had removed her outer coat to reveal jeans and white shoulder-less top both so tight they looked as though they had been painted on. Little was left to the imagination and each time she was required to move or pull a pint, some part of her anatomy would squirm under her skimpy attire. This was splendid entertainment and I have to confess to spending more than a moment or two trying to guess what type, if any, of undergarments she might have been wearing. I didn't think that this was the type of young innocent that Wainwright dreamt of in his account. No, this girl would have eaten him and spat him out for breakfast. During my visits to the bar to order food or another drink I found my-self not knowing exactly where to look to best maintain decency; suffice to say that had it been any colder, I would have known where to hang my cap. There were not too many customers in the Heart of all England that night and it may have only been coincidence that those present were all men and they were all sat at bar stools.

All in all I had thoroughly enjoyed my food, my drinks, my cigarettes and my spectator sport and reckoned that the evening had been, all things considered, the best value for money thus far. I wanted an early night so I left the pub at half past eight to make my way back to my hotel, and as I closed the door behind me there were reflections of lamp lights and shop window displays on the narrow backstreet. For the first time in five days there was a light rain falling – not so heavy as to merit an umbrella but heavy enough to be disheartening for any poor soul who had planned for so long to come this way and see the Wall, and not so heavy as to merit boots but heavy enough to make someone wearing brown deck shoes look like a moron. Still, I decided, I did not care what I looked like and, besides, I was in a town where my presence would be forgotten within minutes of my leaving. In the morning I would be gone and by lunch-time nobody would know or care that I had visited.

As I made my way back to the hotel I passed the entrance to the cinema, which must have been the same cinema that Wainwright had come out of after a performance in the vain hope that some young lady might befriend him. I very much doubted any young lady would even sit near him for by this stage of his trek he must have been unbearably aromatic. I walked toward the entrance to see what was playing and was saddened upon reading the handwritten notice that had been pinned up two weeks earlier advising that the place would be closed until further notice. Another casualty no doubt of out-of-town developments – there was more than likely some multiplex that had been opened which had sounded the death knell for this small slice of history.

Arriving back at the Beaumont, and glad to be out of the weather, I went upstairs to my room and tested my knowledge of the Wall over a final cup of tea. Switching the television on, I waited for the forecast to see if my worsening fortune was likely to continue. It was. The forecast for the weekend was poor and I would rather not have known. I was tired and knew that I would fall asleep very quickly – per chance to dream. One of my last conscious thoughts was being concerned that I might dream of overlarge jellyfish squirming and crawling about in a tight white sack and that they might eat me and spit me out for breakfast. I recall nothing after that.

Chapter 6

Hexham to Haltwhistle

In biblical terms, the sixth day was really rather spectacular. The previous five days had been mere preparation for day six – the big one – the day when all the earlier work came together and people would say 'Wow, that's impressive.' So it was with this walk of mine. The sixth day of this mammoth excursion was also the big one for it was the day that would bear the fruits of the previous five days' labours. I had walked many miles and had seen only scant reminders of Roman remains, meagre traces of their presence, nothing more. There had been evidence of them at Bainbridge and at Bowes, but these extended only to lumpy bits of grass where there had once been settlements. I had travelled along ways that had, all those years ago, been thoroughfares for their traffic, but their original roads had since disappeared under more modern surfacing. If it were not for the fact that my maps had indicated a former presence I would have perhaps missed these earlier sites completely. Not so today though, for I would bear witness to one of the Romans' greatest feats while resident on British soil. Yes, the sixth day was to be a momentous day and gave the whole walk its true objective. It had been uppermost in the heart and mind of Wainwright as he had trudged northwards and had been pivotal to his whole expedition. In the absence of the wall he would have been unable to know where to walk to and from for although he admitted to a desire to further explore the Pennines, he also wanted to reach a definite goal. Ambling aimlessly in the Pennine hills was not of itself an adequate raison d'être and he needed something extra to provide fulfilment. The wall had provided the goal and had become the central point from which all else gained relevance. All the miles of walking, however enjoyable in their own right, would have purpose for they were leading to the pot of gold at the end of the rainbow.

It was, perhaps, the magnitude of this day that caused me to wake early once more or, then again, perhaps it was the sound of rainfall that I could hear in the car park below my room. Equally it may have been my aching muscles that brought me back from sleep, or maybe it was that I awoke with a jolt during a particularly alarming episode of a dream that revolved around jellyfish and a sack. I could not recall any night-time dreams but I was very well aware of all the others. As I limped to the window on legs that ached abominably, the rain was falling quite heavily onto the cars below and I watched the cascading drops in the light of a nearby street lamp for some minutes while the kettle boiled. It was five o'clock and, knowing that any further sleep was impossible, I drank my first cup of tea and read again about Emperor Hadrian and his endeavours.

The wall was built on his orders to act as a northern boundary of the Roman Empire, which had grown so rapidly that the powers that be believed it was high time to consolidate. In addition there were some really rather revolting natives to the north and it would serve also as a means of curbing any unpleasant incursions that they might, from time to time, consider making. It is not my intention to present a treatise upon its history other than as required to expand upon the sheer magnificence of the engineering that was necessary to realise its construction. At over seventy-three miles in length, one was forced to admire the tenacity of these workmen nearly 2,000 years before who had toiled for ten years over its completion, and I was looking forward to seeing the outcome of their industry with eager anticipation.

During the fourth and fifth days I had covered a total of thirty-three miles, twenty-eight of which had been on hard metalled surface that had varied in their degree of usage from quiet lanes to busy roads between dales villages. Too many of them had been too overrun with swarming traffic to be agreeable and it was with great cheer that I studied my route and found that for the larger part of the sixth day's walk I would be in the midst of countryside following footpaths. Although my advance upon the wall would have to be by way of roads, once there I would be able to escape from their verges and tread on softer ground for much of the walk.

I had estimated that the walk to Haltwhistle was around 20 miles and because I feared that my pace might slow as a consequence of my tiredness, I was breakfasting at half past seven, hoping to be on my way forty-five minutes later. This would enable me to average only two miles per hour and still reach The Grey Bull at Haltwhistle well before dusk. I had to assume a lesser pace would be maintained if the effort required in reaching the breakfast room was anything to go by. It was a distance of only the length of a corridor with no steps to negotiate, yet stiff limbs had made it seem like very hard work. Breakfasting alone in the large high-ceilinged room seemed almost too lonely, with other guests not having appeared and places set in readiness for their arrival. Two suited businessmen entered for breakfast and the peace occasioned by my solitariness was disturbed as they discussed the issues that had brought them to Hexham. I could only assume by their conversation that they were to attend some meeting or other and, as they began their day, they discussed the relative merits of this approach or that idea. How very unfortunate that even at breakfast professional travail has to rear its head – it has, of course, become popular to have working breakfasts, the notion of which I find somewhat vulgar. The breakfast table is no place to deliberate problems or difficulties; it should be reserved as a time to charge the batteries ready to do battle with life's trials and tribulations only after the body has been refreshed. I had once, I recalled, been invited to join a breakfast club where business folk would meet and exchange ideas and business cards in the hope of future work. I politely refused believing that drudgery starting at nine o'clock was perfectly soon enough without having to interact any sooner than was absolutely necessary. I glanced over every so often at my two fellow diners to see them making notes and detailing their strategy on a pad that they had brought to breakfast with them. Initially I thought how sad it was that they were so wrapped up in their work that they would do such a thing, and then I remembered that I had brought my map to breakfast and had perused it and wondered whether I was equally enveloped. Of course I was, I thought, but my reasoning had been associated with recreation not work. Could it be, continuing on this train of thought, that these gentlemen so enjoyed their work that they considered it too to be recreational. I was not able to imagine such a concept where a sensation of enjoyment flows from work. It is only the very few who are so lucky as to generate a salary from doing something they adore, and I had never been among their number. Perhaps, I pondered further, these gents' work environment was such that it created, in its workforce, a genuine sense of belief in its structure and its hierarchy to the extent that it had become a pleasure to work. If this was the case, they were an example of an organisation that many other companies could learn from. So many companies' management will sing from the rooftops their own praises as to how they and the staff have a common goal and that they are all members of the same team singing from the same song sheet. Seldom does the actuality of the staff's feeling toward management reflect the declared viewpoint of having common goals and all being a member of one big team. Where the competitive edge has demanded razor-thin margins, there has developed a greater need to assess performance, be it good or bad. To perform relies on decisions being made, and where decisions are made, some will prove to be imprudent. Few would wish to be the team member whose decision had been found wanting for suddenly that common goal seems like just as many words on a page and not a genuine stated management philosophy. The result is that either no one will make decisions, or that when someone does, it is only when there exists ratification from above or an ability to place responsibility for their decisions elsewhere.

This attitude is true of too great a percentage of workplaces, where the style of management has developed into culture of blame. What started (no doubt genuinely) as an ethos of empowerment of the workforce below management level by delegation has, in all too many cases, turned from delegation of authority into abdication of responsibility. The ownership of success remains at management level, but possession of errors lies with the poor sod who actually carried out the work. I recalled working in an environment such as this for three years with my own position having been made even more precarious because I would not look to follow the example of management in transferring blame. It is little wonder that there exists a paranoid workforce. Even greater personal amazement had come when I had read in the press of some rather well-paid researcher pronouncing the result of his or her (or their, because there would more than likely be a whole government-sponsored team involved) survey. The report had concluded that there existed increased incidences of work-related stress. It should be patently obvious to anyone with half an atom of grey matter that there exists increased incidences of work-related stress and that it does not require too much mental agility to see where that stress comes from. Fear is the key – clearly no one wants to reap the consequences of an error of misjudgement, but it is only those further up the ladder who are able to divert any criticism onto the shoulders of those below them. The result is the emergence of a work ethic where the safest form of initiative is not to use one's initiative at all. It should be of no surprise then that as the majority of the workers are forced to spend a wholly unhealthy proportion of their time in such a negative environment that stress is the inevitable outcome. Someone once said with great foresight that the man who never made a mistake never actually made anything. Where a workplace looks to place blame for things going awry and not reward effort for a job well done, it follows that the staff will keep as low a profile as is possible. I never did quite work out what it was that the bosses themselves were scared of, but in some cases I suspected it was their own shadow.

Perhaps, resuming my thinking, it was in such a climate that the two gentlemen were conducting their breakfast tryst. Perhaps they were plotting how best to circumvent the likely repercussions of an error having been made. Whatever was their purpose, they were never once stirred from the discussion that held them oblivious to the coffee having arrived. I left them deep in animated discussion as I finished breakfast. I made my way to reception to collect my laundry before packing and leaving. Limping down the stairs I concluded that it was most likely that my two companions over breakfast had no doubt gradually, over the years, become so engulfed in work that they had lost sight of that other well-known saying about working to live and not living to work. They had given me some small measure of sadistic entertainment over my scrambled eggs on toast, but the diversion had resulted in my forgetting to inquire of the waiter the quickest way to find the road to Warden.

I approached the reception desk with some trepidation as it was only after I had handed my clothes for laundering that I had noticed the standard prices charged for the service. At two pounds for this and one pound fifty for the other, I very much feared that the size of the bill would leave me penniless with six days still to go. Although I had assured the receptionist to whom I handed my clothes that there would be no need to iron them, I still waited with baited breath for the bill. My concerns were unfounded for they suggested five pounds for the whole lot, which I gratefully accepted, settled my account and returned to my room to set about packing. Re-entering my room I noticed one of those questionnaires relating to the quality of the service – I must be somewhere posh, I thought, if I had stayed in a place that had its own customer satisfaction form. It would be the only one I would be invited to complete throughout my travels. I glimpsed through the questions and decided that because I had not used many of the services to which they referred, and because I wanted to be away speedily, I left it uncompleted. Yes, I had been attended to sufficiently quickly; yes, my room was fine; yes, the limited food I had consumed was fine. Apart from these few I could not comment further, and had any of they been poor I would have remonstrated in any case. Customer focus and other such buzzwords have become the scourge of modern service and we are not allowed do anything without someone asking for our feedback. I sometimes wonder who develops these feedback forms and how much of their development is simply a means of keeping someone in a job. I have a sneaking suspicion that higher management use them to help them in their quest to prove to everybody that the organisation is working to a common goal and acting as one big happy team.

I left the hotel reception and went out onto the street at quarter past eight, having decided that I would find my own way to the road heading out toward Warden. As it transpired I walked around three sides of a square before finding it, but my detour gave me a final opportunity of seeing parts of the town I had not seen yesterday. Indeed, quite a lot of parts I had not seen. The rain had eased considerably and was now no more than a fine drizzle that haled from no particular direction and stuck to you rather than fell on you. Nevertheless, it was still wet and had required that my ridiculously expensive coat was being put to good use. I passed through the Market Square and under the tower of the watchful abbey, down the street and passed the Heart of all England. Still I could gauge no clue as to which was the likely building that once upon a time had been the Abbey Tearoom and so I continued on my way down the slope ready to leave Hexham behind. My presumption that it would give up no secrets to aid me in forming a picture of Wainwright's movements had been well founded. I had learned nothing except that the picture house had closed, which was neither stunning nor unexpected, for many other small town cinemas before it had suffered the same fate. A cheery good morning was shouted from across the road, to which I responded, and a brief conversation ensued from pavement to pavement as to the state of the weather and the likelihood of improvement. The ancient couple with whom I had engaged in this brief dialogue were removing the equally ancient timber shutters from a shop that was itself so ancient it must have looked exactly like this when Wainwright had walked by. I could not let this opportunity go by so I crossed the road and spoke to Bill and Vera about their memories of Hexham and whether they could recall the tearoom. They were very apologetic for not knowing its exact location but, yes, one of the buildings adjacent to the abbey had been a tearoom just prior to the war. Yes, I knew that. Although they could not place it they recollected that it provided board and lodging. Yes, I knew that too. Apart from that they were very sorry but such distant memories were a smidgen vague. I thanked them anyway and continued until I finally came to a road junction at which I could turn right, signposted Carlisle, knowing I then must be on the road in the general direction of Warden.

As I walked along the pavement at the side of the busy road I caught glimpses of the dual carriageway over to my right that carried the bypass which had removed most of the passing traffic from Hexham's congested centre.

Looking at the weight of lorries thundering along, it I shuddered to think what the heart of the town must have been like before it was opened. The road I followed out of Hexham would, at one time, have been the main Newcastle to Carlisle route but now it existed only as a feeder road from the cross-country trunk road. It was quarter to nine as I passed the gates of the crematorium and there was a steady flow of cars conveying their occupants to the start of their days' work. I reflected on my thinking over breakfast and my observing of the two businessmen and wondered how many of these travellers would empathise with the working environment that I had mentally described. I suspected that a great many of them would recognise the description as though its subject had been their own workplace. I have often sat in traffic queues, when all lanes have been inexplicably stationary, and wondered as to why all the other cars were there. I had always wanted to get out of the car and ask other drivers to determine what common aim could possibly have brought so many of us all together at the same place and the same time to the extent that none could move. It was exactly the same as I left Hexham behind – I wanted to know more about the people who were now enduring the stop-start journey: what did they do and what would they wish to do. Today I was, I estimated, in a minority for although, like them, I was doing something that I had to do, I was, at the same time, doing something that I also desired to do. We were all in transit on the road to Hexham but I felt substantiation that there was far greater purpose to my progression than there was with the majority of the others who passed along the road on that Friday morning.

This brief digression saw me arrive at the major junction with the Newcastle to Carlisle highway, which required negotiation if I were to proceed north. I could see the unclassified road on the opposite side of the dual carriageway, but crossing to it to continue along my route was a major operation that called for split-second timing. Huge articulated trailer lorries charged incessantly by, but I finally managed to seek the refuge of the central reservation before having to repeat the procedure to see me safely across the eastbound traffic. I had envisaged that, once north of the main road, the narrow road to Warden would be a quiet and little-used backwater with little in the way of traffic to hinder peaceful progress, but upon turning onto it, I discovered I was sadly mistaken. Seemingly most of the westbound lorries that had hampered my crossing had then also turned onto it and I was forced to share it with these huge monsters as they travelled to and from Aycliffe Quarry. At least that was what was printed on the side of most of them. I had no idea of the location of Aycliffe Quarry but I hoped that once we crossed the river then perhaps their way and mine would separate, for the prospect of our paths coinciding all the way to and beyond Warden was too much to contemplate. The sad irony of my debacle with these lorries came when, at one point, I sought refuge at the roadside against a wall and, over the wall's coping stone, I spied yet another disused railway. It had been part of a line that used to weave its way along the valley of the River South Tyne to Allendale and would, undoubtedly, provide a means of transport for quarried waste that was far more efficacious for the company and far less hazardous for the walker. Like so many things, we have destroyed it with no chance of redemption and like so many things, it is only when it is no longer available do we begin to regret an earlier action.

There are many examples of the irreversible destructive capabilities of mans' endeavours, the worst of which is the more modern premeditation with seeing the annihilation of our own country's traditions and heritage. Should it be that you find any difficulty in equating with this statement, you will only have to ask the royal family for they will understand only too well the emotion of being the victims of a witch-hunt under the name of 'Cool Britannia'. There are those who would call for a republic and the abolition of the monarchy with little regard as to a replacement figurehead, the justification being that the monarchy is outdated and costly to maintain. On the matter of expense, those people who promulgate such a view ought to pay cognizance to the massive influx of visitors who come to these shores to share in our traditional royal experience. With regards to the notion of replacement figurehead, for we would surely need a Head of State, enough evidence lies all around us of our tendency towards instating transitory heads who are hired and fired as rapidly as football managers.

For a credible state to exist there must be continuity and an assurance in the mind of its citizens that they are not being governed on a flavour-of-the-month basis. I am always puzzled by the definition of outdated and can only assume that it refers to something that is old, of no use and no longer relevant. Hadrian's Wall is ancient; it can fulfil no functional purpose; its true relevance in a modern world escapes me. Are we then to destroy it? It presumably survives because it has become commercially viable. For these reasons those who would see the destruction of the monarchy would do so at their peril, unless, that is, they believe that the newspaper magnates, for it is they who predominantly influence the minds of the weak, might better be able to fairly govern. I think not. One of the very fundamental changes that Wainwright would have noted had he been here with me would have been the nature of the press and its relationship both with those upon whom it reports and those to whom its reports are aimed. In 1938 reportage was of a much more factual nature, where the issues were reported in order that the public would be kept abreast of items of newsworthiness. In 1998 the meaning of the word newsworthiness has changed to become something sickeningly visual – the public is subjected to anything so long as it is sufficiently juicy enough to adorn the front pages in the apparent name of public interest. I will say no more of the press for I have aired my views before and may well again. Believe and speak only the word that you experience yourself and be guarded about all else, for it is you who will reap the consequences if you are influenced and act while ill informed.

Leaving the wall above the disused railway, I crossed the river by way of the grand stone bridge that appeared to hark back to bygone days when this route had been of greater importance than now, other than for providing a busy crossing point for the lorries that hounded me. Immediately after the bridge crossing, I was pleased to note that they were, to a one, all turning left and I would hopefully be left in peace to make the last three miles to the wall and my first view of its remains at Chesters. Soon I came upon the modest church at Warden with its clock-less tower, still half hidden in trees so that it would have been easy to pass it by unnoticed had I not known of its whereabouts. It did not seem to have changed from the time Wainwright had described it, except today there were no dancing sunbeams filtering through the trees to illuminate the texture of its random coursed masonry. I looked into the gloom around me as I spent a few minutes at the church gate and pondered on the words of Bill and Vera who had been confident that the weather would improve. Admittedly they had given no timescale to their forecast but for the moment, anyway, their prognosis showed no signs of becoming reality. Hexham was now only a memory without visual confirmation of its presence for it had faded entirely into the mist and drizzle two miles across the valley.

Turning, I carried on my journey along the wonderfully quiet byway following above and to the west of the River North Tyne. Giving all credit to Bill and Vera and their prophecy that the day would ameliorate, I had not gone but a few yards when the drizzle ceased and my jacket was stowed. Again I was returned to walking in shirtsleeves and would continue to do so for the rest of the day as the elements became more and more agreeable. Earlier concerns as to the various parts of my body that had been tender now felt as though they were impervious to pain as I strode with great purpose, looking all around me as I did so to admire the tranquil beauty of this shallow valley. Below me lay meadows sweeping down to the bank of the river and to the other side of the valley I could see the settlement of Wall and the sporadic evidence of the old railway line that used to run all the way up the North Tyne valley. At Wall's old station there was even an old Pullman carriage lying forlorn on its trackless site; appearing to be in good condition it was all dressed up but with nowhere to go.

Continuing on my way, I approached the junction with the 'Military Road', which runs in long and unbending stretches across the country with these straight sections separated by definite corners as it adjusts its direction. It is as if the builders had had every intention of constructing a perfectly straight west–east route but had suddenly realised their instruments were giving erroneous bearings, which they then over compensated for and had ended up with this crooked highway. The sad truth behind the course of this road is to be found in the history of its development. In 1745 General Wade was the big cheese in the

English Army and was camped in Newcastle waiting in readiness to give Bonnie Prince Charlie a good seeing to. Charlie got wind of this and bypassed the troops by taking a westerly route via Carlisle, leaving General Wade and his men deployed in exactly the wrong place with no means of rapid transport to intercept him. The command came to build a line of communication connecting east and west and the engineers found that the stones from the old Roman wall, for some part of its length, made for an ideal foundation to their new route. So, before the days of planning and highway authorities and building regulations, great swathes of the wall were simply demolished and put to new use. No matter then as to whether the wall had any commercial worth – it was clearly adjudged to be of no value and ploughed underfoot without a thought for its place within the nation's history. How strange it is that, at a time when the monarchy demanded respect from its subjects, there was no comprehension of the retention of our heritage. In the intervening 250 years the relative status of the two has been totally reversed with little respect being paid to the monarchy but a vastly increasing desire to see all manner of artefacts retained in perpetuity at public expense. I rather expected that I would see a marked change from the informal admission arrangements at Chesters from when Wainwright had visited when he had tried to awaken the caretaker to no avail. Hadrian's Wall is now classed as a World Heritage Site and I suspected that associated with that fact would be a very slick merchandising operation administered under the watchful gaze of the National Trust and English Heritage. So seriously do we now take our history that government quangos have actually been established to oversee redevelopment and provide protection for the remainders of our ancestry. Nailing my colours to the mast, I will express again my consternation that we do not seem to hold as much store in the protection of our monarchy. Like our ancestral pedigree, it stands as the envy of many other countries and should be cherished not rebuked.

I was aware that just prior to reaching the junction with the Military Road I would cross the line of the wall. No trace of it was to be found and I arrived at the end of the road where I turned right following the signs for Chesters, still none the wiser as to what to expect of the previous occupation of the area. With only half a mile to walk, my pace quickened as my heart ruled my muscles and, for all my brain pleaded with me that I still had a long way to walk and should slow, lessening my rate of stride seemed impossible in light of the keen antici-pation of what lay ahead. I arrived at the fort's entrance and rounded the corner into the large car parking area. This must be a very busy place, I thought, on summer weekends judging by the size of the car park. Thankfully, at half past ten on Friday 25 September there were few cars and only small groups of sight-seers entering the slick reception area. My assumption had been correct in that this was indeed a highly polished machine and there was to be no escaping the £2.70 charge, even though I could afford time to stay only a matter of minutes. The smart lady on reception went into her equally polished sales pitch about the benefits of membership with English Heritage. I have to confess that I did not feel disposed to join having just handed over my entrance fee, which would equate to approximately 10p per minute for each minute of my visit. I entered the nicely manicured grassed area from which the remnants of Chesters, the Roman name for which was Cilurnum, protrude as though islands within a be-calmed green sea, each island being set within its own fenced-off enclosure. These fences, although very necessary for the protection of the low residual walling, ensnare the relics and act as a barrier to the imagination, for as much as they restrict damage, their erection also limits the relics' impact. It was not pos-sible to drift in the imaginary world of legionnaires and centurions into which Wainwright had been spirited while he was here, but there was a sense of the magnitude of the undertaking entered into by the Roman forces. There were several other tourists wandering around the site, so I took myself off to inspect the bathhouse down by the edge of the river and sat for fifteen minutes or so in contemplation. I had set about to walk here from Settle and, having passed through various villages and settlements, I had now covered nigh on 100 miles. I was nearly halfway and another three miles would see me at the most north-erly point of my journey, after which I would be commencing my return home. Yes, today was impressive and part of the feeling of euphoria was as a function of the previous five days' effort in transporting me here by foot. Had I journeyed by car, or with someone else, I do not believe that I would have experienced the same measure of satisfaction as I did quietly sitting and smoking a well-deserved cigarette. However smug and self-satisfied I was feeling, I was only too aware that sitting in the bathhouse would not carry me westwards and, as I still had fifteen miles remaining, I retraced my steps back to the entrance, saying goodbye to the polished lady.

Having returned to the roadside I had no choice other than to follow its course for there is no path that follows the wall hereabouts. There is, care of General Wade and his engineers, only the road itself to follow for any remains of the wall are buried underfoot and act only as eighteenth-century ballast. I knew that although I would have to wait before seeing the wall proper, I had hoped to glimpse its other features while tramping up the long incline through Walwick and up to Limestone Bank. To the south of the wall, at varying distances from it, lay a broad channel, the Vallum, while immediately north of it there was excavated a much steeper-sided trench – the ditch. I was aware of their existence both from the literature I had read after my early waking and also from Wainwright's own poetic description of them. I wanted to see them for myself and I hoped that I would not be disappointed when I finally encountered them. Too often we are prepossessed as to the grandeur of an article by an earlier account only to have illusions shattered when we experience the same but first hand. The reverse is also true, where a prior account of critical displeasure establishes an expectation of indifference only to be replaced by a more positive sensation when the subject is witnessed in person. I had already created a mental picture of Teesdale, based on Wainwright's description, as a place with nothing to commend it and to be considered only as a necessary evil in the continued northern trek. I had found, to my surprise and delight, quite the reverse in that the dale was of appreciable attractiveness. My image of Hadrian's Wall, the Vallum, the ditch and the general aura of the area, based on Wainwright's depiction, had me looking forward eagerly in a state of excited readiness for something perfectly spectacular. In his account he wrote of his crossing and recrossing the road to the ditch one minute and the Vallum the next in frenzied excitement, and I was keen to see what it had been that had so set him afire. I have to admit to being a mite wary as to whether I could be sent into raptures over what are, after all, just elongated holes in the ground. Old elongated holes, yes – in fact, very old elongated holes admittedly – but nevertheless, still just holes. Whatever would be my own impression, I did not have much longer to wait, although, as I walked through the village of Walwick, I had to hope that there was more for I had seen nothing of the wall or its accompanying excavations. There was one or two occasions when I detected almost imperceptible indentations in the field to my right, but these were not so grand or so frequent as to have the imagination soaring. Soon after reaching the top of Limestone Bank, I crossed into the Northumbrian National Park and there, directly in front of me, I had my first sight of the wall. Lying just to the north of the road, and on an exact parallel course with it, it ran as straight as an arrow over the crest of the hill that lay ahead. The wall seemed to spring from the ground – perhaps at a point Wade's engineers, finally appreciating their sacrilege, decided to desist from using its stone. At the crest of the next brow I would be at the most northerly point of my excursion and from that juncture, however erratic my route, my general direction would be to the south and home.

After a further few hundred yards I was able to turn off onto a quieter unclassified road from which I could gain access to the wall itself and follow its course for some distance. It is probably timely that I pass on whatever apologies are required to the local landowners for although I followed a fairly well-trodden path, none of these were marked on my map and I suspect that, strictly speaking, I was trespassing. I do not share Wainwright's view that there is no law of trespass for lovers of the wall and I took as much care as possible in ensuring that I did no damage during my encroachment onto private land. I was not prepared, as he obviously had been, to accept that the farmers were used to seeing walkers scaling their walls and fences unchallenged. Making my way alongside the wall, its width was apparent, clearly being constructed of two skins of regular-sized stone with rubble filling between the two outer-facing stone surfaces. Over the years its height has been reduced, partly through erosion at the hands of the elements but mainly by man in his search for walling stone – this first length was approximately 5 feet tall with grass and shrubs having taken root in the rubble filling material. I had talked with my sister just prior to embarking on my journey of her surprise on seeing flora of various types flourishing on the wall during a visit she had paid to the remains. As quick as a flash I told her of the numerous studies I had made of its history and I informed her that the wall had been designed to have greenery atop it. Whetting her appetite for further detail, she inquired as to the reasoning behind such a design feature and I assured her that it was to act as camouflage in the event of air assaults. For a full few seconds, I maintain, she did not doubt my explanation before she finally grasped the ridiculousness of it. She would never dare admit to her gullibility and would tell you that her silence was one brought on by not knowing what to say next and wondering just what research material I had been reading.

Mounting the wall and looking over its northern face, there lay the ditch, its profile softened by years of weathering and now grassed to give the appearance more of a fenceless ha-ha than of a steep ditch. Boulders lay strewn as a legacy to those who excavated it and it was obvious that in places the hard bedrock lay uncomfortably close to the surface for those charged with its construction. Much of the substrata along the length of the wall is of igneous rock with parts of the wall following the steep escarpment formed by the basaltic outcrops of the Whin Sill. Evidence lay all around of instances where the engineers struggled with the severe hardness of this rock before finally conceding defeat and having to accept a less than perfect profile to the ditch. I reached the triangulation point close to Milecastle 30 and rested, thankful for having been off the road for the previous mile and hopeful that I would be able to proceed in like manner for the next few miles. As I left Milecastle 30 not only did I leave the northern-most point but also the halfway point of my walk; I had travelled a little short of 100 miles. This was indeed a supreme moment and the day was shaping up nicely to being truly impressive. Even the weather had continued to improve with the initial haze slowly burning off to give more distance to the views of the increasingly spectacular open landscape that surrounded me.

I walked in the fields for only a further mile until my conscience told me to return to the verge at the side of the adjacent busy road. I had reached the access drive leading to Teppermoor Farm, where I clambered carefully over the fence and continued on my way hoping for an early opportunity to re-establish a route through the pastures. No such opportunity arose and for the next three miles I was compelled to proceed, again, only inches from all manner of vehicles as they sped by me. My only consolation was that for the majority of these three miles I was afforded fine panoramas of the Vallum to my left and the ditch and wall remains to my right. Shortly after recommencing my road-side trek I came to Procolitia, which appeared as desolate as when Wainwright had seen it and now seems to centre largely on the provision of a very fine car park. There was not a great deal to inspect at this site but its point of interest for me was that it was only after Wainwright's visit had further remains been found. In 1949 a drought had caused the surrounding bog to shrink and reveal what was then identified as a previously undiscovered temple to the sun god Mithras. The wall and its environs may have existed for nearly 2,000 years, but even as recently as fifty years ago it was yielding still further secrets of its past. The intervening sixty years between our visits had seen continued investigation and provided more accurate information relating to the association between the wall and the Vallum. Prior to 1938 the historians had conjectured that the Vallum represented an earlier form of boundary and that it was only during Hadrian's tour of the northern extremities of the empire that he commanded the wall and ditch be constructed. It was later established that all three were the brainchild of Hadrian and that the purpose of the Vallum was believed to act only as a boundary to the militarised zone. The forts along the length of the wall were built at regular intervals with milecastles spaced between them at, strangely enough, one-mile gaps. Nothing is ever what it seems though, and I had learned that a mile is not a mile when it is of Roman origin – that would be far too straightforward. It seems that the European game of stamping its administrative authority on us poor Brits had begun many years earlier than I had previously been aware of. The Roman Empire expanded into Britain and with it came their culture, their roads, their education, their drainage, their building skills, their tools and their craftsmen. That's all very well, but what else have the Romans given us, I thought as I marched along in the verge, narrowly avoiding another car as it roared passed. One thing that they had given us was the milecastle, but these were not milecastles, they were 'ninety-two-percent-of-a-mile castles' because the Roman mile was some way shorter than our similar measurement. I suggest that, as a nation, we keep very quiet about this discrepancy of distance for come the day that Italy hosts the presidency of the European Union we may find they are pressing for its adoption. Being cynical, I suspected that when and if they did, it would, no doubt, be introduced into Britain on a trial basis, under some hugely verbose and obscure directive from Brussels, for us to act as guinea pigs.

That is quite enough of technical history, suffice to say that the wall continues to be the site of excavation and investigation and in another sixty years it may be that further conclusions have been drawn as to its formation and use. I passed Procolitia undeterred for I was desirous of reaching the next bend in the road just beyond the farm named 'Shield on the Wall' where I would escape completely the clutches of the traffic and would be free to roam in peace and quiet. There were to be two occasions on my journey where I would walk a fundamentally different route to that taken by Wainwright, and I was approaching the first. He had reached the bend at such a late hour that he knew he would not reach accommodation if he delayed further, so he pressed on in earnest along the road, only swinging north onto the wall at Vercovicium. A purist I might be, but a fool I am not, and to maintain a route along the macadam would spoil one of the most sensational parts of a walk along the wall. I had every intention of parting company with the hurly-burly of the road and its hurried users just as quickly as I was able and, so, our respective routes would separate for the three miles from the bend at the next fort. I had seen enough of cars and was tired of permanently being on my mettle maintaining an alert vigil. I had progressed as recommended, facing the oncoming vehicles, but had taken to looking round when I heard a car approaching from behind me. By now I did this automatically having nearly jumped out of my skin in one instance when a car screamed passed my left side while overtaking another. Choose the road if you must tread in Wainwright's footsteps, but you will be forgoing a breathtaking three miles in exchange for the questionable pleasure of remaining with the cars. By all means go your own way, but be warned: there will be a great many cars to harass you as a result of your purism and you will miss the gloriously solitary three-mile deviation around Sewingshields Crags.

At length I arrived at the stile that would free me from the encumbrance of the motor cars and I paused upon reaching it to allow another lone walker to cross it before me. He thanked me and we chatted for a moment or two about our individual expeditions. It transpired that his wife and children had been left at home and that he had set out to walk the full length of the wall and was, when we met, enjoying the third day. Unless his detailed route was able to bypass many of the things of which I had not been able, I could not be envious of his onward journey for much of it would trace General Wade's Road rather than Hadrian's Wall. He left with a wave as I sat for a few minutes on the top rung of the stile pondering the rolling forested landscape to the north and the prominent ridge that lay to the west and formed the way ahead. I had endured the General's handiwork and could now look forward to experiencing more closely the legacy left by Hadrian. I watched the lone walker as he strode with purpose down the left side of the road – on the road rather than at the side of it – seemingly oblivious to cars as one after another they slowed in the face of oncoming traffic to avoid him.

Stepping down from the stile I was immediately behind a field boundary wall, which provided instant relief from the noisy road, and I undertook to walk as far as Milecastle 34 where I would lunch. The relief my spirits had felt was shared too by my feet and legs for they were also mightily pleased to be again in contact with the softer ground. At half past one I arrived at the rock-scattered site of Milecastle 34 and sat gratefully on a tumbledown part of the wall where the height of the residual coursing of the stonework made a perfect seat to be able to take all weight off my legs. I sat in this leg-dangling manner for thirty minutes while devouring the rather meagre daily ration I had allowed myself and decided that all was well with the world and that God was in his Heaven. On the subject of God the thought occurred to me that whilst the Romans were slaving over the construction of this magnificent barrier it would have been only a couple of generations after the last years of Jesus Christ's life. It seemed incredible to believe that these two events were, within 100 years or so, contemporaneous. I cast aside the inconsequential thought as quickly as I had considered it and looked instead at the mile upon mile of forest that now swept across the undulating uplands to the north-west. I knew from old maps that this tree-scape of Wark Forest was less than sixty years old. Had Wainwright sat at this milecastle and peered north-west he would have seen only hundreds of square miles of barren moorland with barely a track, path or settlement to provide any break from the otherwise vast desolation. I sat on a flat stone that had lain unchanged for nearly 2,000 years beholding the other immense changes of which man had been capable of within such a short span of time.

Turning my gaze westward, I studied the impressive promontories that were part of the Whin Sill and I knew that the wall followed the highest point of each. The loftiest of them all reached 345 metres above sea level and although only six miles away, looked to be much further with its impressive outline faint in the haze that still persisted. Beyond its summit I would have a further four miles to hike before I would arrive at my stopover. I was, I calculated, at half-distance for the day and it had taken me five hours. As I had thought might be the case my pace had slowed and as my watch showed two o'clock I knew I must again be on my way, with some determination. Not a soul did I see during the entire three miles after my escape from the road until I reached the tourist magnet of Housesteads, the modern name for Vercovicium. All extraneous sounds had been blotted out and I was able to savour alone the silent delights of this magnificent open country and the equally imposing remains of the wall, milecastles and interspersed turrets.

I progressed well along the line of the wall and soon I was staring up at one of the scree-ridden crags on top of which the wall was constructed to make maximum use of the natural features. This was the beginning of Sewingshields Crags and a few minutes passed before I realised that I should be looking down from it, not up at it. I had found myself on the wrong side of the wall in the lands of the Barbarians whereas I had wished to be a Roman. The only Roman I was now was a-roamin' about – somehow wildly off-course. I decided that the chance would arise to correct my error and, for the time being at least, I would follow the path that trailed indistinctly through the bracken and the heather until I was able to climb the crag and rejoin the wall. I was to discover that these engineers in whom Hadrian had entrusted the building of his wall were not stupid and my only way up involved a dexterous scramble and negotiation of a near-vertical final stretch. My navigational error had cost me some time and I had been frustrated when my auto-everything camera suddenly refused point blank to allow me to load a new film. I tried several times with several films all to no avail; I would have to rely solely on the manual camera I had brought with me, which was loaded with black-and-white film. No sooner had it decided to not to allow film to be loaded than the last remains of the cloudy haze thinned noticeably and the ridges ahead stood out in bold relief, with more remote hills layered behind them as an impressive backdrop. This was a scene of delicate shades and hues that I would have to recall from memory alone for I had no means of capturing it. There was nothing I could do other than to be thankful I was here on such a day as this.

Once I had completed my somewhat precarious ascent of the crags, I made my way back to the path I could see running adjacent to the wall. From this elevated position Vercovicium was visible, sited on the dip slope with the steep escarpment appearing almost as a continuation of the fort's northern rampart. I had often seen photographs of the wall majestically riding the crest of Sewingshields Crag with the dark, forbidding cliffs topped by the wall as it snaked its way across the isolated Northumbrian landscape. Imagine then how disheartening it was to reach the structure of the wall to find that it was no more than a single-skin construction and more a flimsy façade than the massive stone edifice, as I had expected. I felt let down and as though I would not be able to admire the photographs of the serpentine wall in the same light again. This was more a field wall than a monument to a former civilisation. My disappointment turned to humour as I mused that maybe the local farmer was called Adrian and that this was his wall – I was then, for the moment, following Adrian's Wall. Having found my way back to the path, I began the rollercoaster ride that would last for the rest of the day, for the wall from here on hugged closely to a ridge that dipped and rose. Much of it had survived, with this unyielding topography being its saviour from General Wade's destructive mission to link east and west. It would have been unpractical and nigh on impossible to construct an effective line of communication along such a switchback ridge and so the course of the highway was forced to run half a mile south, traversing more gentle slopes.

Vercovicium is sited at the top of a particularly stiff climb and it was with a fast pulse and heavy breathing that I stopped at the north gate. Looking west I could see the small copse of firs with the wall disappearing into it and the path on top with the drop to the north face that would pitch the unwary over an alarmingly sheer precipice. Looking to the north I could still see only the rolling tree-lined landscape beyond the dark waters of Broomlee Lough. Looking to the east I looked back at Adrian's Wall and the splendid vista of its rising and falling route, spoilt slightly by the fact that I no longer considered it to be the genuine article. Finally, looking to the south and into the heart of the settlement on the other side of the gatehouse, I watched various groups of tourists – there were Japanese and English and other accents that I could not readily identify. The majority of these trippers were milling about seemingly uninspired. If only they had travelled here on foot then perhaps they might have been more able to appreciate the fantastic arena in which they now walked. Their presence deterred me from staying longer – and I promised myself that I would indeed return. When I did I would do so on a clear and cold winter's day, which would serve as a harsh reminder of the endurance that must have been required of those who were stationed here. I could well imagine that a very sharp wind would whistle up a short Roman tunic in the days long before thermal underwear, or, more likely, any underwear at all. The thought did not bear dwelling upon and I shivered as though someone had just walked over my grave.

Wainwright exulted in this place and was enraptured by the sight of the wall to the east, writhing its way like a living reptilian across the hills. I could comprehend his excitement but, at the same time, wondered whether he knew that the eastern section of the wall was but a sham. I doubted it for he described it in his account as a colossus and a massive barrier – I now had been made aware that however much it looked the part, it was not the real thing. Still, I speculated, we are often fooled by appearances. If something looks the part then we will, more often than not, assume that it is genuine with the converse being true where a doubtful first impression is created. Door-to-door salesmen have used this human tendency for many years to gain access by generating a belief in their appearance. Wainwright believed that he saw a substantial wall because he assumed it to be so, basing his assumption on what he had read. I, on the other hand, had experienced the wall to the east for myself and could perceive it for what it was. Had it been a door-to-door salesman he would not have crossed the threshold. This was one of those occasions when possession of the truth was undesirable for I would rather have proceeded in blithe ignorance.

Proceed I had to do and I climbed on to the top of the wall where the west bulwark of Vercovicium intersects with the main wall as it continues its westerly course. The broad Northumbrian farmer who had doubled as caretaker for the fort when Wainwright had called here had allowed him free range of the wall and permission to walk where he chose. Many must have done likewise in the ensuing years for not far beyond the copse a sign instructed me to dismount the wall and take the path to reduce the damage caused by erosion. The wall ahead stood at its full thickness but it was evident that years of walking on it, however carefully, had taken their toll and a deep rut had formed in the less durable rubble-filled centre. With a slight disappointment but an understanding of the problem for the wall's guardians, my short walk along it through the copse was to be my only chance of patrolling its ramparts as the legionaires and auxiliaries would have done so many years earlier. It was the same understanding that I had for the Lake District's severe difficulties with erosion. Many might balk at the prospect of hill paths being protected by the laying of formal foundation slabs and think that such trails should be left as nature intended. Regardless of whether a path may lose its naturalness by the introduction of very apparent paving, the greater concern must surely be for the future walkers to whom we have a responsibility and to whom we owe a duty of care. Perhaps nature did not intend to have so many pairs of feet passing the same way so often and in so uncaring a fashion. It is not possible for the hills to accommodate the amount of people who would wish to escape from time to time without there being untold and irreversible damage. Leave things as you find them and take care while you have them for, for the greater part, they are only on loan to you. Wainwright was a lucky man for he had roamed the Lake District unhindered and he had wandered on the wall with a free spirit, to do as he pleased, in the days before the major onset of damage. Some have held him singly responsible for the popularising of walking and for the subsequent harm caused. One man alone cannot be held entirely answerable for it is by those who followed that the injury has been caused. While he may have been a catalyst, he surely could not have foreseen the mass exodus that would ensue. The Footpath Commission and the Ordnance Survey must also accept some responsibility for it was they who showed the paths to the masses. In the days of Wainwright walking alone along the wall, many paths now shown on maps would have stayed protected simply as a result of their anonymity.

The further west I travelled the fewer were the throngs of tourists and it was a little way beyond Hotbank Crags that I found myself looking both ahead and behind and seeing no one. The sun was now shining quite brightly. The view from Hotbank over Crag Lough was arresting and I was hungry and thirsty and fancying a quiet sit down. The hunger and thirst I could not assuage for my sparse rations had been used at lunch, but I would, I decided, take a break in any case before I progressed toward Steel Rigg and onward to the highest part of the ridge, which I had seen hours earlier. It was now half past four but I had no wish to hurry. Moreover, I simply wanted to take in all that I could of this glorious place and my mood turned to one of total calm as I sat on the steep west-facing slope slowly smoking my first cigarette since lunch at Milecastle 34. I was now almost as far west as the site of Milecastle 38 and my sojourn with the wall would extend until I reached Milecastle 42, where I would turn south for Haltwhistle. I cared not that my advance had been laggard for today was not a day to be rushed, especially as it at last had deigned to show itself in all its beauty with lengthening views and clarity improving with each minute that passed.

Getting slowly to my feet, I continued down Hotbank and began the walk up the ridge at the side of Crag Lough. Up and up I tramped until I reached a more level and stony path, which skirted perilously close to the edge of a dizzying vertical drop into the water below. I am never overly ecstatic about being in close proximity to such severity of cliff faces and my feet found their way as far as they were able away from the exposed edge. I recalled a walking holiday on the Isle of Arran in Scotland when Sue had had an urge to revisit one particular peak that she had climbed some years earlier. I had been knee-tremblingly nervous about this desire for the peak in question was Cir Mhor, which I had only ever seen from a distance and that had always looked nigh on vertical. We had approached from a direction from which I not previously seen the mountain and I satisfied myself that it did not look hopelessly insurmountable. We had set off from the summit of another peak and had to cross the head of a corrie following a well-trodden path that ran altogether too close to the edge of the corrie face for my liking, with the steep drop having me walking a respectable distance away from it. Sue, meanwhile, and as ever, calmly beetled along, hands in pockets, with her left leg almost dangling over the edge.

Passing the crags overlooking Crag Lough without incident, I then followed several sharp descents calling for delicate steps and steep and tiring ascents before I came to a depression known as Sycamore Gap, named after the large tree that grew at the base of the hollow. This I recognised instantly as the dip that had been featured in the remake of the film Robin Hood where Kevin Costner, accompanied by his Moor cohort, had done battle with a band of the Sheriff of

Nottingham's men. The two heroes had come ashore on the south coast with the somewhat Americanised Robin of Loxley exclaiming they would dine with his father that night in Nottingham – some going to get to the East Midlands by nightfall! Their trek north was smartly interrupted when they came to the aid of a young lad who was being hunted by the sheriff's ruffians for killing deer and the contretemps that ensued was undoubtedly at this dramatic depression. So their route to Nottingham took them by way of Hadrian's Wall, and all in the same day to boot for they reached the burnt-out shell of his father's castle that night! So extensive was the erosion around Sycamore Gap that the path had been diverted and major reparation works were underway, and all was draped in bright-orange warning tape that marred the gap's aesthetics.

The diversion over, the path and the wall again ran side by side and the next long ascent began to Steel Rigg. I have to confess to a second breach from Wainwright's route as it was at about this point on the wall that he said au revoir to it and made directly to Haltwhistle for dusk was fast approaching – and the wall was no place to be when darkness had fallen. He had descended to the military road at the inn at Twice Brewed and had then followed it all the way to Haltwhistle – his exact route was not clear from his account. I was not disposed to leave the wall until the last possible minute and wished my association with it to continue for as long as I was able. In his travels Wainwright had already omitted one superb section and then compounded his felony by accepting an invitation to join General Wade's road. Having apparently timed my walking more efficiently than he, I had reserved the crowning glory for the last part of the day. Puffing and panting my way up to the highest point, I arrived to behold grand scenes all around. Wherever I looked there was majesty and magnificence and a clearness to the light that made me forget completely its earlier inclemency. I felt as though I was the master of all I could survey and I could survey a lot from the triangulation point on the high ridge. I could see Haltwhistle nestling on the lower ground to the south-west in the valley of the River South Tyne and I could look back whence I had come at the wriggling line of the wall as it twisted its contorted course over the crags and hills. I could also see the road below me to the south, which was a very poor substitute for being up high on my lofty perch. I was not aware whether Wainwright ever revisited this place, but if he had not then it must stand as his one sad omission, one he took to his grave with him. At half past five I smugly sat where he had not and cared not whether I had strayed from his route, for the loss was abundantly his.

To coin a phrase I had heard somewhere not long before, I could have eaten a scabby horse I was so ravenous. I left the triangulation point and walked briskly heading for Cawfields with my desire for food and drink beginning to be greater than my wish to see more of the wall. I would leave it at Cawfield until tomorrow when I would again be refreshed and more able to appreciate its splendour. The fine late afternoon weather had brought out more visitors and in the car park near the small lake were several cars with occupants spilling over the remains of Milecastle 42. Their presence had me bidding them good evening but not lingering long for my abiding memory of the day had been its stillness and the accordant sense of solitariness – that was how I wished to remember the day so I passed by these noisy few quickly. With the exception of where there had been scope for car parking at Chesters, Housesteads and Cawfields, I had seen very few people all day. There had been the lone walker and I had met a couple of bearded men who looked like throwbacks to the 1960s and I had chanced upon a runner near Steel Rigg. Apart from those, the day had been mine to share with no one. Just the way I like it.

Almost as soon as my feet hit the macadam of the road I would have to tread for the last mile or so, they began to ache again, a malady that was not helped by the steepness of the slope down to Haltwhistle. They clomped one after another on the unforgiving road surface and I was only too happy to find myself on the final approach to the Grey Bull, following the directions from a passing cyclist. There was one last hill to climb though before I could claim sanctuary and I mounted it with tired limbs and an empty stomach which had sapped the last of any energy I might have had in reserve. Wainwright's description of the Grey Bull as being a rambling and architecturally uninspiring building was not far from the truth, but it was a very welcoming hostelry as I struggled through the harshly sprung double-entrance door and found the bar. There behind the bar stood Mrs Morpeth who, with her husband, had owned the place for some years after Mr Morpeth have left his job as a brewery chemist. At least the beer should be good I thought, and I proposed to waste no time in ascertaining its quality. Introducing myself, I asked for a pint of whatever she would recommend and she hand-pulled a fine-looking pint of bitter. Not only had the beer benefited from being kept in an excellent cellar, but when I handed two £1 coins over the bar, Mrs Morpeth handed one back and confirmed that it was only a pound a pint. By way of celebration I downed the first in fine style and ordered a second. I had arrived at half past six and had rather forgotten my tiredness and hunger. It was only my willpower that dragged me away from the bar, although the prospect that I would be returning to it shortly thereafter meant my parting would be only temporary. I had arranged that, after having a bath and sprucing myself up a little, I would eat in the bar at eight o'clock – I had inquired of Mrs Morpeth as to whether there was a restaurant in town, to which she replied that I could eat at the inn if I wished. When she asked me to name what I fancied and immediately responded yes to all my first requests – namely chicken pie, chips and vegetables – I was smitten in an instant. The final decider was the price: £2.95 for a meal that, I was to find out, must have been prepared by a chef not trained in the art of nouvelle cuisine or of portion control. If there were to be a downside to my repast it was that in agreeing to take it in the bar, I returned at the appointed time to find the room much more populated than it had been. I gained the impression the new faces were all locals well known to Mr and Mrs Morpeth and the majority had sat around the perimeter seating in the small bar area. There had been one or two customers when I had gone to my room and these were still in situ. This spread of customers left only one small circular table free in the very centre of the room and it was at this table that my place had been set with cutlery, crockery, condiments and napkin. I felt very much as if I was the attraction to be observed during any lulls in conversation. I had, by this time, remembered my hunger and did not much care who saw me eating and how uncomfortable I felt. I was eating purely because I was starving and I must have given that impression for when I was finished, one of the locals quickly broke off his own conversation and, pointing to my polished plate, suggested I must have been ready for that. I had used a knife and fork; I had resisted temptation to simply ram my face in the food as if to suck it off the plate. I did not ask why he had considered my eating habits but could only think that it was the speed at which I had eaten. Barely was one forkful masticated that another was being prepared, ready for insertion, the very second the first was swallowed.

I quickly found that I need not have been concerned about being on show at the Grey Bull. The customers were down-to-earth types and made me feel welcome, including me in their conversations. There were, unfortunately, too many discussions into which I had been welcomed for much too frequently I seemed to be in need of a refill. My willpower was at low ebb, especially as both the price and the quality of the pound-a-pint beer continued all evening. What willpower I had left took a firm hold at half past nine and told me to retire immediately before I did something I would regret in the morning, like order another drink. For once I listened and, in a slightly doddery fashion, found my way out of the bar as composed as I could and lugged up the flights of stairs to my second-floor room. I was glad I had left when I had, but even having done so the room swam as I lay down on the bed and trying to watch the television caused my head to spin.

There was nothing else for it but to lie down with the lights still on to give me something to focus on. I doubted whether there would be any dreams tonight, or if there were I doubted whether I would recall them in the morning. In fact, I doubted whether I would recall my own name in the morning. I had allowed myself to be carried away in the bar, but, I argued, I was exuberant for the day had been a very spectacular one. The type of day where people would say 'Wow, that's impressive.' Yes, it had been one of those sorts of days.

Chapter 7

Haltwhistle to Alston

My name is Andrew, I thought as I woke. Well at least I had gotten that far. Upon first awakening I wondered whether I would get much further than being able to recall who I was. The light was still switched on but my brain felt decidedly as though switched off, with my head having been stuffed with cotton wool during my slumbers. My eyes, if opened any wider than the slightest of cracks, sent painful messages to remind me of my excesses the evening before. My mouth felt as though it had been open all night and had provided ablution facilities to a nomadic herd of camels; the surface of my tongue was as arid as a desert wadi and its texture was that of a cat. I chose not to deliberate too closely on what my breath must have been like but I suspected it would not have been dissimilar to a previously unknown condition brought on by French-kissing with a few too many of these camels. This, and a general throbbing of my head, did have one blessing: I had forgotten all about any other aches and pains that might have plagued me on previous days. My name is Andrew, I remembered. Thank goodness. At least my hangover wasn't getting worse as so often is the case. As I have advanced in years I have developed an increasing misfortune of believing that I can still drink beer with the best of them and still surface unscathed the morning after. It is sad that my maturity of years has not been accompanied by any noticeable expansion in wisdom so far as my misguided drinking habits are concerned. It is also sad that I usually suffer worsening after-affects as the day after progresses, and rather than experiencing a steady improvement, I invariably develop the most disagreeably bilious symptoms. It is an illness that must be endured alone for it secures very little sympathy – only belittlement from females and ridicule from males. In moments of extreme suffering through my distressing malady I generally satisfy myself with the fact that there are many others with the exact same illness and that I am not alone. As I awoke in Haltwhistle (I remembered where I was too, which was a good omen for an imminent recovery) full consciousness was aided by focusing on the thought of there being someone somewhere worse off than I. Time is more usually the only cure, although, in extreme circumstances, an alternative remedy comprising a huge and greasy fried breakfast can sometimes alleviate the worst of the symptoms. If the alternative treatment proves not to be a success, there can be only one outcome: at some unspecified time in the not-too-distant future the sufferer will be talking to God on the big white telephone. This creates further belittling and ridicule and not a little embarrassment if walking alone among the hills of Northumberland. I had not the luxury of time, so I decided I would have to look for salvation in the greasy cure-all.

This was not the first time my willpower had been found wanting and I doubted very much that it would be the last. I could only hope that there was no repeat of a walk I once took late at night following a kind invitation to friends for an early evening chilli con carne and bottle of wine. I had wined and dined admirably, in fact so admirably that at gone midnight I had the unwise notion that the four-mile walk home would be a good idea and I indicated to them my plan in lieu of the more usual ordering of a taxi. This would do me no end of good, would burn off the calories and, more importantly, would reduce the impact of any hangover. This last matter had become a serious point of consideration for I had exercised little restraint in respect of drink and I was distinctly squiffy. More accurately, I was completely ratted and had begun to sit very quietly not saying much, more judging how many seconds it would take to get upstairs if the need arose. I rather think the chilli had been cooked with wine for I am sure, like all men, that it must have been something I had eaten.

I duly set off walking on a very pleasantly warm July evening and estimated that I would be home by two o'clock at the latest – I always like to set a goal in my own mind as to when I will arrive at a destination. After half an hour or so I was striding purposefully past some school playing fields and decided, with the weather being so clement, that a cigarette break would be in order. Although this meant clambering through a low hedge, this did not dissuade me and I sat on the dry grass. (This was the year of the drought when Yorkshire had seen little rain and the Yorkshire Water Authority chief executive hadn't had a bath for three months.) I lay back for a few minutes' rest having discovered that I had smoked the last of my tobacco before leaving to walk home. After a few moments I began to contemplate the Heavens for the stars were very clear: surely in all that space there must be other life forms somewhere; how is it that all the satellites that have been sent into space don't collide; if they did collide would the wreckage fall to earth or spin out into space. I pondered on these and other profound matters for several minutes until the need to relieve myself became of greater concern, after which I recommenced my late-night walk. On arriving home I was able to roll a cigarette from my supply of tobacco and decided to have a cup of tea before going to bed. Only when I sat in the armchair did I notice that the time, rather than being two o'clock, was half past four. This was one of those moments where the first reaction is to disbelieve the clock – I looked for a second opinion. My watch also was showing half past four. Two clocks being wrong I knew to be unlikely, and when a third, on the oven, also showed the same time, I knew I had not only sat in the field thinking profound thoughts but I had actually dropped off to sleep for two hours! I had been dressed in my work suit and must have looked a very strange site had anyone seen me.

Of the two requisites of the alternative hangover remedy Mrs Morpeth did not disappoint – the size of the portions were enormous and my plate was as full as my dinner plate had been in the bar the evening before. It would seem rude to suggest that her repast was greasy, so suffice it to say it was satisfactorily well fried. Everything was more piled than arranged on the plate before me – fried eggs, bacon, sausages, tomatoes, fried bread, mushrooms and, if I recall correctly, hash browns. After only the first few mouthfuls I knew that I was ravenous and that this cure would work. I might see a return to full health given one or two large mugs of strong coffee to boot. No sooner had the thought entered my mind than a cafetière of dark coffee was delivered to my table. My prescription was complete. I savoured breakfast and, thanking Mrs Morpeth profusely, inquired as to my debt for my night's stay. I nearly choked on my coffee when she replied that the total bill, including the gargantuan dinner, was less than £18. My accommodation had been basic; there had been no en suite facilities except for a washbasin and there had been a distinct shortage of tea-making accoutrements – my room being milk-less and spoon-less. Any short-comings had more than been made up for by the hospitality I had received however, and if you ever have reason to pass this way and need a bed for the night, you could do a lot worse than spend it at the Grey Bull.

As I left the inn and made for the centre of the small town I reflected on what Wainwright had described as a depressed place dying in direct relationship to the slow demise being suffered by the local mining industry. The town had, he felt, known more prosperous days and the inhabitants appeared to have heard the tolling of the bell of death and had accepted their inevitable fate. The people were sullen and dejected but still lingered and loitered in the streets as though waiting for something to return them from the commercial precipice. From his impression it was difficult to imagine why any traveller would wish to deliber-ately pass through the town and his narrative would certainly not be snatched by the local tourist board as a testimonial to the town's attractions. In 1938 many cross-country wayfarers would have been forced to at least see Haltwhistle for the main road ran through its heart, but sixty years on even the willing visitor is whisked away to the south of the town's centre. As at Hexham, the main Car-lisle–Newcastle trunk road has bypassed it and can only have served to reduce passing trade to a trickle. My own impression, gleaned from only the most cur-sory of inspections, was of a town that has long ago fallen off the precipice but whose inhabitants have accepted the fall with a certain modicum of self-effacing humour. This sweeping summation had its somewhat unreliable base in the various discussions I had been party to in the bar the night before, where even the locals talked jocularly of the greyness of the town. Admittedly I walked in early morning drizzle at half past eight on a Saturday morning, but I detected an air of desolation about the place, manifested in the array of boarded shop windows that were clearly not to be opened at nine o'clock. More than likely they would never open again and would provide one more reason for visitors and locals alike to look for their provisions elsewhere. The mines that were closing when Wainwright had visited are all closed save for one at Blenkinsop. The bell was still tolling. Haltwhistle has a skeleton of roads and it has flesh, but it lacks the coursing of blood through its veins and any impression of vivacity could probably only be gained from reference to old picture books.

Perhaps it was also my own physical and mental attitudes that were not fully attuned to appreciating Haltwhistle. Physically I continued to suffer at the hands of the head cold with which I had started my venture. In addition, my hangover, although much improved for having had a splendid breakfast, was still occasionally battling for attention. I also recalled from the Bible that the seventh day should have been a day of rest, a day in which one should take stock of earlier achievements. Instead of that I was following my predecessor, walking a further eighteen miles, my goal being to reach Alston. I would have walked in Northumberland for the greater part of three days until, some two miles short of Alston, I would pass into another new county, Cumbria. When Wainwright walked into Alston he did so with Westmorland under his feet. Cumbria had been the brainchild of another job-securing boundary change and had devoured both Cumberland and Westmorland, much to the chagrin of the proud inhabitants of both counties. Of more concern than any physical ailment was a sense that I had passed the halfway mark and that I was now counting down my remaining days of liberty. A total of 90 miles lay ahead, yet somehow those miles felt to be no more than a formality to be completed only in order to return to my starting point. Earlier eager expectation seemed less acute and my appetite for the scenery I would witness was less intense. It was in this frame of mind that I saw Haltwhistle, so I must apologise if I have been entirely unfair to the place or its denizens.

I reminded myself that I still had five days left and reprimanded myself for even momentarily entertaining thoughts of any future concerns beyond those five days. It is so often the case that we allow the present to be marred by thoughts of what the future holds. Seldom does a two-week holiday, in truth, provide more than a week's rest for the first few days are spent unwinding and the final few are cursed with increasingly intrusive contemplation of work and other problems that you mistakenly believed had been left behind. I was not prepared to succumb and would strive to cast out negative thoughts, concentrating only on each day's target. Only by taking on the challenge of each individual day could I hope to achieve my overall goal.

We spend too long looking only at the end with little time expended considering the means. We have grown to expect almost instantaneous results and very soon does our patience become exhausted if the perceived result is any further removed, and this want-it-now attitude starts at an early age. I remember well as a child having to save and save for what seemed like an eternity to acquire some new toy or other. Perhaps I have a slightly skewed view but I have gained an impression that modern juveniles are not required to suffer the same interval between arousal of their desire and it being satisfied. I am convinced that the enjoyment of an acquisition is directly proportional to the efforts made in achieving that acquisition and that there is much less pleasure in simply being provided with everything we could want in total absence of any enterprise on the part of the recipient. This want-it-now culture runs deep and establishes itself very firmly in adulthood in the form of the buy-now-pay-later philosophy. The fact that the means to make the purchase out right might not exist appears to be ignored, the inevitable result of which is uncontrollable credit card debt. There are always those who are eager to feed off our inability to resist spending, which a brief look through the Sunday newspapers will affirm, bombarding the reader with tempting offers of loans or a new credit card to consolidate payment of the old one. I recalled my own struggles to save and reflected that, in retrospect, it was those struggles which heightened the ultimate gratification. So it was with my walk, where each day was a challenge but each was also an integral part of the whole and the overall and climactic satisfaction could only be appreciated by the successful completion of the separate elements of it. Yes, I thought, the end might be in sight but that did not need to reduce in any way the sense of achievement to be relished in successfully surmounting the challenges of each day.

With such positive thinking, I set off in earnest in a northerly direction following a minor road that would lead me high up above the Haltwhistle Burn, across the Military Road and back to the wall. The road became little more than a track as I passed several farm buildings before finally hearing the sound of traffic ahead. I had to rely more upon my ears to warn of traffic for the weather had taken a distinct turn for the worse, with poor visibility and a fine drizzle that would severely restrict any views the wall might have to offer. As if to rub salt into an already open wound, my camera, which had refused point-blank to allow me to load film yesterday when the weather had been far more clement, had now gladly accepted my latest attempt to load the cassette. What an annoying shame it was that when I most needed it to chronicle my endeavours I had stubbornly been denied, but now, when the weather precluded any meaningful record, it condescendingly agreed to operate. I comforted myself with the thought that it was running true to form of most technology, which has a nasty habit of working wonderfully well in theory but leaves much to be desired in practice. Like so many technologically advanced pieces of apparatus, we are entirely reliant on them and are utterly lost if they malfunction. I had not the vaguest notion of how I might attempt even a makeshift repair – there was no manual override, it being totally automatic. The boffins that sit behind their desks thinking of all these newfangled bits of equipment have a lot to answer for, for the upshot of their labours is that instead of surrounding us with great convenience, they have, at the same time, introduced far greater stresses. When Wainwright made his way to the wall the rate of growth in technology was in its infancy, with any advances taking place in small and comprehensible stages. At each stage it was more than likely the consumer would appreciate the relatively marginal improvements, thus allowing the user a greater degree of control. When technology was maintained and controlled by the user all was well, but now we live among machines that begin to have their own thought processes, which can be far more powerful than our own. The self-training computer pro-grammes that now abound will be improved upon and put to use in other applications and will ultimately maintain and control us. Such fantastic im-provements will be heralded by most as the way forward, but I could not help but wonder whether, one day, there would be tears for we will have opened Pandora's Box and there will be no opportunity to close it. It has been predicted that the year 2000 will see a breakdown in computer-driven technology, and perhaps on entering the fourth millennium the entire foundation of our relatively new society will be laid waste for we will have learned to rely too entirely upon our mechanised cousins. If they were to choose to become inoperable mankind will surely face ruination for machines would dominate and the need for human activity would decrease. There will be no skilled craftsmen or trained workers for the machines will have built and trained themselves. There will be no pilots or drivers as all transport will be entirely automated. There will be no police force as its role will be fulfilled by the electronic tagging of all citizens, their behaviour and conduct monitored by machine. There will be no agricultural workers for their labours will have been replaced by synthetic food manufac-ture. There will be no postal service for all forms of communication will be via electronic links and matter-transporters. I feared especially for the demise of the postal service as there was I about to start in the job – I could only hope to get in a few years before the electronic age rendered me hopelessly out-performed.

I reached the wall at a point near Great Chesters. It may have been great at some point in the past but all it consisted of now was a few grassy hillocks and the shattered remnant of its western rampart. Even the wall over this stretch of country appeared little changed from Wainwright's description. He had noted that it was, for the most part, nothing more than a mound running east to west and now, sixty years later, the wall remained as, well, nothing more than a mound running east to west. A long green mound on a day when the physical environment existed only for approximately 50 yards in any direction is, I had to admit, not overly interesting and I progressed westerly along the mound without delay. Very little happened of note along the length of the wall west of

Great Chesters – I saw some sheep only half visible in the mist. Then, at one point, I saw a herd of cattle and a small wood away to my left. Both of these were also only half visible in the mist. I saw very little masonry but an ever-present green mound guided me westwards towards Thirlwall and the nine nicks about which I had read earlier while nursing my hangover. I had a strong suspicion that they would also be only half visible in the mist. The nicks formed a switchback course for the wall with steep slopes and the wall, on occasions, constructed in precarious locations to make best use of the natural buttresses offered by the escarpment of the Whin Sill. I had no warning of the severity of any of the slopes for I was on them before I realised, puffing and panting my way up a series of ascents and gingerly finding my footing down an equally steep series of descents. Never once was I allowed to see the adversary that lay ahead for each time it lay hidden in its misty shroud, which had worsened as I had gained altitude.

I had already seen considerable commercial extinction, much of it leaving a sad reminder of its former presence and a permanent indelible mark upon the landscape. Where people had worked and the local settlements had thrived, all that was left were the hollow memories of what had once been. Most of this was very saddening and my thoughts were of those who had been affected by the passing of the various enterprises, whether it was the railways or the lead mines or the quarries. At Walltown, as I descended and enjoyed improved visibility, I was actually pleased to see that the quarry workings had been abandoned. My pleasure stemmed from the thinking that its abandonment had at least curtailed any further damage to the wall. The quarrymen had been presumably permitted to excavate horizontally into the face of the steep sill regardless of the fact that to do so meant inevitable destruction of the wall above. Wainwright would have been very pleased too for when he had passed Walltown Quarry it was still be-ing worked and was slowly eating its way along the line of the wall. Now all that remains is a cliff face, slightly concave on plan, with the truncated faces of the wall appearing at either side seeming lost for never again can they rejoin. We have destroyed the wall forever at Walltown but, for once, the destroyer had been destroyed. The biter had been bit and fatally wounded. I gained a certain pleasure in the knowledge that the wall had had its posthumous retribution, albeit that the assailants, at the time of their actions, were no doubt acting within bounds acceptable to society. It seemed likely that there would have been no anguished voices crying out for the protection of the wall as the quarry slowly extended ever southwards into the escarpment and begun to threaten and devour its foundations. Long before the quarrymen had undermined the entire wall and its footings, much of the regular-sized facing stones had been removed for use as walling stone for local buildings. Theft of the stone had even extended to members of the clergy for the majority of Lanercost Priory had been constructed using stone purloined from Hadrian's much earlier endeavour. All that remains in many places is the shattered random stones of the looser central core lying unclothed and bereft of their outer garments. As I walked by the naked remains it was interesting to think again of our monarchy and heritage and to ponder on the apparent reversal in our attitudes that has taken place in those intervening years. All those eons ago the monarch was venerated while the wall was ransacked unchallenged and now we treat the wall with a damn sight more reverence than the present monarchy can perhaps ever hope to attain again. I drew no particular conclusions as I stared forward into the mist but could not help but wonder whether there was also evidence of a disheartening swing in attitudes displayed towards other people relative to their standing. The basic premise, I recalled, was to generally feel sympathy for those worse off than yourself and, presumably, to respect those fortunate enough to be better off or, if not to actually show respect for them to at least recognise their possessions without coveting them. We now appear to have developed into a society where the doctrine has changed from sympathising with those worse off to downright resentment of those better off and for all that they represent. Perhaps this is only an impression stemming from the English love of the underdog and that it is only the press that has hyped this apparent society of aggressive envy out of all proportion. Then again, perhaps the French thought along similar lines prior to the revolution. Perhaps as an extension of the want-it-now mentality there is a reaction that, should it begin to become apparent that our sought-after possessions might never be attainable, why should anyone else be allowed to enjoy theirs. If we judge ourselves by our own materialistic gains, it is all too easy to view others' successes with jealousy and harbour a wish to witness their downfall or to see them fail.

The destruction at Walltown Quarry was partially forgotten by the fine sight of the superbly preserved Walltown Turret, and as I prepared to part company with my stony companion, I could at least be assured that there would be no further devastation. I said a quiet goodbye to the wall. Wainwright had left it and proceeded into Greenhead before walking back along what is now the main Carlisle–Newcastle trunk road. I had braved enough traffic on the quieter roads without doing battle with endless juggernauts, so I made my way south from the wall to find a minor road that facilitated my minimising an unpleasant altercation with speeding civilisation. I had enjoyed the last few miles free of the noise of lorries and the smell of diesel and had no desire to lengthen any re-exposure. As I turned onto the quiet byroad and found my way across the Military Road, I followed a path that led me as directly as possible to the road up to Blenkinsop Castle, which required only the crossing of the main road without actually walking along any part of it. I was fortunate enough to see one sight that had been rare during my seven days of walking – a railway line that was still in use. I had seen an abundance of lines that were now only memories for those old enough to recall their use. Tree-lined embankments and buttresses of former bridges I had seen in abundance, but very few that still saw the passing of rail traffic. They all stood as reminders of a time when the main road that I was avoiding would have been quieter and our towns would not have been choked or needed unsightly bypasses to reduce the traffic's impact. However, here was one that had escaped the axe. The only other that I would encounter before journey's end would be that linking Settle with Carlisle, although I knew from my maps that I would come upon the husks of many branch lines where Beeching had turned his thumb downwards and sealed their fate. I crossed the railway and was soon on the south side of the main road heading up the steep side road toward the castle.

In earlier days I had headed generally north and I had headed generally west but now I was southbound; I was using the return part of my ticket. Each day would take me further and further south until finally I would re-enter Settle and my quest would be complete. I had now covered approximately one hundred and twenty miles and, barring mishaps, had banished all thoughts of failure. I was in control and had only one day of walking that gave any cause for concern – my way tomorrow would lead me over Cross Fell, which I knew to be a devil of a place if there were to be a mist. As I had walked away from the wall I had been aware of a shift in the strengthening wind to an easterly direction and with it a worsening of visibility. Were Cross Fell to be so shrouded, it would be a challenge indeed to safely navigate my way over it and I would most certainly receive a severe battering for there would be no protection from the wind on its exposed and rounded bulk. Subsequent days were predominantly going to consist of lower-level walking through the Vale of Eden except where I would skirt the Howgill Fells and make the crossing from Dent over to Ingleton. Wainwright admitted that he largely felt his adventure to be at an end as he left the wall and paused for lunch in Greenhead, and this sentiment is possibly reflected in the choice of his route over the last few days. He accepted that his mission was completed and set his course south with little apparent regard other than to get back. With the exception of his intention to walk over Cross Fell, much of his route over the remaining four and a half days was on roads. His account does not make it clear as to whether he planned his route in such a way or whether it was that once beyond the wall he simply took any route that gave him the most direct course. He perceived his freedom to be at an end and saw no benefit to prolonging the inevitable return to a more mundane existence in Blackburn. He had been transported to great emotional heights by his dalliance with the wall, but they had had to part and the sorrow of that parting had left him deflated and demoralised and ready to accept that his destiny lay elsewhere. He had been given a glimpse of his own yardstick of perfection and all else would pale by comparison. For my own part, visiting Hadrian's Wall had been the culmination of my challenge and as such it represented the pinnacle of the walk's achievements, but I could not say that I was so awestruck by it as Wainwright clearly had been. His words of description flowed in great prose and I had a mental picture of him skipping about at its base in a manner not entirely unlike Toad of Toad Hall skipping about having just acquired a new automobile. Where Toad wished to show off and share his acquisition with his friends, Wainwright wished to act in similar vein only in words – as regards his proclaimed love for his newly found sweetheart. But now she had left him and he was bereaved and could only look to the future as holding nothing of interest for him. His love had departed and the sooner he returned to work the sooner the sadness would be reduced, or at least masked by the familiarity of his working environment.

So it was that Wainwright set his course up the valley of the River South Tyne towards Alston, some fourteen miles away, there being little in the way of accommodation prior to reaching the town that could boast of being the highest market town in England. In his account he only referred to his route as following the Maiden Way where he was able. The Maiden Way was a Roman road, the course of which is still marked on the Ordnance Survey maps. I learned very quickly as I struggled in vain to locate it that where the map indicates the course of a road, it means exactly that with absolutely no surface trace of it whatsoever remaining. I was forced into abandoning any attempt to follow any part of it over Featherstone Common and begrudgingly accepted defeat insofar as I would have to continue my trek along three miles of a, thankfully, deserted byroad. As for the remainder of Wainwright's course, it could only be assumed that he walked along the roadside until he was able to turn off and cross the river to Kirkside, only two miles short of Alston. This would entail a return to jostling with traffic for ten miles, a prospect that, however purist I might have been in wishing to follow in his footsteps, I resisted, knowing that the course of the Pennine Way lay along at least part of the length of this valley. I would find it, I decided, and hang Mr Wainwright and his toddling along at the side of the road.

He was lucky; he walked at a time when these black arteries were not clogged and hardened. In 1938 the lifeblood flowed smoothly through them before the years of overuse began to take their toll. The road is a metaphor for the pressures of society – the demands placed upon it far outweigh its ability to permit a smooth throughput to the extent that we exist in a permanent fight to progress and can only do so at the expense of others. In 1938 there was less pollution, but now life on either side of the road's course is strangulated. It is as a path through a moorland bog where the driest route can only be found via an ever-widening course if we are to keep moving – in much the same way as we extend our motorways only to find the need for further widening ad infinitum. There had been a railway running the length of the valley but I already knew that this had closed in 1972 and the tracks long since removed. What a shame it was for if it, and others like it, was to have had continued use they might now have reduced the pollution and congestion which have sentenced our roads and their environs to a slow and lingering demise. No, I had no wish to follow the road.

The only physical record that I came across of the Maiden Way was on the nameplate of a house that I chanced upon as I weaved my way through a maze of twisting side roads. Reference to the map showed this short stretch of the tarmac lay on the course of the old Roman Road. Finally, upon reaching the remains of an old disused lead mine I was able to cut across the main road and strike out once again along the Pennine Way. I had already toyed with the most famous of England's long-distance paths on a number of occasions and now it provided me with respite from the hard road surface under my feet. Instead of unforgiving macadam I was able to squelch and slither for the next three miles through equally unforgiving ankle-deep moorland bogs that epitomise the Way. I had encountered its course at various points each day, except on my walk from Blanchland to Hexham, and I would meet with it again for one last time tomorrow as both it and I climbed to the highest points of our respective walks at the summit of Cross Fell. After that final concurrence I would bid it farewell for our paths would not cross again upon my leaving the radar station atop Great Dun Fell. It was on this stretch of the Pennine Way that I discovered a fourth use for my monopod. As well as it acting as my weirdo-hitting stick and cattle prod, these in addition to acting as a firm base for a camera, it also satisfied perfectly the requirements of a bog-poker. Where the morass that passed for a path gave no indication as to its depth, I found I could gauge the shallowest point by jabbing ahead to test the firmness of the ground underfoot. This process undoubtedly slowed my progress, but it meant I would be less likely to leave a boot as a permanent souvenir of my passing.

The Pennine Way, as it skirts the shoulders of Hartleyburn Common and Glendue Fell, represents a visible section of the Maiden Way and carried me as far as Knarsdale where I left it to find refreshment at an inn marked on my map. Although the environment underfoot had become most disagreeable, the earlier drizzle had all but cleared and the valley ahead was randomly bathed in sunlight, which gave an effect like that of a patchwork quilt laid out before me. The surrounding fells still looked forbidding however, as they remained veiled in a low and gloomy cloud cover that, when set against the sunlit valley, gave a heightened impression of their potential malevolence. It was half past two and as I carried no food with me, having assumed that I would find a suitable lunch en route, I made for the inn only to find that it, apparently like so many I had been told of on the 'Inn Way', operated strict lunchtime opening hours. I arrived at the Kirkstyle Inn barely in time to order a drink but the landlord took sympathy and allowed me to order two simultaneously. The first was quaffed even before the second was pulled and even before I had finished rolling my usual cigarette. I had the rare luxury of time and was able to dally over my second pint for Alston was little more than two hours' walking and I was advised that I could follow the old railway line for most of the way. This seemed altogether very fitting for I had seen so many disused railways – it was as gratifying to think that I could make use of one as it was pleasing to contemplate a lack of any steep ascents. My thirst was quenched but satisfaction of my hunger would have to wait, although I was jocularly offered a leek as I had visited the pub on the day of the local leek competition. Believing I must be the butt of some prank, I glanced as requested around the doorjamb into the back room to where

the group of locals had indicated I would find the vegetables. To my amazement, laid out in rows on cloth-covered trestle tables were the largest leeks I had
ever seen and although on reflection I can't recall actually seeing that many,
they did, nevertheless, make for an impressive sight. Not sufficiently impressive
however to keep me from my drink, which the landlord was now looking at
politely as if to let me know my welcome had expired. I took the hint, took up
my bags and took my leave, retracing my steps until I came to the five-arched
railway viaduct where I had, forty five minutes earlier, left the course of the
Pennine Way to seek my late lunch. The locals had told me of a way onto the
track bed at this point, but I have to confess that I found myself having to clam-
ber carefully over a barbed wired fence and slip and slide climbing a
steep embankment before the level course of the railway stretched before me.
They had also told me that although the path was well trodden, it had a
tendency to become a quagmire after a spell of rain. While splashing through
lengthy secuutions, which were more like tarns than a path, I was still trying to
recall when it had rained sufficiently hard – perhaps this was what the local
folk would term dry. I would hate to have been here when it was thoroughly wet.

On my way from the inn I had studied the map and was slightly concerned
that the disused railway was not designated as a footpath. I need not have worried for once on the wide track bed it soon became apparent that it had found a
new and dual-purpose use. Neat fencing had been erected at intervals to act as
extensions to adjacent fields and through each of these fences was a gate sufficiently wide for the track to render its use as a bridle way. My course along the
railway extended for four miles and over most of the distance it jockeyed for
position with the main road, both vying to follow the contours of the valley on
the western side of the river. For the majority of those four miles I found myself
intermittently splashing through the waterlogged track bed, sometimes taking
detours up the embankment to avoid the worst of the mires. This unpleasant
aspect of the railway did not detract from the tranquillity of the walking however. I saw only one other lady out with her dog and a farmer who confirmed
that there was a way off the railway and onto a track that would lead over the

river and on to Kirkside. Apart from those I was entirely alone providing, that is, that cows do not count. I met plenty of them and thought of Wainwright for he confessed to having a fear of bullocks and how, from the front, a cow and a bullock were hard to tell apart. I was in their environment and, worse still, when we did meet it was invariably in the narrow and confining corridor created by the railway, whether it an embankment or a cutting. There was no avoiding the creatures and I skirted around each of them gingerly, thankful that all those I had encountered were cows. Many of them were with calves, a fact that worried me greatly for I was only too aware that the female of the species could become very protective of their young. Cattle prod at the ready, I marched confidently, speaking kindly to the animals as I drew alongside. I cannot recall the nature of my conversation but I remember it was always very one-sided – they did stare at me as I approached and watched me carefully as I departed, so perhaps they were considering their response. I feel it may be more likely that they thought I was something of a lunatic and could not take their gaze off me for they had seldom seen anyone so overtly stupid. All such confrontations passed off without incident and after each I was left once again to my lonely rambling. I was now well progressed onto my fourth map and close to saying farewell to Northumberland as I came upon the splendidly named settlement of Slaggyford. The locals at the pub had firmly but amiably reminded me that this was still Northumberland. Cumbria would be the last of four counties that I would traverse. Yorkshire had been the first and would be the last and I had travelled north through County Durham and on into Northumberland. The meandering course I had taken through this northernmost county of my route would end after just three more miles and I would be nearing yet another change of maps the next day when again I would follow the route of the Pennine Way up Cross Fell.

It was at Slaggyford that I noticed what must have been the station which served the hamlet. It had ceased to function many years earlier yet its timbered ticket office still stood as a monument to what had once been. Instead of a platform edge where the railway staff would assist ladies to negotiate the step into the carriage, all that remained was a grassy bank to either side of a short length of derelict masonry. It was difficult to imagine the tiny ticket office bedecked in late-summer flowers as it no doubt would have been when this stopping point was the domain of a proud stationmaster. No time for flowers now at stations; the only art seen within modern stations seems to be the crude daubing found in the witless graffiti that adorns the walls and glazing of the characterless un-manned stops. The only voice heard would be that emanating from the disembodied loudspeaker announcing that the next train is the delayed arrival from so-and-so place. Silence usually accompanies modern stations, except for the sound made by accidental footsteps treading on the shards of glass that have not yet been swept up from the vandalised shelter. As I gazed at the tatty but unmolested remains of Slaggyford station, I wondered why it was that certain sections of society had taken to the wanton destruction of our environment. I pondered on what it might be that motivated the actions of those who chose to destroy whatever they encountered and I questioned whether it was so prevalent in 1938. I wondered whether Wainwright might have waited for his train at Blackburn station amid irreparable evidence of wanton destruction. Perhaps I have an overly nostalgic view of the past, but I doubted whether the mentality that drives the total disregard that we have come to accept as the norm in 1998 would have existed in those pre-war days. As I contemplated further along these lines I could not help but recall the stocks at Bainbridge and consider that while some may believe it barbaric to mete out such sentences upon transgressors, was it not true that their deterrent power was undeniable. Who are the 'some', I thought, who would believe those stocks to be entirely brutal and unjustifiable. They are the liberal but vociferous few whose noisy rantings have influenced greatest the conduct of our society for too long. Their voices have travelled far, through the press and media, and have been listened to altogether too seriously by those who make our laws. It is the same few who appear to care more for the perpetrators of crime than for those who suffer at the hands of those who perpe-trate. It is the same few who seem to believe that we could live in an inherently civilised society without clearly understood and enforced codes of conduct. I remain convinced that were it to be that the silent majority was allowed to form the basis of our penal codes, and that if its voice was heard, the penalties for violation would be very different. Where the deterrent is meagre then so too is the will to remain within the law. We all have a choice: to act in accordance with society's rules or to selfishly ignore them. Blatant ignorance of them might well create greater wealth or aid and abet an earlier accomplishment of one's goals, but these will, almost certainly, only be achieved at the calculated expense of others. A society with no rules would, sooner or later, see the emergence of a class system where power was held by those most willing to operate in a fashion that would have absolutely no regard for anything other than for their own gain. It is high time we revisited our rules and listened very carefully to the victims while casting only an occasional ear toward the criminal. If there are those who would act outside the law then so be it, but let us make sure that they do so safe in the knowledge that when ensnared they are not released without recalling most vividly their time in incarceration. This had still not answered my question as to why it was that there exists such disregard for property, but I am not so moronic as to be able to comprehend such behaviour and could not lower my mentality to that exhibited by those who would commit such acts. Accordingly, I utterly fail to see what pleasure can be gained through the destruction of someone else's possessions but wonder whether it might all be part of the want-it-now society where those that have are hounded by those that have not. Oh, dear, I thought, what a sad place we live in, and decided to think of something more refreshing on an afternoon that was brightening by the minute.

Slaggyford station had lain disused since the early 1970s when the line had closed and there I was walking quietly along the track bed where steam locomotives would have plied their business up and down the valley. Wainwright would have looked up every so often to watch a train pass as he wearily continued toward Alston. He was tiring as he found a place to eat in Slaggyford village and perhaps wished that he could climb into one of the passing coaches and hitch a lift for the remainder of the day. He had left his elderly host as the sun was setting and once again was destined to arrive late in the evening at his stopover for Slaggyford was still five miles from Alston. My walk along the railway took me two miles south of Slaggyford where, at a bridge over a track, I scrambled down the embankment following the directions that the farmer I met earlier had given me. Once onto the unmade track I was back on the same path as Wainwright for he had left the main valley road and had found his way via this rough path down to the river. He had been attempting to find a fording point across it that was marked on the map only to find that the voluminous waters rendered impossible any pedestrian crossing. Whether the ford is ever passable on foot is debatable for the river is of sufficient maturity at this point to suggest that only a fool would make any attempt to cross other than on horse or through some other means of solid transportation. I had walked up this valley for the past three hours and certainly had no wish to be swept back down it again having got so close to my destination. It was fortunate that the bridge that Wainwright had been relieved to find remained intact. Although Kirkhaugh Bridge is a footbridge, the structure is of some size, of concrete decking supported on steel girders spanning the shores between three large stone stanchions. I gained the impression that its current fabrication was the result of major refurbishment works carried out only after Wainwright had gratefully crossed it. Most bridges are built to connect two places rather than simply one side of a river to the other, but this bridge seemed not to make any meaningful connection. The track to the west of the river led only to the farm buildings at Kirkhaugh while on the east bank there was the church with its steep and slender spire. Beyond that there appeared to be no reason to have erected and take on the maintenance of a bridge of such magnitude. It seemed slightly incongruous that something that would carry so little traffic while still commanding considerable upkeep had not simply been allowed to fall into decay when only fifteen minutes earlier I had walked along the last remains of the railway that had been culled in the name of efficiency. It is not that I believe that the bridge should be wilfully ignored until its closure were to be the only option, it is more that it seemed a crying shame that the railway link had been irreversibly destroyed. Once across the river the path crossed level grazing meadows whereafter it soon became a track before joining a metalled road for the final stretch of walking and the first signs of a return to civilisation with the rooftops of Alston visible two miles further up the valley.

The first building I came upon was the church at Kirkhaugh that still sits on its modest footprint half hidden among trees and behind other buildings with only its interesting spire to herald its presence as the walker nears it from the north. It is the steeply sloping pitch of its roof and incredibly narrow spire that stand out in the memory and give the building a sense that its designer must have been of foreign descent. As I passed I wondered whether the spire's dimensions might have been scaled down as a requirement of needing to contribute toward the erection of a nearby footbridge by way of planning gain in much the same way as supermarkets have to pay for access-road improvement schemes. The map symbol indicated the church as having a spire but this was no Salisbury Cathedral and it must have been a close decision as to whether the Ordnance Survey classed this flagpole-type construction as a spire or merely some out of place phallus. The trees that afforded the church's hiding place continue as the road and the river converge and the valley meadows are squeezed as the eastern fells close in. The trees of Kirkside Wood cling to the steep slope and the road winds a twisting course along the narrowest of shelves hemmed in between the precipitous valley side and the river. Wainwright may have been more fortunate than I for he only arrived at this wooded riverside avenue late in the evening and perhaps after its predominant inhabitants had retired for the evening for otherwise he would surely have made mention of the insect life. As I entered the tree-lined avenue so I entered the lair of a myriad of insects all hell bent on my providing them with a late-afternoon snack. As breathing through my nose was still proving difficult as a result of my little-mentioned affliction, I was forced to draw breath through a partially clenched hand placed over my mouth to avoid inhaling great lungfuls of the persistent creatures. Those that weren't investigating around my face were proving equally awkward elsewhere, encircling my head and any other exposed parts. In their absence it might have been plausible to imagine the tranquil romantic rendezvous that

Wainwright had witnessed, but as it was, half-eaten by a variety of miniature winged monsters with voracious carnivorous appetites, I could imagine nothing. All I could think was the relief it would be to escape from their clutches into the relative peace of the open ground that I could see further ahead.

Finally I reached the open ground and, on studying the map, realised that as I crossed the Ayle Burn at Randalholme I had left Northumberland behind and was now walking within Cumbria's borders. I was becoming tired and was all too ready to reach the haven of my overnight accommodation in Alston. Although I had ached the evening before as I neared Haltwhistle, I had not suffered the same level of fatigue that I experienced as I entered Cumbria. I longed for an easy end to my day but to my chagrin my route was not to be a straightforward and flat valley walk for the last two miles. The road began a steady ascent immediately after Randalholme, which continued in its relative severity until I joined the main road from Allen Dale, which swung down from above me and to my left after its crossing of the fells to the north-east. Only when I rejoined the traffic of the main road did I begin to descend. The consolation for my efforts was that I was afforded fine views of the dale and of Alston that was nearing with every laboured stride. I could see below the preserved railway that has been reinstated to give the tourists the briefest of tastes of the days of steam. Although the largest part of the South Tynedale Railway was killed off, a short section from Alston to Gilderdale Halt has been reopened as a narrow gauge line. As with the majority of these lines, the railway relies on the manpower of keen volunteers to keep it running and it is a credit to people like these for so often their undertakings are simply taken for granted. There are innumerable examples where the efforts of the few are taken as read by the many and it sometimes amazes me that they retain the energy to continue in the face of what must seem like total indifference. Their enthusiasm must come out of pride from a job well done not unlike, perhaps, the old stationmaster at Slaggyford as he might have tended his hanging baskets and colourful borders. Did anyone turn to him and commend him for his enterprise, I wondered, or was it that he was driven by his own sense of pride. If the motivation behind an enterprise is a narcissistic desire to earn praise then the spirit will surely flag for unsolicited testimonial is rare indeed. Only where the desire exists to carry out such work with the sense of achievement being a personal one will the undertaking be completed and maintained with a sense of vitality and enthusiasm. I returned, momentarily, to my earlier contemplation of vandalism and destruction and wondered why such good people even bother to strive in an environment where wider society seems to not care about their surroundings. Perhaps I had answered my own question when I thought of the volunteers who take care of the modest railway that I looked down upon as I approached Alston. Maybe it is they who realise that while it would be all too simple to accept unsociable behaviour as the norm, this would be to reduce society to the level of the lowest common denominator where no one cared because there was no point in caring. While there remain a few who will lead by their own profitless examples, perhaps the rest of us might wish to follow. I still could not get away from the thought though that for those who did not heed such good examples, a night or two in the stocks at Bainbridge might refocus their public-mindedness. It is not enough to live in the hope that the good deeds of some will be emulated, or at least appreciated, by the rest; there remains the need for a clear code of conduct that would be strictly administered for those who ignore its edicts.

The road continued to descend and when I entered what was clearly the beginning of Alston I did so at an area of the town known as Townfoot. This concerned me for I had noticed that my accommodation was at the Albert House, situated in Townhead. I had the sinking feeling that having been commanded to walk up one long hill only to once again descend, my reserves were likely to be tested one more time in carrying me from Townfoot to Townhead. I inquired at a service station and the attendant confirmed my worst fears. If Alston were to be situated on the Norfolk Broads my anguish would not have been so great, but as it was my eyes followed the attendant's directions up the horribly steep incline to which he pointed. When I further inquired as to whether he knew of Albert House his smile broadened even further at my look of discomfort as he went on to explain that Albert House was one of the last houses up the hill. Slowly making my weary way through the quiet streets of Alston, I was struck by its modest beauty with its cobbled market square and tastefully presented shops and cafés. No garish fast food outlets or brightly illuminated signs of building societies or estate agents. No plethora of charity shops or unsightly discount stores. There was a sensation that although the shops sold modern wares, they did so within a trading environment that had changed little in sixty years. No doubt there were more cafés serving increased numbers of tourists and no doubt there were craft shops where once there may have been the cobbler or the farrier, but even so, on first impression Alston was a place that had survived the ravages of commercialism. My stay was to be brief and I would see little for the shops were closing and I would have to leave early the next day, but I would return to Alston to sample its delights at some future time.

As I ascended the main street the town was very much quieter than it had been when Wainwright had climbed the same street with tired legs and flagging spirit. He had arrived at the town on the day of the Alston Show and had found himself among a revelling melee of local folk who jostled and partied and had, it seemed, saved their energy all year for the occasion of the fair. He had felt as out of place as I would have had I been surrounded by merrymakers – I was struggling to concentrate on putting one foot in front of the other as I came to the final climb and would not have invited joviality. My hosts, the Pesters, seemed to understand my exhaustion for they quickly and courteously showed me to my room and indicated that there would be plenty of hot water. They must have read my mind for all I wished for was to drop everything where I stood and sink into a hot bath. As a mark of general decency I waited for Mrs Pester to leave the room before I did so, but within minutes of her leaving I was being re-energised by the comfortable massage that the hot, lapping water of the bath was providing. Albert House had catered for travellers since before the turn of the century but never can one have been so ready for relaxation and recuperation as I was as I lay with the bath water gently returning my body to a state where it might carry me to some local hostelry. Taking heed of my hosts' earlier recommendation, I found a pleasingly warm welcome at the Turk's Head Inn some little way down the main street and it was to one of the barstools that I proceeded almost before all my little parts were dry. The barstool and I remained in close proximity for the following hour or so and I only moved away from it twice: once to eat a fine helping of scampi and chips and once as to not have done so would have led to an embarrassing incident.

The Pesters had not been able to help in my quest to identify my predecessor's hosts, the Richardsons. They had suggested that I might ask at the pub but I very soon discovered that the surname Richardson had long and numerous connections with the town and no one could recall the man to which Wainwright had referred. Mr Richardson had been heavily involved with the fair and was secretary of the poultry section, but I suppose I would have to accept that sixty years is a long time in poultry and once you've seen one chicken you've seen them all. I had learned my lesson the evening before in respect of alcohol consumption and I moderated my drinking for I had no desire to feel as I had done during the earlier part of the day. I still had notes to write and still had the decision to make as to whether a crossing of Cross Fell would be possible. I knew only too well what the tops could be like in intemperate weather and although this seventh day had ended more amiably than it had begun, the tops of the surrounding fells had been still deep in cloud cover as I had looked out of my bedroom window. The onset of dusk had concealed whether the earlier improvements had continued, but the forecast was not promising and I had no wish for an abrupt end to my walk as a statistic.

Bidding the landlord goodnight, I sluggishly returned up the main street and back to my room where I did not complete my chores for no sooner had I laid on the bed for a few moments than I had dropped into a deep sleep, a sleep so deep that it was best likened to a coma, unlikely to be interrupted by anything other than the loudest of disturbances.

Chapter 8

Alston to Knock

The only sound to disturb my repose, and I was pleased that it did for otherwise I might have missed breakfast, was the alarm clock sounding at seven o'clock. There was no waking at five o'clock to adopt some ungraceful position at the window in which to smoke a cigarette. There was no leisurely cup of tea while checking whatever it was that I had to check or clean whatever it was that I had to clean. There was no scanning of the relevant chapter from Wainwright's account (although our paths in any case were to seriously differ for the first time. What there was, though, was an overcast dankness to the day with the consequence that all surrounding fells were concealed in a grey veil and as I peered through the glass of the bedroom window I questioned the wisdom of my proposed route. I was strongly averse to proceeding the way that Wainwright had had to for he walked mile upon mile on what would now be a very busy main route connecting Alston and Penrith. I had thought long and hard about the spirit of my adventure, vis a vis whether the route should be over or around Cross Fell. I had satisfied myself that although I was parting company with the man, I was following my route-plan, which only accommodated what he had wished but did not dare attempt in the adverse weather. I had planned my eighth day to end at a farm near the village of Knock and if I deviated then the only alternative entailed a further six miles being added to the day, which was already sufficiently quite long enough thank you at eighteen miles. So it was that I began to imagine with every passing minute that the cloud base had lifted ever so slightly and that perhaps the forecasters were wrong and that by lunchtime I would be basking atop the fell in shirtsleeves and shorts. If my belief in amelioration were flawed then it would not be the first time that I had set out with the conviction that things would pick up by lunchtime only to find that not only had they not improved but they had worsened alarmingly. More than once Sue and I, while being drenched by rain in nil visibility, had exchanged words not too politely regarding my parenthood having earlier convinced her of the prudence of our endeavour. If you are speaking to her she will always recall the same two occasions: the first was when I genuinely believed that the clouds would lift and so we proceeded to walk the Fairfield Round and the second was an ill-fated traverse of Bow Fell. I admit there was little to enjoy on either trek except for the fact that we saw absolutely no one all day. Mark you; if there had been any other walker on the fells, had they been more than thirty yards distant then they would have passed unnoticed in the appalling visibility. They would have passed unheard, too, for on both occasions the wind propelled the mist with a cruel velocity that stung exposed skin that had been tenderised by the bitter chill, for it was also cold enough to freeze the what-nots off a brass monkey. I have lied in my brief recounting of these journeys for on the Bow Fell excursion we did see another walker. He was, in fact, good enough to give us a lift the thirteen miles back to our car at Dungeon Gill for we had descended in the wrong place entirely. I maintain that we would not have erred were it not for the break in my navigational concentration as a direct result of being shouted at for being a total moron for having suggested such a walk in the first place. Sue continues to maintain that whatever my excuses might be I was still a total moron for having suggested such a walk in the first place. At the time I consoled her by assuring her that we were not lost, we simply were not where we should have been. She inquired in a shrill scream as to what the hell was the difference, a question that I chose not to answer fully for I could not satisfactorily explain the relative nuances of each. I did try to deflate the situation by advising that one day we would laugh about our predicament, but she failed to see how this helped and continued to shout about me being a moron etcetera. I was correct in that there have been times since when we have laughed about it but not all that often and not all that loud it has to be said.

It was this brush with unpleasantness that had provided the impetus to purchase the GPS, which, using some whiz-bang technology, provides the walker with a grid reference for present location. The principles of its operation are not for inclusion in my account, partly because there is no reason to expound further and partly because I am not absolutely sure as to how it works. I am, frankly, completely reliant upon it performing its function – I charge myself only with changing the batteries and making sure I have spares for these machines eat battery power in much the same way I drink beer if it is on special offer.

One of the dangers of being an enthusiast and at the same time an optimist is the ability to convince oneself that no obstacle is insurmountable. The enthusiasm provides the drive and the optimism provides the belief that things will be fine. Without enthusiasm surely nothing would have been achieved by anyone and without optimism, however strong the enthusiasm, failure would ensue at the onset of the first problem. There are times, however, when a more circumspect outlook might be considered wise and as I sat at breakfast looking out and pondering my route I thought back to those previous ill-advised treks. I think I knew only too well that the summit of Cross Fell, at almost 900 metres, was likely to be so inhospitable that attempting it was near madness, but I was refusing to allow admission for such thoughts. I persuaded myself that while the past few days had all dawned somewhat grisly, they had all later developed to become perfectly gentle and entirely suitable for enterprise, such as I proposed as I sat contemplating over my second bowl of cornflakes. After all, I thought, I had the GPS so at least I would know where I was at any point. I had the correct walking attire to keep warm and dry. I had rations and makeshift shelter in the shape of a bivvy bag. I had map and compass and I had advised people of my plan so that rescue might follow in the event of my not arriving at my next destination. More than these, though, I had a single-minded pigheadedness that was not about to allow defeat at the first sign of a tiny bit of inclement weather. No, Cross Fell it would be and besides, I thought, the clouds just might have lifted ever so slightly even in the time it had taken to eat the second and pour a final bowl of cornflakes.

Over breakfast I regaled the Pesters with my abject failure to find any trace of the Richardsons of which Wainwright's account had related. Prior to my visit they had also asked in the town as to whether any of the older residents could recall the small, wiry, moustached man with large nose and thin facial features. Although Wainwright's description of him was undoubtedly his most extensive of any of the hosts on his journey, no one had been able shed any further detail on the man who had been so involved with the Alston Show. I had drawn a blank in the town where I had felt confident of being able to glean a very clear image of the family that had acted as good Samaritans all those years ago and had left a mark on Wainwright that he no doubt remembered long after his journey ended. He wondered, as he left Alston, whether he might ever return for the Richardsons had invited him to call again. He considered that a return was unlikely but probably did call again for Alston is sited en route of the Pennine Way. The best part of thirty years would have separated the visits, so perhaps he had been correct in concluding that he was not likely to see Mr Richardson again. Wainwright spoke well of Alston, and deservedly so for it is a grand place and my first visit will most certainly not be my last. I will certainly return – the only difference is that my hosts did not invite me back for they had sold the house and were about to embark on an altogether longer venture. They, and their toddler son, were to up sticks and go travelling the world just as soon as the paperwork was finalised for the sale of their fine guest house. I thanked them for their hospitality, wished them well, paid my bill and hoped that the new incumbents would provide as pleasant a stay as the Pesters had done. One day I shall find out.

As a consequence of my somewhat relaxed start to the day it, was half past nine before I retraced my steps down Front Street toward the Market Square and down to the river. As I crossed the River South Tyne I did so for the third and final time; I had already crossed it as a mature adult at Hexham and again as an adolescent at Kirkhaugh. Eighteen miles lay ahead of me, much of which would be up the long ascent of Cross Fell with a fair proportion following the Pennine Way across the roof of the Pennines, so I was anticipating slow and boggy progress. If I were to average only two miles an hour, I could not expect to arrive until half past six, which left precious little time for any unforeseen eventualities. There would be barely any time for pauses or rests and it might even be necessary for lunch to be taken on the move. This was not too great a frustration because, however much I told myself the weather showed signs of improvement, it seemed most unlikely that I would be tempted to stop frequently to admire long-distance vistas. If the visibility in the valley was poor it was a fair bet that at the altitudes that I was to attain there would be nothing to be seen in any direction, unless, of course, my optimistic hopes for a magical improvement proved most unusually to be correct.

If leaving the Roman wall had marked the beginning of the end of Wainwright's eagerness for his trek then his eighth day of walking sealed its fate and flushed out any last vestiges of optimism at the same time. He had awoken to a cold, clear morning but he had no sooner left Alston than the elements sallied against him and it started to rain, driven by a cold wind straight into his face. He stated that it had been his intention to make his way to Appleby via Cross Fell, a wearying twenty-three miles, but with enthusiasm at its lowest ebb he did not need too great an excuse to simply give up his goal and yield to the conditions. It was apparent from his account that for a great part of his final four days of walking he found his way by road and made little attempt to take more challenging routes. He had peaked when he had reached the wall and all after that was undertaken he resigned himself to his imminent return to normality. The verve had dissipated from his mission. His cup had runneth over upon reaching the wall but, in the horizontal rain outside Alston, that same cup had emptied noticeably. His zest had all but gone and he was only too ready to accept the easier option of following the Hartside road even though to do so would dramatically lengthen the walk to Appleby. I would not wish to cast aspersions on his efforts for as I approached the tiny hamlet of Leadgate it was difficult to imagine my own attitude had I been facing conditions of equal severity. Although uninspiring, the weather remained relatively benevolent as I too found shelter in the doorway of a barn. Rolling a cigarette and studying the map I realised that if I chose to follow Cross Fell then it was at Leadgate where our sixty-year-separated paths would deviate for the next ten miles or so. It took me less than the time it took to light the cigarette to decide that it had to be Cross Fell and I refolded the map for I knew that the following three miles entailed a straightforward road walk as far as Garrigill.

Where Wainwright had taken the right fork at Leadgate I took the road to the left, all the time looking down to my left on the much smaller River South Tyne. I had seen it in all its stages and now I witnessed its infancy. The river that I had first encountered just north of Hexham as a great torrent that was then only possible to cross where it had been bridged would soon be little more than a dale stream that might be forded by some nimble and careful footwork. I had travelled many miles since crossing it near Warden and had traced it almost to its source, which lay only five further miles upstream. Along the valley floor, running adjacent to the river, lay the course, again, of the Pennine Way. For a large part of both yesterday and today the route I had taken mirrored the long-distance walk with which Wainwright's name had become synonymous. Our loosely parallel courses would only separate, for the final time, upon my descent from Great Dunn Fell. While I proceeded with a spring in my step, Wainwright's melancholia had continued unabated as he pressed on upwards into the driving rain over Hartside and his totally depressing day was complete at having to forego any further plans of walking upon reaching Gamblesby. He had covered only nine miles. He arrived at the inn in the small village and could then only sit and watch the deluge outside and wait. He waited and waited but finally had to accept that his only option was to stay overnight and replan his route for the following day. It was in the light of the knowledge of his frustration that I chose not to laboriously follow him for it seemed like madness to omit Cross Fell, solely for the reasoning of retracing his steps. Failure is difficult enough to cope with when its onset is unforeseen but I could not reconcile myself to deliberate failure purely for the sake of apparent accuracy. I substantiated my decision to digress from his route for exactly the same reason as we might modify an earlier design in the name of progress. It is surely only a fool who continues to send messages by carrier pigeon when advances in communications can realise the transmission of the same message much more quickly. There are times when change is not only preferable but is essential. Besides, he had wanted to bag the fells and I would do it for him, albeit posthumously. It would not be until I left Slake's Farm on the ninth day and, after half a mile, rejoined the Milburn to Appleby road that his and my paths would once again converge.

I noticed a sign indicating that refreshments could be secured at Garrigill and at once began to relish the prospect of a pot of tea. I had made good time and could afford a brief rest to savour the delights of tea and a locally made sticky bun. The road twisted and turned as it followed the contours along the valley and Garrigill remained hidden until I finally rounded a corner where, from my elevated position, I was looking down on the last village of the South Tyne valley. Reaching the more level valley floor I was joined by the Pennine Way at a stile over the wall from an adjacent field and I wondered whether I might now join the slow procession to the summit seven miles distant. If the activity in Garrigill were to be a measure then I might never have seen another living sole again. The place was still asleep except for the odd car that slowly drove around the village green, presumably seeking out the same place of refreshment that I sought. It quickly became apparent that the tearoom was at the waterfalls which lay a quarter of a mile over the bridge on the other side of the river. I had no desire, nor really the time, to recross the river so I rested for ten minutes on a bench under a mature tree on the green looking at the inn to see whether there were any signs of life there. There were not, so, undeterred, I got back to my feet and set off on what had to be classed as the most hazardous part of my journey. I walked respectfully slowly through Garrigill for I gained the impression that nothing would ever be hurried in the village. The village gave an impression of serenity that I ruined by loudly blowing my nose as I made my way along its quiet street. Wainwright would, I decided, have liked Garrigill. I liked it but would have found it even more pleasing had I been able to obtain a cup of tea and sticky bun. I left the village at half past eleven on a Sunday morning and wondered at what time the residents might stir. I suspected that opening time at noon might see an increase in pedestrian traffic but I had not the time to confirm or deny the supposition if I were to keep to my schedule.

I am something of a stickler for schedules and I gain considerable satisfaction if arrival at a particular destination is close to my own estimates. Sue has never understood this predilection with timely arrival and it drives her to distraction for she appears able to saunter about with no predetermined programme in mind. This seems, to a greater or lesser degree, to be true of most women who will wander in and out of shops with no firm proposal for any specific purchase. I have always thought of this type of amorphous shopping spree to be a waste of time for it is entirely lacking in purpose, which means that any achievement or accomplishment by way of acquisition is immeasurable against the objectives, for there were none. I fail to perceive any gain in risking the action of a purchase where there is no planned benefit – this is basic risk – and does not appear to figure highly in the minds of female shoppers. Then again, perhaps my observation is fatally flawed – it may well be that the hidden agenda of these apparently purposeless trips is to ensure that any item bought does not match anything already in the wardrobe, thus entailing subsequent excursions to ensure correct colour balance. Maybe the aimless meanderings are all a part of a ploy to make sure that subsequent trips would always be necessary.

My next goal was to find the track on the edge of the village that had once upon a time served the lead miners as they went about their business into the high hills. Both Alston and Garrigill had evolved on the back of the lead-mining industry and I knew from the map that there was plenty of evidence of the long-deserted workings scattered in the hills all around. The activities of these hardened workers had ceased long ago and all that would be left now would be the relics of their labours in the shape of spoil heaps and derelict shacks. The track that had served the mines would provide me with a clear route to within a mile of the summit, so I remained reasonably confident that whatever the weather threw at me I would still find my way up and over the fells. Leaving the relative sanctuary of Garrigill, I soon climbed the valley side to look back on a grey and gloomy scene below. Not, though, as grey and gloomy as what lay ahead as I peered upwards into the murk of low cloud, mist and drizzle. I had not travelled far before I came to the corner where the Pennine Way was indicated as branching off to truncate the otherwise longer route taken by the track. At the corner I saw no sign or indeed any obvious path through the heathery upland – all I could see was a boggy morass leading off into the mist, which would require navigation to be by way of compass. I decided that as I had no desire to become lost so early I would maintain my progress up the stony miners' road and rounded the corner ignoring any temptation to veer from its more obvious course.

Walking a little further I folded and stowed my fourth map as my venture carried me onto my fifth and final new map. All subsequent maps required for my return would be those to which I had already referred on the northern leg of my journey. Any greyness or gloom of the valley had disappeared as I considered the five miles remaining to the summit. In actual fact, the entire valley had disappeared, concealed totally as I had entered an arena where my surroundings extended to only fifty yards in any direction. The severely limited extent of my visible environment created an increasingly eerie sensation as ghostly shapes loomed at me from the mist. Boulders that had been strewn at the side of the track began to take on strange and sinister shapes and gave an appearance of being alive until their true form and size could be established. Isolated pools of peat-blackened moorland water gave no indication as to their depth if one were to stray off the path. Between the pools lay great swathes of deep heather that would slow all progress to a crawl if the track were to end. I would momentarily start as the occasional boulder moved before I realised that it was nothing more than a sheep. All sense of scale had vanished along with the visibility and what might have seemed like a sheep only ten yards away was, in fact, another boulder at the very limit of my perceptible world. With the increasing altitude came a still further worsening of visibility and an amplification of the inability to sense scale and form. I had become accustomed to walking with my monopod as a walking stick and, as I walked, I noticed that I was holding it tighter as though in readiness for retaliation against some spectral assailant. I am not generally superstitious or prone to irrational fears, but as I carried on up into this shrouded world of long-dead miners' country I would be lying if I did not confess to a little jumpiness. A bird would fly from the undergrowth or a previously unseen sheep would suddenly move and I would catch my breath and smile nervously to myself as I looked again forward and continued on my way. This sensation of uneasiness was not improved by the emergence of greater evidence of the ancient mining workings. My way passed through great fields of shattered stones lying as permanent memorials to the primitive mining techniques of rock breaking and ore extraction. Every now and then a more recognisable shape would gradually develop as I came upon the tumbled down walls of old buildings and I passed their remains with a slightly tighter grip on the monopod. I smiled also as I thought back to schooldays and the meetings with the careers advisor – I wondered how many schoolchildren might ever had had the desire to become lead miners and whether such an occupational aspiration would be met with approval as being a proper job. Had careers advisors existed in the last century they might, no doubt, have believed a pupil's desire to be perfectly normal and representative of a wish to secure well-respected employment. It seemed hard to imagine though, as I continued through the desolation, that men would put themselves through such a solitary and harsh existence unless there were no alternative.

Climbing through the occluded and deserted landscape, trapped in my restricted realm of grey with all points of reference completely obscured, I was struck by how much my ascent might be likened to that of life. We struggle blindly forever upwards, not knowing when our goal has been reached, not knowing when we might actually be assailed, not knowing if the chosen path will carry us to our destination and not knowing exactly what we are doing and why we are where we are. Regardless of knowing whether a chosen path might lead to fulfilment, many pass through life unaware as to what their destination is. Life becomes essentially nothing more than an aimless meander that starts with birth and ends with death and all that happens in between is pure incidence.

If we are not aware of where we are going we will never know if we have arrived, and if we are unsure of our arrival then our purposeless and empty chore will persist unceasingly. The only reminders of the span of life are the materialistic trinkets that are acquired along the way and the only relative measure of success lies in the greatest number of these trinkets being secured. The seeking of the trinkets is fruitless if their acquisition is based purely upon an apparent need to be perceived as successful – it is of no greater purpose than random shopping sprees. If our actions are without purpose we may as well stay motionless. In all my digressive thought, as I questioningly maintained my upward course, I at least had one advantage in that I knew where I wanted to be in the short term. I wanted to be sitting in the lea of the cross-walled summit shelter that I knew existed from pictures I had seen. The wind was picking up from the east and the temperature had plummeted and the mist had begun to scud across the moorland, blown by increasingly squally winds. In addition to multiplying the effects of the already eerie landscape, I had to accept that, as ever, my thoughts for more benign weather had stemmed from a degree of optimism that was proving to clearly be sadly overactive. Far from lunchtime seeing an improvement, it had begun to look rather more likely that my eighth day would develop very much as Wainwright's had done. I was too far advanced toward the summit to contemplate a return to Garrigill. I was only a little over two miles from the top with two hundred metres of climbing; once I had reached the top of the highest Pennine hill I would descend its escarpment slope making a return to a more civilised environment far more quickly than I had left it. A little way further advanced along the increasingly less apparent track I decided to make the best of the minimal shelter afforded by a stile over a timber post and wire fence and pause for lunch. I doubted very much whether there would be much in the way of refuge after the point where I stopped for the map showed the track ending after another mile and I guessed beyond that I would be on open and tempestuous moorland. As I sat on the wet timber plank of the stile I noticed that it was one o'clock and I congratulated myself for I had made good time to what was approximately half-distance. I would arrive ahead of my schedule if I were to be able to maintain my earlier pace, a fact for which I was not sorry because the sooner I was off these unfamiliar hills the better.

It is all well and good entering into a challenge when all factors are known, or can at least be estimated, but as I sat in the relative calm of my resting place I pondered whether my decision to proceed had been taken in absence of some alarmingly material facts. I had not bargained on the extent of the reduction in visibility and, in the peace of the valley, I had not considered fully the consequence of the vastly increased wind that made map reading nigh on impossible were it to become necessary. While I could follow the track I was unconcerned but I knew that soon I would lose its aid, after which the walking would be very little better than blind. The map and compass would then be my only passport to the western side of the hills and without them I would be liable to stagger about in circles with all sense of direction being disabled by the conditions. My GPS might act as my crutch but without reference to the map from the information it provided I would be as lost as though I did not have it with me in the first place. I began also to worryingly question the life expectancy of the batteries – I had used the spares on day one of my journey and had not thought to buy a replacement set. Although I had kept the old ones as emergency back-up, I wondered whether I might live to regret not having bought fresh ones. Regardless of living to regret things I was, in fact, beginning to wonder whether I might not live at all – I had brief thoughts as to exactly what I would do in the event of being totally lost. My hill-walking mettle had never really been tested to the extreme and, although I knew that panic would always more than likely be the final killer, could I be sure that I would maintain my composure if and when tested by the ferocity of the elements? These ponderings over lunch provided a rather strange cocktail, laced with equal measures of self-doubt, anticipation and pumping adrenalin. The anticipation and adrenalin did not give any worry but my self-doubt was of concern. Most normally balanced people can walk along the 3-inch-wide kerb at the roadside, but introduce the fear factor of the same kerb being raised 6 feet above the surrounding ground and the previously straightforward task becomes altogether more difficult. The significant danger of an error of judgement is heightened with the senses concentrating less on the job at hand and more on the consequences of a foot being put wrong with an increased probability of calamity. It is not dissimilar to the pessimist who enters into a venture with the attitude that something is sure to cause the undertaking to fail. With such an approach the likelihood of defeat is increased. Presumably though, in such instances the pessimist will not experience disappointment for the enterprise will have performed as it was expected to. I could not afford to enter the final pull to the summit in such a frame of mind so lunch was a fairly brief affair, as the sooner I continued on my way the sooner my thoughts would turn to more pressing and, hopefully, more positive matters.

The mist thickened as I climbed and visibility worsened as I neared the point on the map shown as Greg's Hut where the track would end and I would have to fend for myself on what was marked as a bridleway. The hut's vague bulk appeared menacingly from the mist and as I approached I half expected a wizened old miner to emerge and warn me of the foolhardiness of further upward progress. There were no sheep at this height and all earlier sounds had deserted me, so I was left in a world of silence except for the gusting wind and the steady rustle of my clothing as I walked. But for those noises it was as though I had been struck stone deaf. I paused for a moment on the leeward side of the hut and studied the map once more – I had studied it quite a lot since I had lunched, but however much I looked there was no easy solution to the crossing of Cross Fell. I chuckled nervously as I concluded that the fell seemed indeed particularly cross today and I hoped that it would allow me the liberty of treading on its summit without taking malevolent retribution. With the GPS switched on and, thankfully, accurately reporting my position, I plotted the length of time it would take to reach the junction on the path marked on the map as half a mile ahead. I was skirting the head of the valley of the Black Burn and following a gradual cross slope – I estimated that a maximum of fifteen minutes should see me to the junction at which point I had to bear left southerly to remain on the Pennine Way. Were I to miss the junction I would soon have found myself on a descending course that would mean I had completely missed Cross Fell. After fifteen minutes following the distinct path, and with eyes glued to the GPS, I was pleased to come upon a signpost that showed, at least, that someone had been up on these fells since the abandonment of the mines. Any concern I had harboured as to whether I might join a caravan of walkers was misplaced for I had not seen a soul all morning. This fact did not altogether astound me because most might well have taken the more circumspect view that perhaps I should have taken and stayed away until Cross Fell was a little less so treacherous. One of the arms of the three on the signpost confirmed that I should turn left to continue along the Pennine Way and I did so with a renewed calm for I had satisfied myself that such a prestigious route would not allow the lone walker to become lost. Why, I thought, I would not be surprised if there were to be service stations en route that would provide for the weary wayfarer.

As the mist turned to rain my new-found confidence dissipated horribly quickly as I very soon found myself wandering up a gentle incline of boggy grassland dotted with intermittent boulders and no particular waymarked path to guide my steps. I had the compass bearing but I had turned south so that the wind-blown rain was at my left and within seconds my glasses were covered with a fine film of moisture that rendered meaningful study of the compass impossible. I took my glasses off but, and it pains me to admit it, my naked eyes are not what they once were – by the by, there are a number of other areas of my body that when seen naked are not what they once were, but further detail on that note can wait perhaps for another time. Devoid of glasses I was completely devoid of vision, so, putting my glasses back on to make the best of a bad job, I tried again to track my way following the bearing toward the triangulation point that I knew to be approximately half a mile away. Either the softness of the ground underfoot had absorbed all evidence of boot prints or I had strayed from the path and I arrived at the logical conclusion that if I were to be blind then all I could do was to keep heading in a direction whereby I was travelling uphill. The previously sporadic boulders had become prolific in number and the chances of refinding the path were reduced to nil while I teetered about among their great mass. Maintaining my theory that so long as I was still ascending then I could not be going too far awry, I scrambled over the boulder-strewn landscape and continued upward. This simple expedient worked extremely well until I came to the more level plateau of the summit area itself. There, in the thick mist and blustery wind and rain, judgement as to which way was up and which way was down became almost subjective and I found that I was growing uncomfortable in trusting my senses.

I stopped and took stock of my situation; I wasn't entirely sure where I was; I had to find the triangulation point to be able to fix my position and take a bearing for the descent to Little Dun Fell. It was now after two o'clock and I had three hours of good daylight left. These factors alone might not have been too alarming, but when the matter of my not being able to see through my glasses was taken into account, I was beginning to think that a helpful solution might be to run about the plateau in ever-decreasing circles shouting 'Don't panic'. Resisting the startling simplicity of this suggestion, I arrived at the conclusion that it was essential to restore my vision to a point where I could actually see something. It was not until this stage in my predicament that I considered how useful it would be if I were to put my hood up – I had for some inexplicable reason ignored the fact thus far that my ridiculously expensive coat had an all-singing, all-dancing hood. Turning my back to the howling wind and fastening it tight around my cheeks, I reached into a pocket for a clean handkerchief. Cleaning the water droplets and condensation from my glasses and keeping my back to the wind, I was able to contemplate the map, compass and GPS. Looking at a map while exposed to a screaming wind that would do its utmost to whip it from a cold-fingered grip is hard enough, but trying, simultaneously with compass and GPS, to determine a course in such conditions becomes almost laughable. I did finally establish the direction of the summit and walked in a series of zigzags over the grassy plateau to help ensure I found the trig point. I had progressed in such fashion for what seemed like an eternity but, in truth, was probably little more than ten minutes when I spied a mass to my right that proved to be the cross-walled shelter. As relieved as though this had been a service station when an extremely urgent call of nature was required, I snuggled into a cosy alcove on its western flank and rolled a cigarette. This was, without any doubt, the most pleasurable cigarette I smoked in the whole of my eleven solitary days. I was relieved to at last find shelter after the previous hour of being battered and near-beaten by the wind and lashing rain and I knew that shelter must be very close to the actual summit itself.

I was in no hurry to leave my temporary peaceful haven but knew that I did not have the luxury of time to spare for I had no idea how problematic the navigation might prove after leaving the summit. I then remembered that in my haste to enjoy the benefits of my masonry shelter I had not actually found the summit, so throwing my cigarette to one side, I got to my feet to continue on my way. I gingerly raised my head above the wall and, catching my breath as the full force of the wind hit me, I peered in all directions to espy the trig point. In the swirling mist to the south-east I could see occasional glimpses of the monolith that I knew was the concrete block that would mark the end of my search. As briefly as it appeared so it disappeared again, shrouded in the incessant mist that had been in my company for too long. Some mists are pleasurable and allow for quiet reflection, but this had a mean streak about it that demanded constant attention lest its evil intentions be realised. I made my way out from behind the wall and into the full exposure of the wind and, as I did so, I could have imagined that I heard a sound carried on the wind that was alien to my environment. I imagined that above the roar of the gale I heard a sound of that of an engine. Like the vision of the trig point, no sooner had I heard the noise than it was gone and I was left to ponder on the extent to which the hills on such a day can play tricks on our senses. Taking what minimal shelter I could from the column, I noted my direction for the start of my descent and decided, without delay, to set about a return to what I hoped would be the more clement environs of the Vale of Eden. As I stood again and set off south-east I nearly walked headlong into a young man on his motorbike. My senses had not deceived me. I had heard the sound of an engine, and in a bizarre greeting we cheerily waved at one another before he vanished into the mist in the direction from which I had just come. I had grappled with map and compass to safely see me thus far and there was he on a pleasant Sunday afternoon excursion with, seemingly, not a care in the world. I suddenly felt rather inadequate in that I had been in the throes of what I considered to be a near-death experience while he was calmly tootling about on his Yamaha enjoying the great outdoors. Perhaps though, his facial expression, concealed by his helmet, would not match his cheery wave and that, in reality, underneath was a panic-ridden rider who was totally lost but could not bring himself to inquire as to where the nearest service station could be found. Whatever was the truth I did not discover for he was gone as quickly as he had appeared and I was left, bemused, to follow my bearing away from the highest point on the Pennines.

Wainwright had looked with envious eyes at the Lakeland hills as he proceeded south for he missed them and wished that he might have been among them. He was fast becoming disillusioned with his venture and had begun to treat each step only as a means to an end. Over his last four days he gained a vastly reduced measure of fulfilment from the journey itself and sought to be back by a warming fire, away from the Pennines and their great propensity for bog and rain and wind. His account does not hide the disappointment that he felt for he had set a target which he failed to achieve. I had aimed to achieve what he had not and I had succeeded in attaining the first part, and now all I had to do was find my way back down. From the flat summit of Cross Fell the views over to the west and the hills of Cumbria would be spectacular and, had I been able to see anything at all, then perhaps I too might have wished to be elsewhere. As it was the views afforded me did not even extend to seeing whether the path was marked, as so often they are, by a series of cairns. The consequence of the lack of visibility was that finding my way off the plateau became, more or less, a reverse procedure to that used in reaching it. So long as I was walking downhill, roughly in a south-east direction, I would not be too far off course. I saw no indication of a path and was continually being tempted by some disbelief of my equipment to head on a bearing that was too southerly. After several corrections I did finally find my way to the crossroads of two paths and re-establish contact with the Pennine Way whereupon I turned right along a very user-friendly pavement made up of great slabs of sandstone laid end to end to help protect the surrounding moorland. As the path descended into the col between Cross Fell and Little Dun Fell, the presence of these slabs assisted progress greatly. Without them I would have been wading through ankle-deep mud and to either side of the pavement oozed the evidence of what the Way must have been like for so many walkers before their being laid. The compass and GPS were pocketed and, in a greatly more relaxed frame of mind, I strode out with good speed for I had broken the back of the challenges that the day would throw at me and it was now all downhill.

For the second time in two hours my pride went before a fall as the path began to bend noticeably. I had been heading south-east and needed to maintain a south-easterly course to remain on the Way, but now the route was turning north and was, I feared, about to return me to the windswept summit from where I had set out from thirty minutes before. I could only think that I had misunderstood the markings at the crossroads and had, somehow, proceeded along the wrong path. I will happily admit to being close to panic because, for a moment, I was utterly lost and in the absence of the assistance of modern technology I cannot begin to estimate where I may have ended my day. My senses had been fooled completely for the sensation of heading north was entirely fallacious – the compass told me that the correct course was being maintained and the GPS confirmed that the gentle incline was the lower part of the northern flank of Little Dun Fell. The ability to use a compass and to interpret its reading is all very well but if you are lost in the first place it is futile endeavour to attempt to steer a course leading to safety. Without the knowledge of your current position the compass is of no use and although on a clear day it may be possible to triangulate the present location from known landmarks, on such a day when visibility is so restricted, once you are lost you are lost good and proper.

As in life we can only judge where we are in the present relative to where we have previously been and what has been previously experienced. Our reaction and conduct to a given set of parameters will vary dependent upon our experience – what we prefer to call upbringing. It is these experiences that mould the way in which we behave. Where a stimulus is unlike any other encountered earlier the response can only be based upon an amalgam of reactions to similar incidents. It is the memory of these individual events that form the basis of future response, regardless of whether that response is simply a knee-jerk reaction or is in the form of more complex premeditated conduct. If we have no recollection of our previous responses we have no starting point upon which our actions can be based and no yardstick by which we can evaluate those actions. It is entirely similar to being alone on a fog-addled moor with a map and compass. While the means exist that would enable the walker to extricate himself from his dilemma, if he has not maintained a regular exercise of taking stock of his position then he may as well throw the compass into the nearest morass, sit down and wait for spring. Only by this frequent study of our retrospective locations can we have any confidence in our estimate of our current position. If we don't know where we are it becomes increasingly difficult to know where we are going – hence the benefit of taking stock and valuing what is the present, regardless of what has been in the past or might be in the future. Live for today, learn by the experience and tomorrow will take care of itself. As I slowly re-gathered my composure I satisfied myself that these three edicts were all very true. Perhaps the next time I decided to hike over a bleak moor on a foul and inhospitable day I might be better prepared for the loss of sensory perception that had so taken me by surprise. Then again, perhaps I would have learned to know that the altogether more circumspect view might be to stay indoors and hide away in some comfortable cocoon. I rather doubted it though for I was sure my enthusiasm and optimism would always reassure me that the cloud base would lift by lunchtime.

The disorienting effect of the mist was further emphasised when, all at once, the fine pavement upon which I tramped ceased. Not long after the path had started to ascend the natural ground had become firmer and the need for an expensive flagged pavement became unnecessary, so my guiding stones were left very quickly in the murk behind me. Without warning I was cast adrift in an ill-distinct sea of grey-green grass interspersed with tufts of slightly different coloured grey-green grass. All around was grey-green. I was only too aware that good fortune had been running with me so far, so I stopped, took stock, confirmed my bearing and maintained my direction with a concentration that would not have been broken even if the barmaid with the tight clothing had appeared. I had no desire to brave a similar experience to that of groping my way about on the summit of Cross Fell and I never took my eyes off both the compass and the ground directly in front of me simultaneously. I am convinced that I must have rapidly developed abilities similar to those of a chameleon with one eye looking straight out in front and one looking down. The ground levelled and then began to fall and I realised that I had passed the summit of Little Dun Fell. Although I was growing in confidence I was still gratified to find the recommencement of the slabbed footway in the next col between the Little and Great Dun Fells. As I crossed the more level terrain of the pass I breathed an audible sigh of relief for I was only too aware that the radar station lay less than half a mile away and all I needed to do was continue on my heading to collide with its perimeter fence. The prospect of the collision pleased me for once clinging to the chain-link mesh I would be able to feel my way around to the station's southern side and locate the service road that ran down into the vale below.

The two domed-topped neighbours of Cross Fell are no pushovers themselves for the altitude at the summits of both is near to 850 metres. I could therefore not expect any improvement in my ability to see the station ahead and I was commanded to navigate by compass all the way up to its boundary fence. Only when I was within 30 metres of it did I begin to notice its slender, regularly spaced vertical posts. No sooner had I begun to tentatively accept that these were likely to be the haven I was seeking than I was convinced for out of the mist above me and to my right loomed monstrous shapes of the buildings and other associated paraphernalia of the radar station. Their outline could only be the fruits of mans' labours – there was no way that something of natural formation could take on such obscure forms. The time was twenty minutes to four as I found my way off the Pennine Way and up to the fence that would lead me to the road and away from this barren world of misleading images and of sensory deprivation. It was with a feeling of great relief that I followed the line of chain-link fencing around to the southern entrance of the station stockade to find the black narrow ribbon of macadam that would ultimately lead me onto the lower ground far below. Initially I could barely see from one side of it to the other but as it descended with a severity that caused me to wonder what type of vehicles might be able to use it I could very soon see for distances that counted, relatively, as panoramas. Visibility could be measured in yards rather than feet and the vicious rain that had for so long thrashed at me from the east eased as I was increasingly afforded shelter on the western side of the fells. What wind there was now blew at my back and no longer tried to rip the hood from my face. What rain there was now fell as no more than a light drizzle that gave no impression as to the malice it had shown only a few moments earlier. Even the mist began to disperse so that its previous uniform consistency was replaced by occasional maverick bands of loose itinerant hill fog that were swept along above my head where the wind still retained its force. Within minutes any prior difficulties were as memories and my previous concerns now seemed awfully melodramatic. For all that, though, at a corner where a path leading off back onto the moor was signposted 'The Pennine Way' I had no wish to chance my arm further and ignored its invitation to return to open moor. My aim was to arrive at Slakes Farm as soon as was reasonably possible so that I might spend some time counting my blessings.

I had earlier speculated as to my hill-walking mettle and, as I walked down the steep road with paces that clomped first left then right, I decided that the eighth day of my journey had tested it more than sufficiently. I had, accordingly, learned something about myself – my composure had remained intact, albeit only just. I felt that I ought to consider myself very fortunate. My good fortune was not because I was still alive to tell the tale but because we live through very few days where we are offered and accept a challenge. Whether occupied in arduous or painstaking or repetitive tasks, the vast majority of days for the vast majority of people are spent carrying out largely the same arduous or painstaking or repetitive actions. There is no challenge and the days are often very similar. This is our acknowledged view of normality and we have come to accept that each day holds very much the same in store for us as the last, and as the next, and so on. By its very nature normality shares the same bed as boredom. Familiarity breeds contempt, and as most of our days are filled with the same mundane and, more often than not, meaningless activities, it is hardly surprising that there exists in so many a feeling of a lack of fulfilment. Many have become lazy and even if offered the chance to undertake some new activity would probably decline for in difference there is risk and where there is risk there lies the potential to fail. Security can be maintained by following the safe route along the line of least resistance, along a course where the wake will be least noticed. No one likes to fail and, increasingly, no one can afford to be seen to fail. The best method of avoiding failure is not to try something in the first place. While the logic of this thinking cannot be doubted the creditworthiness of it can insofar as the character shrinks in direct proportion to the number of times the safe route is taken. It is only where there is an inherent risk connected with a task or an activity that we can enjoy the sensation of achievement relative to our own estimate of our abilities – all the better if the success is witnessed by others and receives their plaudits. Only when we take some risks can we stretch ourselves and only when we stretch ourselves do we develop. If life could be represented by a graph charted by achievements it would, for most, be a flat line with few high or low points, perhaps with the odd blip either way when something moderately good or bad occurred. Sue has often maintained that providing money was of no object she would be perfectly content simply spending each and every day clothes shopping (a sentiment shared, I suspect, by a fair proportion of other women). We have discussed the point at length and never yet agreed – the fact is that any activity carried out as the norm, however seemingly pleasurable, will still generate a relative flat line with few blips and will create a feeling of ennui. To gain a sensation of fulfilment the graph has to show a peak in its charting that is higher than the surrounding – the high point stands out in the mind and provides an oasis in an otherwise desert landscape.

Fulfilment exists as a relative sensation, where success feels good only because we recognise the feeling of failure. If we have never failed then our sense of fulfilment would be less and, conversely, if we have never succeeded then our sense of despair at failure would also be reduced. If there exists a fear of failure and a deep-rooted desire to avoid it, we also must, to some degree, accept that we lessen the pleasure of reaping success simply because we would never dare to do anything. It is easier not to do or make anything but, as someone famous once said (probably Confucius or some other luminary), the person who never made a mistake never made anything. I felt as though I had achieved a success in the face of some hostile adversity and my sense of satisfaction could be measured in proportion to the feelings of fear I had experienced while lost in the mist. But for the vivid memory that I had been in some danger while traversing Cross Fell my sense of achievement would have been greatly reduced and my thoughts of living for today came back to me as I continued my somewhat ungainly walking pace down the road. I would learn by my experience in readiness for the next time and I would, at least, make sure I had those spare batteries.

I had learned something too about Wainwright – notwithstanding the fact that he had been absolutely right not to attempt the summit he had, nevertheless, from the moment of his decision to circumvent it, begun to criticise himself for taking the easy option. He knew he was right to not accept the challenge but he still regretted not having the inclination to put the bit between his teeth and make his way to the summit. He would have perhaps found too great a danger for if the tops had been bad for my journey, then in the days sixty years earlier, when the path would not have been so well marked, he would have done well not to have become entirely lost. His later wishes for his ashes to be scattered on Haystacks might well have been thwarted by the fact that he had ended his days in 1938 face down in a bog in the middle of nowhere. It was probably only the intervening years of increased pedestrian traffic and the fact that the path had had to be made into a flagged pavement that had secured my safe passage. I also had the added advantage of modern technology to help me with finding my locations, without which I might well have floundered and ended up face down in a bog in the middle of nowhere. Much had changed since Wainwright had glanced a displeasing eye over the Vale of Eden and I may have given the impression that most of the change had been for the worse. While a fair percentage has been of questionable benefit to society, there are one or two aspects that have been positive boons, one of which is undoubtedly the GPS. It was likely that its services would not be required again for the remainder of my journey and it had been seldom used during the first seven days, but, like all good insurance, it was ready to assist when quite desperately needed. Wainwright would probably have rebuked me for accepting the help of such wizardry for it only served to lower the essence of the challenge. So, call me a scaredy-cat, but at least I was a live scaredy-cat.

I walked the last five miles from Great Dun Fell with growing evidence of human population and agricultural activity, although any fears that I had held of being a member of a procession remained unfounded. I had seen but one other person since leaving Garrigill and even he had been hidden under a crash helmet on his motorbike on the summit of Cross Fell. This was one of the advantages of choosing to venture out on a day when the weather was questionable – there would be few others daft enough to share the same desires. The narrow macadam road gradually became wider as I rounded Knock Pike and I could see more fully the expanse of the wide and sweeping plain through which I would walk for the next day until I reached Soulby, just short of Kirkby Stephen. Only after that would I return to any form of higher ground, as I would pass to the east of the Howgill Fells. I had, though, for the moment, had my fill of the fells and a day of lower-level walking was more than a little welcome. I was only half a mile short of my destination when I exchanged a cheery greeting to a man out walking his dog. These were the first words I had spoken since leaving Alston eight hours earlier for the time was now half past five. I turned the last corner and entered the farmyard at Slakes Farm at twenty to six to be greeted warmly by Mrs Braithwaite before being shown to my room and advised that dinner would be ready at around half past six, if that suited. It suited me very well for my rations had long since been depleted and my rapacious hunger had, I could only think, been exacerbated by the nervous energy I had expended. Retiring to the delights of the cavernous bath I did not immediately appreciate that I was selfishly engaging the house bathroom and precluding other members of the family from their pre-dinner ablutions. Dinner was a slightly strange affair, taken as it was in an anteroom to the main family lounge where I could hear the conversations within the adjacent room but could not be part of them, sitting alone in the guests' dining room. Strange it may have been, but the extremely generous proportions admirably outweighed any strangeness, with all courses of sufficient portion to feed an army. I arrived at a point where my appetite was satiated long before I had finished eating but, not wanting to appear ungrateful having told my host how hungry I was, I struggled with the enormous dessert until all that remained were some pieces of fruit. Gorged, I decided that it might be prudent to take an evening constitutional to the nearest pub – a mile away, toward Milburn. In fairness I would probably have reached the same judgment even had dinner comprised a dry biscuit and a bit of mouldy cheese, but I used my stuffed condition as a lame excuse to substantiate a pint or two. I also justified my decision as a result of believing that I had earned a drink before collapsing into deep sleep.

In the twilight I found my way to the inn to join the small number of customers who stood around one end of the bar. The rest of the large bar area was empty, although through into the dining area I could see one or two diners. Had I not brought my book with me for company I would have been very lonely, so I took the opportunity to read Wainwright's account ahead of the following day's walk for tomorrow he would catch me up again as I made my way into Appleby and on toward Soulby. Returning to Slakes Farm by torchlight I entered into some discussion with the Braithwaites' before taking my leave and making the one last climb for the day up to my room. Chapter read, notes written, map studied, boots cleaned I said goodnight to a day that, although supremely exhilarating, was not one I had any wish to repeat too soon.

Chapter 9

Knock to Soulby

Perhaps it was that my enthusiasm was waning or, then again, perhaps it was as a result of being just absolutely knackered. Perhaps it was the shortness of the day's mileage that lay ahead or, then again, perhaps it was the rather uninspiring nature of those miles with all of them being road walking. Whatever the explanation, I remained dead to the world for the second day in succession until I was rudely awoken by the alarm at eight o'clock. I had no need for an early start because the entire day only extended to thirteen miles, second only in brevity to the ten miles from Blanchland to Hexham. While I welcomed the opportunity of a gentle stroll with a distinct lack of risk, the fact remained that there was no real urgency to the day's venture. My pith was definitely not rising to the challenge for there was none and, accordingly, my spirits only moved at a snail's pace as I mooched to the bathroom and mooched back again some minutes later. Most of my actions were carried out in a moochy type of fashion, all bar one. I had received some interest in my journey from a television company and it had been agreed that I should telephone their news desk at half past eight. Although I must confess to having decried the media and the press, and have extolled the virtues of lone walking, I would be lying if I did not admit that I found the prospect of television coverage more than a little attractive. In truth I was as keen as mustard and was dialling on the stroke of half past eight. I returned dejectedly to my earlier mooching upon being told that their schedules were full for the day and that they could only ask that I try again the following morning. I agreed of course and tried to sound excited at the promise that they would do what they could tomorrow. I have never been good at waiting for tomorrow. I am like everyone else – once I have an idea I want to implement it right away. I know that I have preached about others demanding instant results and being unwilling to accept delay in acquisition … well I never said that I had any intention of practicing what I preach. Tomorrow it would have to be and I mooched back to my room to slowly finish my packing.

Breakfast was to be at nine o'clock, taken in the anteroom where I had eaten the gargantuan evening meal the night before. I held back on my usual temptation to gorge the cornflakes because I guessed that the breakfast would be of equally generous portions to those of dinner. I was not wrong and I waded through all that was laid before me, more out of courtesy than of hunger. Mrs Braithwaite was very clearly of the opinion that a hearty breakfast sets the body up for the day. Her breakfast set me up for the remainder of my walk and I could almost have survived upon my reserves all the way back to Settle. Fifty-five miles remained, I calculated as I sat back in my chair with my cup of coffee. Today would see thirteen more under my belt and the last two days approximately split the remainder between them. Only three days left – I was beginning to have that depressingly engulfing feeling that can spoil the last few days. I could counter its effects to some degree for like Wainwright I could look forward to reliving these days as I mentally revisited all the places en route in the writing of my account. I was returning to an entirely uncertain future, and one that was so totally divorced from what I might have expected only months earlier. I had, for the greater part of my adult years, made what had proved invariably to be unsound assumptions as to the directions that my life would take. It seemed peculiar to have to accept that at the grand old age of forty-two I had, in terms of my career, come to a grinding halt and had probably ended up on what most term the scrapheap. It seemed equally peculiar, however, to think of life only in terms of the furtherance of a career and why it should be necessary to judge our success or failure by the measure of what we earn – there has to be more to life than the amassing of wealth. This not only applies to the accumulation of wealth for its own sake but also where such amassing becomes the be-all and end-all of being able to substantiate a fruitful existence by means of outward and material possessions. The volunteers on the South Tynedale railway had found a sense of reward far greater than that which could be generated by material gain. Life's scrapheap is a self-imposed sentence and if you feel that you are on it, then that is exactly where you are – more than likely looking for sympathy from others or at least wallowing in self-pity. I remain convinced that there are many who could escape the dismal existence that they feel has been dealt out to them if only they could recapture their enthusiasm. It is when enthusiasm has gone that self-worth makes an exit soon after. People are too ready to concentrate on complaining about their lot or on the negative aspects of their lives and they take completely for granted those things that, with a moment's thought, they should be thankful for having. Instead of thinking of what could have gone wrong, they carp at the slightest setback that they perceive as wholly unfair and typical of their ill fortune. I had complained of my cold and had damned my dogged luck for having acquired it in the days before I set off but never stopped for an instant to contemplate how lucky I was not to have a broken leg. I had taken my health for granted and only stopped to complain when a minor setback had occurred. So it is with career progression: we make certain assumptions and only stop to think when the whole plan begins to derail. I had come to accept that whatever else lay in store for me – unforeseeable and beyond my ability to control – I could revel in the anticipation of being able to return to these days of freedom that were fast drawing to a close; I could govern that part of my future at least.

Breakfast was an unhurried affair and I was finally standing in the Braithwaites' hall ready to set out by quarter to ten. I was tired as I stood looking out on to a flat and dismal landscape, damp under a light-brown sky that held no promise of brightening. Even I could not convince myself of the likelihood of brilliant sunshine by lunchtime. All trace of the high hills to the east had vanished in a low mist that enveloped them and concealed any evidence of their existence. A persistent drizzle was falling on the farmyard outside the door, and as I talked with Mrs Braithwaite I was in no particular rush to leave the confines of her hall. We talked of farming and of how the meagre marginal returns had forced her husband from his livelihood on the land to seek alternative employment. I had wondered why there had been no family gathering around their breakfast table, a fact that was explained as a result of Mr Braithwaite having gone off to work hours earlier at five o'clock. To supplement the diminishing income from the farm he had found work as a ready-mix concrete delivery driver and each day drove to the cement works near Penrith to shuttle back and forth with load after load of concrete for construction projects. Every day began at five o'clock in order that he might be assured of work, for loads were allocated on a first-come-first-served basis. For her part Mrs Braithwaite took on the role of administering the guest house, tending to their paying guests. As to the farm activity itself, that had become an increasingly small part of the equation and I gained the impression that the animals were more a part of the family than of financial security. There was no security to be found in working the land and the forecast for the future did not give any measure of hope – government regulations had seen to that. In light of various scares that had hit the headlines, public confidence in our own produce had been at an all-time low. With that, and the fact that cheaper European products had flooded the marketplace, the very people who had been his customers for so long were effectively forcing the British farmer out of business.

As I moved to the back step to don my boots I looked over to the cowshed where a few bullocks took an interest in my activity – I was relieved that they were behind half-height barn doors and not allowed free run of the yard. I explained to Mrs Braithwaite of my cowardice in the company of cattle, especially bullocks, and how I had been fortunate that so far I had not encountered any on my travels. Other farm animals do not concern me, although after an altercation with goats some years previous I tend to be more wary of them than their size alone might command. She thought my apprehension was misplaced but I recounted to her the story from where my disquiet stemmed.

My cautionary tale related to an otherwise idyllic afternoon spent messing about on the water in the Lake District. On Grasmere Lake there is a picturesque island which can be easily reached by hiring a rowing boat – that is, easily reached on the proviso that you don't have Sue with you doing the rowing, for she may look just the part on the rowing machine in the gym, however when once set the challenge of manoeuvring the real thing (even moving away from the jetty) the boat-keeper only avoided personal injury by ducking and dodging as though a wasp were chasing him. From his expression it was clear that he wondered whether he would ever see the boat or us again. After some minutes we decided it would be more expeditious if I were to take over the rowing and Sue the navigating, a decision that was made all the easier when we thought of the hourly charge for the hire of the boat. Having completed the delicate task of changing positions, we then made for the small island and moored the boat around the far side on a small section of shingle beach, securing the painter to a tree branch. It was April and the island was particularly beautiful with great swathes of daffodils in full bloom and fir trees lining the perimeter of the island giving a great sense of isolation from the madding tourist crowds. This being the start of the season, the village of Grasmere would be just beginning to become throng with tourists, but out on the lake all was calmness and serenity. To complete the scene there were two swans quietly swimming some 20 yards offshore, obviously enjoying the afternoon sun for it was entering the time of year when the sun begins to have some strength and there is a sensation of warmth when the sky is predominantly clear of cloud. With the boat moored we set out to reacquaint ourselves with the island where, six months earlier, we had become engaged. I trusted in my recollection thus far that the scene was set as painting a truly romantic and very special moment and was happy that Mrs Braithwaite acknowledged that it all sounded perfectly marvellous.

Central on the island is a large sloping grassed area on which we were very pleasantly surprised to find no-one picnicking. I use the term picnicking out of general decency for I suspect that many other activities have taken place in the isolation of that island. In truth I wasn't too far away from having those sort of thoughts myself, tempering them, however, with the fact that I would need some energy to row back. We then began to discover why it was that the island was devoid of holidaymakers. Atop of the grassy knoll at the centre of the island stood two goats, one a small kid and the other a larger billy. They had ignored us as we looked up at them from the foot of the bank and they continued to ignore us as we approached them. This did not surprise us and we assumed that they were well used to human beings and had probably been put out to graze on the island as a way of keeping the grass down. We walked very close to them and still they simply carried on with their grazing.

We slowly explored around the central part of the island and smiled as we realised that we had followers – the two goats appeared to be glad of the company and wherever we went, they went also. Now this was fine up to a point but the billy was beginning to become what could only be described as over-friendly and took every opportunity to follow me about altogether too closely for my liking. It soon became clear that we were being pestered by the world's first over-sexed homosexual goat and that it most certainly wanted to give me a good picnicking. I found myself having to push away the goat and his intentions. We decided to retreat toward the boat, with the goat in rapid and alarmingly hot pursuit. Although it may sound ridiculous, we gave the goat the slip and enjoyed a few moments sitting on a large branch of a tree growing in a downward curve for part of its length near the water's edge, making for an ideal seat. I had begun to roll a cigarette and on raising it to my mouth was nearly overcome by the stench of billy goat – both my hands felt as though they were covered in a greasy lanolin similar to raw wool but very much more pungent. My thoughts of a cigarette were interrupted by Sue telling me that we'd been spotted. The goats were now approaching the tree, and although we assumed that the foliage had kept us concealed, they were making straight toward where we sat. Being just the sort of tree that was easy to climb, we decided to move to a higher branch while they lost interest. How the goats could sense our smell above that of the billy's horrendous personal hygiene problem I had no idea, but they indubitably could for when they reached the base of the tree they stopped momentarily, and then proceeded to walk round and round its trunk. These goats meant business I thought and I started to wonder whether the bloody things could climb trees! I should point out that by now Sue was beginning to find this whole episode increasingly amusing as she could sense my uneasiness but had no sympathy for it; after all she had never been on the wrong end of a rampant goat's amorous desires. The animals did not think to look up until Sue made a noise, at which point they stopped pacing around the tree and looked up (the billy, pretty longingly I noted) and continued to stare, never once taking their eyes off us for a second.

Before we could reach the safety of the boat we would have to negotiate approximately 50 yards of undergrowth of one sort or another, with the first obstacle being the goats, particularly the billy. His own undergrowth appeared, by this time, to be in a state of extreme arousal (I say appeared because I am no judge when it comes to knowing the state of arousal of goats). It was clear that we would have to leave the tree, and on so doing the plan was that I would walk ahead to untie the painter, throw it to Sue who would get straight into the boat, after which I would push it clear of the beach and climb in from the bow. The first part of our cunning plan went swimmingly insofar as we dismounted the tree from the other side to the goats – they were, however, quickly on to us and recommenced their following our every step. At this point our relating of the saga would vary. I maintain that I walked with purpose, while Sue prefers to describe my movement as more 'running in a blind panic'. Whichever was the truth, we reached the boat and, as far as I am concerned, left the island a little wiser, a little wetter and a lot smellier.

The afternoon was to end on a much cheerier note. Navigating past the swans, we had not rowed more than 50 yards from the shore, with both animals now standing slightly above the small beach, when a second rowing boat slowly appeared from around the other side of the island. The three occupants were clearly looking to also enjoy the tranquillity of Grasmere's island on that fine afternoon and I suppose, on reflection, we could have hailed a warning to them. However the thought of calling to them in a raised voice to 'beware of the goat' was altogether too embarrassing (especially if they asked why) and, secondly, it would have spoiled what turned out to be the next few minutes of unbridled hilarity. They moored on the same beach and were met by a gaze from the two goats, who by this time had returned to grazing. The boat's occupants made off up the grassy slope to be slowly, at first, followed by Mr Personal Hygiene Problem and his young cohort. After a minute or so, their pace was quickening as they too found that the goat was anybody's (and everybody's if he'd had his way). They made, with some speed, toward a derelict barn with the goats hard on their heels. If I had to be entirely fair, I would estimate that the billy was now moving with even greater speed than during our own contra-temp, and if anything was gaining on the boaters, who by now were in full flight. No thought-out plan for them as to whom should untie the boat and who should push off from the shore; their retreat strategy was quite evidently formed out of sheer terror – and very amusing it was. By this stage, Sue and I were both in danger of personal accidents, but the other boat had one last climactic episode with which to entertain us still further. In their haste to get from the island smartly, they all failed to notice that the two swans had now swum quite close to the beach, not at all far from their boat, and were continuing to quietly mind their own business. That is, until they were rudely interrupted by the antics of the three panic-stricken occupants of the boat, who were more concerned in looking where they had just been rather than where they were going. So, to complete their afternoon, two very irate swans then harangued them for having disturbed their peace. How I wish I'd had a video camera for those few minutes. Meanwhile we quietly rowed around a small wooded headland to settle ourselves before rowing back to the jetty and to the boat-keeper. He seemed pleased, and almost surprised, to see us and I wondered whether he might have known of the fate that awaited us if we were to set foot on the island. Since then I have always assumed that all goats have rampant sex drives and are best kept at a respectable distance.

I was not convinced that Mrs Braithwaite did not believe there to have been some exaggeration in my account and I assured her of its accuracy in retelling. Thanking her for her hospitality, I left her door and made my way down the side road for half a mile to join the Milburn to Appleby road. Turning left toward Appleby saw me reacquainted with my erstwhile walking colleague after his unhappy detour over Hartside. Our separate ways had come back together again and would remain so for the rest of the day for his account was comprehensive as to the route taken. He had lost time and his dark mood had blackened further and he again chose to walk on roads with the intention of reaching Kirby Stephen by evening. His sole objective over the last three days was to progress with all speed to put an end to his torture and only once did he walk on anything other than macadam road. He left Gamblesby and proceeded as directly as possible via Melmerby, Ousby, Skirwith, Blencan, Milburn and Long Marton to Appleby with the entire fourteen miles being summed up in his account in one paragraph. From Appleby he continued to march with the hope of reaching Kirkby Stephen but more foul weather stopped him short at Soulby. From Soulby he followed the Kirkby Stephen to Sedbergh road before swinging around into Dentdale and on to Dent. His final day saw him pass over into Kingsdale and via Ingleton Falls (his briefest of returns to paths) and Clapham Station back to Settle. As he walked between Milburn and Appleby his longing to be in the Lake District returned for he could see the great peaks away to the west, and to darken his mood even more he came upon, not for the first time, an encampment of gypsies. He had no time for their indolent lifestyle, viewing them as leeches living off the nation – he was not a man to mince his words and would find himself in varying degrees of trouble in the politically correct England of the 1990s. His attitudes were, more than likely, representative of many people, whether they referred to women, war or gypsies. He would be lambasted if he were alive to make such utterances in modern England and in some cases, perhaps, with good reason. Of the many things that have changed since Wainwright despondently made his way into Appleby there can be no doubt that one of the greatest has been the enforcement by regulation of what we say and do. His forthright views with regards to the place of women in society are scattered throughout his account. I could only hazard wild guesses as to how he would view the shifting roles of the sexes and as to what he might think of the legislation that enforced the rights of women. Removal of discrimination by enforcement, whether the regulatory control be in respect of sex or race or disability, in reality had heightened any tensions that might have pre-existed. The sector in receipt of protection under such legislation is viewed by some as having received a benefit that the remaining populace has not enjoyed, particularly where the benefactors of the lawmakers is a minority group. People do not react well to being told what they may or may not say in a democracy where free speech was the presumed right of all. Undoubtedly, where discrimination exists it lives as a cancer eating away at the core of a mixed society, but equally over-legislation can only serve to amplify the voice of those who would seek to question the validity and fairness of the establishment. There are times when our legal system appears to bend over backwards to avoid upsetting some group or other. There is a sense that certain sectors have been provided with megaphones, giving them disproportionately loud voices that cannot fail to be heard above the more muted tones of the rest of society. Equal rights for all is a most splendid objective but care must be taken if the finely balanced scales of impartiality are not to be tipped in favour of one group at the expense of another. There is a very fine line between anti-discriminatory measures and positive discrimination and I could not help but feel that Wainwright would have been disparaging of some of the enforcements taken in the name of supposed harmony and equality. I do not believe that I am either a racist or a sexist but like many others have become somewhat weary of the rantings and ravings of the small minority who seem to think that their lot is a bad one and that they are permanently down-trodden. The ardent feminists who demand that God is a woman or that study of the past should be referred to as 'herstory' ought not to be given coverage in the press. The disabled authorities that formed a lynching mob and bayed for the resignation of the England football manager ought to question their motives, for is it not reasonable for any person to be allowed to speak their beliefs, however bizarre others might find them? The anti-royalists who hurled tirades of abuse at the royal family for their apparent uncaring at the death of Diana, Princess of Wales, ought to ask themselves whether there is not, in fact, a God-given right to mourn in an entirely personal way. Surely we are not to see laws introduced outlining the various requirements that constitute correct and proper reaction to bereavement. The civil liberties champions who protest against apparent infringement at the very mention of identity cards should consider why they are objecting, for if there exists the slightest opportunity to curb society's transgressors then they should surely be welcomed.

It is so often that the actions of a minority are allowed to influence the majority. I have no doubt that social do-gooders would seek to ban all corporal punishment and can claim to want to do so by making examples of instances where children have been persecuted persistently. A picture is then formed of all parents systematically thrashing their offspring with great regularity until the powers-that-be become convinced that this is the norm and finally wield to the actions of the minority. The result is that hordes of undisciplined and uncontrollable children run riot, safe in the knowledge that no one can do anything to stop them. I apologise for making this sweeping comment in the absence of expertise in the field but I suspect that many teachers will, under their breath, concur as to their powerless status. I have no doubt either that the memory of the children of Dunblane saddens many hearts but to simply ban all handguns is a knee-jerk reaction that will not suppress ownership for those willing to operate outside the law. I also have no doubt that so called joy-riders have become viewed as an unavoidable evil and a bane of the modern community, but are we to contemplate banning all cars to put a stop to the occurrences? It is not the gun that inflicts injury, just as it is not the car and just as it is not the leather strap. It is the state of mind of the possessor of the gun or the car or the leather strap that guides the hand to its cruel practice. The actions of the minority should not be allowed to force limitations on the freedom of the majority. For some reason I remembered my schooldays and the bullies that gathered in the playground at break time: perhaps we should close all schools and keep children cosseted away so that no harm can possibly come to them. I continued this train of thought and recalled a story that I had heard of drug taking by athletes. The answer was simple and had been staring the authorities in the face; all competitive athletics should be banned, thus removing the need for cheating. My last and rather irreverent thought strayed to the Ten Commandments. There was clearly a percentage of the population that paid no heed to their instruction, so are we to scrap them as well, I wondered.

After a little over two miles I arrived in the village of Long Marton. This would be the only village I would visit of those that had been swept asunder by Wainwright's pen in his general malaise. I have to admit that the village held little of interest but, in fairness, I was making for Appleby and did not pause to search out its delights, if indeed there were any. The only point of noteworthiness was that at Long Marton I arrived back on the route of the Settle–Carlisle railway and that I would loosely and intermittently follow its course during the last three days. Seeing the embankment upon which it ran somehow indicated that I was nearing my goal. I had seen many embankments over the course of my walk, but very few railways. All that had so often remained now were the odd moraine-like mounds that stood as memorials to a bygone age. They were now home to overgrown shrubs and nettles and brambles. I must have been slightly unimpressed with my surroundings because at some point I actually bothered to calculate that I would cross the route of the railway four times before I reached Soulby. This seemed, at the time, to be of some keen interest but for the life of me I cannot now imagine why. The gently undulating road through the rolling country of the Vale of Eden was another example of how much busier our thoroughfares are from when Wainwright had referred to it as a lane. It was well used and without footpath, so walking entailed a frustrating mixture of looking, listening, standing back and being extremely cautious on corners.

Al least, I thought, I was more fortunate than my predecessor had been: as I approached the famous old market town of Appleby I did so with the firm belief that the weather was getting better. Perhaps today I would be basking in afternoon sun. He had been pursued by dark and threatening clouds that held within them a great maliciousness that would visit him before the day was out. I passed under the bypass and was pleased to note that the town's welcoming sign retained its historic link with the fact that it was once the county town of the now-defunct county. Appleby-in-Westmorland welcomed me and just as it did so I crossed the Settle–Carlisle railway for the third time (you might care to check your map if you are as sad and boring as I clearly had been). Appleby is a further instance of the road builders' desire to take traffic from the centres of towns and to steer it around the periphery in a sweeping new road pattern so that the heart of the town might return to life. One of three things will happen with the opening of a new bypass: the town may stagnate from lack of passing trade as Bowes appeared to have done; it may evolve into a collection of awfully pleasant desirable residences; or it may flourish having been allowed to return to a former time. Appleby had flourished, the only blot on the landscape being the necessity to construct two monstrous concrete bridges, one to carry the new road and one to carry the railway. Once in the town itself there was an atmosphere of modest affluence with a number of high-class clothes shops and a plethora of cafés and inns and associated tourist trappings. Thank heavens, I thought; I might at long last have that pot of tea and sticky bun that had proved so elusive on previous days. It was half past eleven as I crossed the eastern side of the large loop in the River Eden that served as a natural barrier surrounding three sides of the settlement. The castle supplemented the town's defences, sited at the southern end of the gradually rising main street, Boroughgate, and closing the only open aspect not otherwise protected by the river. I was positively spoiled for choice as to which tearoom should have my business, but with selection made I entered and ordered my pot of tea and cake. The waitress headed out from the kitchen laden down with an enormous pot and, assuming that she was making for a table that had three or four customers, I returned to studying my books and map, which I had laid out on the tablecloth. A polite 'excuse me' followed a few seconds later and I realised that this veritable urn was intended for me. It was as well that I had taken the precaution of buying one or two more postcards for I could fill my time while drinking the seemingly endless cups of tea. There was not very much I could write to people that could not wait until I would see them upon my return – my journey was three-quarters complete and I would be chasing the postcards home. Nevertheless, there was something rather soothing sitting and watching the world go by writing all the usual things that is written on postcards. I sat and watched the world go by for more than half an hour before sidling up Boroughgate to see more of the town. There was actually not much else to see and before very long I was sidling back down Boroughgate beginning to wonder what I could do with myself for I had time to kill. For the first time my schedule was generously empty and I knew that Soulby was no more than three hours distant, even at a casual pace.

I had started the day mooching and was in danger of doing so again, finding myself aimlessly wandering up and down until finally deciding, as I passed an inn, that I would adjourn for a lunchtime beer and bowl of soup. I watched the world go by some more and relished the cigarette that accompanied a very reasonable pint, the brewer of which I cannot recall. I was beginning to relax with the newspaper I had borrowed from the bar and I cast a cursory glance over the headlines. The world's press was still hounding the president of the United States over his sexual misdemeanours and clearly would not relinquish their inquiries until all the sordid details were spread out for all to see. Before I had left on my travels they had reported day after day every minutiae of mind-numbingly boring rubbish as though there were nothing else in the world worthy of mention. This was the sum total of what might be classed as the modern day crisis – no war-mongering dictator could possibly find his (or perhaps her way onto the front pages while the air was heady with the scent of sexual scandal. Hitler's antics would have been destined for a few lines on an inside page. Sex sells. War only sells when it's the real thing, a graphic image of a mutilated body adorning the front page alongside a clever headline and witty play on words. All this seems to overlook the fact that the subject of the picture is dead. I put the paper down having become bored of whatever it was that the president had allegedly done and took Wainwright's account from my pocket.

Our relative temperaments were very different. I sat slowly drinking the remaining half-pint of bitter and rolling a second cigarette, having consumed a pleasant bowl of pea and ham soup. He had sat staring once again at heavy rain falling in the street. Although I was conscious that my liberty was nearing its end, I remained in a positive frame of mind and was proposing to savour these last few days. He had sat wishing it all at an end and having regrets that his quest had not been completed upon reaching the wall. My final thought as I left the inn was of my keen enthusiasm to recount my journey. He had used all his reserves of enthusiasm and could think only of arrival back in Settle in line with his schedule – he was marching, not walking, over these last days, which is no way to enjoy a walk. To further aggravate his depression he had no sooner left Appleby and turned off onto the narrow Soulby road than the headwind began in earnest and accelerated until he found himself battling to propel himself for-ward – he could have opened his cape and succeeded in winged flight all the way back to Appleby. As if the wind were not enough to blacken his day, the rain that he had watched from the café developed into a torrential downpour. Both wind and rain kept him company for the seven miles to Soulby. Any hopes of marching to Kirkby Stephen were doomed to failure just three miles short and instead he found the rather dubious overnight accommodation offered by the Black Bull in Soulby. His adventure seemed destined to end on a note so sour that he might have harboured a wish never to return to the Pennines. My own progress was made under a hazy but increasingly warming sun and as I left Appleby, having delayed my departure until half past one, I was able to walk in shirtsleeves for the first time since walking on the wall three days earlier. Leav-ing behind the predominantly red-sandstone architecture and busy affluence of Appleby, I proceeded slowly past the settlement denoted on the map as Slosh. There was something almost fitting about the name as it reminded me that this would be my only evening where a public house was not within reach for the partaking of liquid refreshment. The Black Bull had been demolished in the 1960s having been pronounced structurally unsafe. No replacement hostelry had been forthcoming in the village so the nearest inn would only be found in Kirkby Stephen. Not even I was willing to entertain the prospect of walking the additional miles for the sole purpose of getting a drink, so I had resigned myself to the face that my ninth evening would be a dry one.

The hedges that lined the road and gave Wainwright some shelter from the worst excesses of the wind and rain still line it thus, only allowing any vistas of

the surrounding landscape at gaps where gates give access to the adjoining rip-
pling fields. The scenery hereabouts comprised in its entirety of one undulation
after another and although all very pastoral, it began to become a smidgen repetitive and I soon found myself uninterested in things other than the way
ahead. The rolling topography extended in all directions as far as the eye could
see, which in actual fact was not that far because the persistent haze precluded
long-distance views. I could just make out the vague outline of the hills to the
east of the vale that were the Pennines and had formed my windswept battle-
ground of some twenty-four hours earlier. To the west all I could see were more
undulations. Ahead my way lay before me in the form of long straight stretches
of road that were, unfortunately, a damn sight busier than when a very wet and
windblown Wainwright had struggled along it. To either side of the road there
were, unsurprisingly, more rolling drumlin-type mounds.

Wainwright had wished for respite from the rain at Helm Beck; I desired an
escape from an altogether different assailment of the senses – in my case from
the smell of the slurry spreading from Helm Farm. I had approached the farm
and was greeted by the foul stench of what could only be the ripest of manures.
As I passed the entrance the farmer appeared from the yard driving a tractor and
trailer unit and proceeded to make his way into the field opposite having obviously called back at the yard for a fresh consignment. He stopped after some
yards, alighted, carried out one or two adjustments and returned to his cab, before moving off at walking pace and switching on the rotary device that flung
semi-liquid excrement high into the air. I had not seen so much shit spouted
from a single chamber since accidentally switching the television over to live
coverage of Parliament. The smell followed in an instant and the air was full of
the most repugnant of odours. To make matters worse, the tractor's slow pace
matched mine and was in the same direction and continued for the full length of
the field adjacent to the road. There was no escaping the noxious fumes and had
he been any closer to the road there would have been no getting away from
them for days to come for I would be covered. I might have ended my journey
as foul smelling as Wainwright must have been by his ninth day with his mini-

malist attitude to changing clothes. The tractor and I finally parted company when it reached the end of the field and the farmer returned to the other end with his disgusting cargo being spewed out elsewhere. I received frequent reminders of the farmer's recent labours for the next mile or so as what gentle breeze there was wafted the slurry's pungent scent in my direction. Wainwright could only find scant shelter from the wind at the beck because the swollen waters prevented him from tucking himself neatly behind the parapet walls of the bridge. At least he was able to stop – any thought I had of pausing at Helm Beck for a brief rest was rapidly forgotten as I was not sure that I could enjoy a cigarette while retching and I had no wish to see an early return of my four cups of tea, pint of bitter and pea and ham soup. I had paid good money for them and did not want to see them drift quietly downstream at the bridge. My pace lessened as I cleared the bridge and left the stench behind, and with lunch still intact I progressed up the gentle slope of the shallow valley and away from the beck.

I drifted quietly along for around 200 or 300 yards and was approaching a cottage when the deep barking of a dog rudely interrupted my thoughts. The tone and volume were of sufficient magnitude to cause me to sincerely hope that there was a stout gate between the animal and me – I had visions of becoming an early afternoon snack for some enormous carnivorous canine creature. Having recovered my composure and managing, just, to hang onto my lunch for the second time in as many minutes, I walked confidently toward the cottage practising my greeting in the event that the brute was roaming free. Half the battle with dogs is to show them you have no fear and to let them know by your tone just exactly who the top dog is. Nice doggy, nice doggy, I practised. My voice quavered and I knew only too well that the issuer of the fierce barking would have no doubt as to which of us was top dog. My fears were allayed as I saw the fastened gate, behind which was a huge Alsatian dog that stood on its hind legs barking very menacingly as I neared. The solid timber gate that formed the only barrier between it and its early afternoon snack was around 4 feet 6 inches high. Having seen video footage of police Alsatians showing them to be eminently capable of clearing such a height, as I passed I sincerely hoped the dog had not seen the same film and did not fancy his chances. I thought forward to days when I would be delivering post and wondered whether I might be able to develop a more determined canine greeting. Perhaps I needed to practise some more. Nice doggy, I said to myself. Better, but still not wholly convincing. I pressed on with the sound of barking becoming more intermittent and fading as the distance between us grew. Usually I am very good with dogs but I like to believe that I can sense when they are unapproachable. I was taught, as a child, not to be scared of dogs but to be wary of them for their reaction might vary dependent on circumstances: whether they were, perhaps, defending their territory or feeling cornered. It always annoys me that there exists such a gulf between the way we are allowed to treat animals and the respect that is demanded in our relationships with fellow humans. If the dog in the garden near Helm Beck were to have bitten me there would be no inquiry as to whether its upbringing might have had an influence on its behaviour. We live increasingly in a society where a human perpetrator is perceived as the victim, only having acted in such a way as a result of a deprived childhood or as a result of being from a broken home. Care and concern and counselling are piled upon the violators in an attempt to ask them awfully nicely if they would mind not repeating their crimes. There seems little point in treating them in any other way for even where some measure of relative severity of sentencing is meted out to them avenues exist whereby they will no doubt be able to claim their sentence as an unjust one. There is little apparent thought of the true victim, whose life they may have scarred forever. The worst violators of our laws laugh at such inane treatment and judge being apprehended as only the most minor of inconveniences. The rule of law used to be innocent until proven guilty but it has changed to become closer to that of being innocent until proven not guilty for their will always be some aspect of the perpetrator's life that can be latched onto to provide them with immunity from their misdemeanours. If many more of the would-be criminals held the law in great fear there would be many fewer would-be criminals in the first place.

The dog in the garden near Helm Beck would not have been the recipient of such in-depth concern – it would quite simply have been put to sleep. I've never been quite sure as to why I feel so strongly regarding this blatant inequity other than for the reason that generally I have a greater inclination towards animals. I find it of extreme irritation that humans seem to feel that a completely different set of ethical standards can be applied in the treatment of our animal cousins to that we would apply to our own kind. I excuse here the need for food and aspects that may be viewed as being within the bounds of the balance of nature. I recalled several years earlier when I had a dog, Joe, a well-behaved collie-cross, and I was manning a stand within a craft show marquee with Joe sitting quietly under one of the trestle tables with the cloth partly concealing him. While I was talking with a customer (a fairly rare event for customers were hard to come by) a most unpleasant child noticed the partly hidden dog and made efforts to pat him. Nothing wrong with that – I used to do the same myself – but when Joe showed little movement the ill-mannered little brat then began to prod and poke the snoozing dog, presumably to gain a more animated reaction. I only noticed this after my customers had sidled off (without buying anything – par for the course) and, as his parents were close by, I politely invited the child to cease. The parents then remonstrated with me, pointing out that the boy was only playing, without any words of parental advice for their dear offspring. Two thoughts struck me about the incident. Firstly, the parents were oblivious to the generally unruly behaviour of their child even though they had seen his actions. Secondly, it is a fair bet that had Joe reacted territorially and bitten the young so-and-so, any provocation would be ignored and I would have been lucky if he weren't subsequently put down. Before we believe that we have the right to judge the behaviour of others, whether man or beast, we first ought to establish that our own conduct, or that of those for whom we are responsible, toward others is acceptable. Too many people, increasingly it seems, take the attitude of the parents of the spoilt brat and look after their own without a moment's thought for the effects their actions might have on others.

While this instance related to a single event, on a more global scale similar rules apply, whether it relates to the treatment of individual animals or of whole species. It is surely hard to reconcile that there can be a truly fair and equitable God watching over us for if he (or she, sorry) did put all the animals on Earth, he seems to have turned a blind eye, rather like the parents of the little boy, to the treatment of a great many of his subjects. The parents did not for a moment contemplate admonishing their son but chose instead to denounce my efforts at authority and reprimand me for chiding their son. I can recall a time when if a policeman gave a misbehaving child a clip around to the ear then returned the child home, a more severe chastisement would more than likely follow from the hand of the parents. If such an action took place now the cry would be only from the policeman's family as he lost his job. Wainwright himself must have shared a empathy toward animals, for in later life, when his relatively modest needs were satisfied by his income, he established a sanctuary close to Kendal. The great majority of his earnings were invested in the refuge and it still bears his name in 1998. He would, I am sure, be mystified to know the differing views that have developed between what is reasonable in the treatment of ani-mals and what is just in the treatment of humans. It is not that our strategy toward animals had hardened; it is more that our perceived justice for human misconduct has become softened, especially where the lawmakers have listened to the loud hailing do-gooders and the sentencing authorities dare not offend them. The lunatics are very close to taking over the asylum.

My tangential wanderings had distracted me from studying my surround-ings for a little while. I looked around me again to see yet more undulating hillocks. I was becoming a little wearisome of their endless similarity and would be pleased to cover the remaining three miles. I decided that an extra-long soak in a bath would be of greater benefit than an extended stay among the low hills of the vale, and I strode out with a view to arriving at Hutton Lodge as soon as was possible. Mrs March was to be my host and I had telephoned ahead to ad-vise her that I might be early. She had indicated that an early arrival would cause her no problem and that she looked forward to seeing me, although I suspected that she might well have held a different view had I been any nearer to the farmer in his slurry-spreading tractor.

A little way further on I came upon a flock of sheep being herded down the road by another farmer, an activity I had not witnessed in several years. The drivers caught in the hold-up simply turned their engines off and waited for the farmer to complete his manoeuvres. There was something slightly incongruous about the sight for there was no impatience, no horn-blowing, no action of any sort to indicate annoyance on the part of the drivers. I had become too used, perhaps, to beholding intolerance and was genuinely surprised by the restraint of these road users. They had time or were, at least, wise enough to know that their journey would not be any the faster for them losing their temper and harassing the herdsman. They recognised his right to use the road as they were doing, only somewhat more slowly.

Clear of rank smells and at a considerable distance from any ferocious dogs, I took the opportunity of the slow-moving convoy to pause, roll a cigarette and take in the fresh air. I sat on a boulder at a road junction and as I did so one of the drivers in the stationary queue inquired as to whether he could give me a lift anywhere. Thanking him I declined his offer as I was nearly at my destination. How refreshing that not only did these people not lose their tempers at such interruptions to their progress, but they retained the courtesy to see whether they might be of assistance to others. It was also slightly uncanny that it had been at about this point on his travels that Wainwright had been offered a lift by a passing driver, an act of even greater courtesy for Wainwright was absolutely soaked and dripping from every orifice. As I perched on my stony resting place I did so under a pleasantly warm but still hazy sun and I waited for fifteen minutes until the farmer, his dogs and their charges had disappeared to wherever it was that they were heading. It was a far cry from the howling wind and lashing rain that had thrashed Wainwright into submission and compelled him to fall short of Kirkby Stephen.

I set off with a vigour that saw me arrive in Soulby a little after four o'clock, keen to find my lodgings and sink into a hot bath. I had passed the farm at Bonnygate where Wainwright had been forced to wade through knee-deep floodwater – I was later told that even sixty years later the road still floods after heavy rain. I had unknowingly passed the site of the Black Bull Inn that had provided Wainwright with his rather unsatisfactory accommodation, the pub long since demolished and now just a grassed area home only to a solitary road sign. Finding Hutton Lodge, Mrs March welcomed me into her very fine Georgian home and showed me the palatial bathroom that would be at my sole disposal for I was her only guest for the evening. We agreed that my meal would be prepared for half past six and with that she left me to my own devices, to relax in the equally palatial bedroom. They don't make rooms like these anymore, with their high and ornate ceilings. Everything about it was of generous proportions, the floor area being the equivalent size of that of two or three rooms in a modern house. Without delay I climbed into Mrs March's bath, which was as ample in proportion as the room itself – a huge cast-iron relic of a bygone era that was of sufficient length to allow the entire body to be submerged. It seemed to me that there existed the distinct possibility of drowning had I dropped off to sleep for I could have quietly slipped below the surface before my feet would reach to tap end, halting any forward motion. The extreme tiredness of the first few days of my walk had abated as I had grown more accustomed to my daily exertions, but as I reclined my feet were thankful for this final short day. Only forty-two miles lay between Soulby and Settle but I was required to cover those miles in two last long days, which would test my remaining energy reserves.

The very size of the bathroom curtailed my stay in the bath, for the high ceiling meant that the room soon began to feel chilly as the heat dissipated from the water. I had already run off enough water to float a small ship just in filling it and had not the cheek to demand more, so stepping high to clear the rim of the bath, I draped myself in the bath towel, the proportions of which matched all else, and returned to my room. The evenings were closing in noticeably, so any scrutiny of the tiny village would have to be before dinner, which I knew was to be three courses and would, I guessed, be as large in portion size as befitting everything else. Mrs March looked like the type of host who would not allow her guests to leave her anything other than fully replete, so it was fair to assume that it would be dark by the time I had stuffed myself full by dessert. With an hour to spare before the agreed dinnertime, I was dressed and rolling a cigarette to smoke during my saunter around the neat array of houses in search of anything of interest. I doubted whether there would be very much to arouse curiosity for the inn was gone and it would have been beyond its portals where any singular interest lay. My previous four evenings had all drawn blanks in respect of my predecessor's activities. At Hexham I had been correct in that there had proved to be no chance of validating any part of Wainwright's visit – the tearoom was no more and there was no sense of any trace of his calling. At Haltwhistle, although I rested in the same inn, there was no recollection of his staying – sixty years is a long time and I could perhaps not expect anything other than ignorance of such ancient events. I had hoped for better at the smaller town of Alston but had been afforded nothing. I could not expect other than to draw a blank on my eighth day as I had made the deliberate choice to deviate from his route and stay elsewhere than Gamblesby. At Soulby I did not expect to be able to reconcile any part of his description with events that were so old and as I slowly ambled toward the main street, I resigned myself to the fact that my early successes had been pure flukes. Turning left from the side road and retracing the route I had arrived upon along the Appleby road I soon came to the end of habitation and turned about to search for a friendly-looking local who might assist me by pointing out where the Black Bull had stood.

I came to a house where the owner was in the throes of clearing away gardening implements and I inquired of him as to whether he knew of the Black Bull. He was a little vague in his response but would call his wife for she had taken a keener interest in all things local. She appeared presently and a brief conversation ensued not only with regard to the Black Bull but also as to why she had become so intrigued with the more recent history (or herstory for those that way inclined) of the village. By an incredible coincidence she had known of a proofreader who, in the 1980s, had been given the proof of a book to read in advance of publication. The book was none other than Wainwright's Pennine

Journey when it was finally published some forty-six years after his writing it. When she and her husband were to relocate to Soulby the proofreader recalled the episode in Wainwright's account pertaining to their new village and she purchased a copy out of intrigue. Well, I was like a pig in muck for I had finally met a person whose local knowledge had been honed out of polite investigative nosiness following the reading of the very account I had followed for nine days. We chatted over her garden gate with her husband still clearing away garden tools. By a second extraordinary coincidence she confirmed that the harvest festival sale, which had been held on the evening of Wainwright's stay, not only still took place but that it was to be held in the village hall the very night of my visit. I was in danger of being late for my half past six dinner appointment so I excused myself and agreed that I might see them at the sale – I was first to speak to Mrs March though to ensure that my presence might not be inappropriate as an off-cumden. I hurried back and arrived with only enough time to sit myself down at the table before the first of three courses was brought to me, each of which proved to be as substantial as I had anticipated. Mrs March returned to the dining room during coffee and confirmed that she had spoken with a gentleman by the name of Arthur Bainbridge who was the auctioneer for the evening and that he had indicated I would be welcome to join the gathering. She also explained that he might be able to help with other details of Wainwright's stay. I did not recall mentioning to my host the specific nature of my inquiries so I was slightly bemused that she was aware I had come in search of answers. Mrs March also appeared to know that Betty Wainwright was Wainwright's surviving spouse. The two original Wainwright drawings of Soulby, along with their printing plates that hung in the dining room, also intrigued me. I could not help but feel that there seemed to be an acquaintance between the March family and the Wainwrights but it was not my place to pry. I never did find out and as Mrs March did not offer I would forever remain curious. By an apparent never-ending set of coincidences, when I explained to Mrs March that I knew something of Soulby from a booklet I had read the night before she explained that the author, Douglas Birkbeck, was her next-door neighbour. It was Mr Birkbeck, a local historian, who had published the booklet that Mr Braithwaite had lent to me – his interest had stemmed from the fact that it had been his father who was the vicar at Soulby between 1947 and 1951. She promised to introduce me to Mr Birkbeck at the festival sale for he might also add some detail to my quest.

In essence the village, two and a half miles from Kirkby Stephen, was like many others insomuch as it had seen indigenous craftsmen and services die out, never to be replaced. In 1938 the village boasted two grocers, a joiner, a miller and sub-post office in addition to the Black Bull Inn. The local school closed its doors for the last time in 1971, nine years after the closure of the Eden Valley Railway. All trading activity had long since ceased in the village and all that remained was a collection of well-to-do houses. The sense of foreboding that I had feared for the traders in Muker did not recur at Soulby for there existed no businesses upon which the life of the village depended. Soulby's more recent evolution had centred upon it providing a place of domicile for people whose business activities lay elsewhere. I was surprised, in the circumstances, that a feeling of cohesive community still survived to render the festival sale an annual success.

Torch in hand, I set out following the instructions that would lead me to the village hall. Any doubts I might have had as to the popularity of the event were quickly dispelled as I tentatively opened the door to be met by the stare of what must have been the entire village's population looking round to see who the newcomer was. All were sat except the old boy that I knew must be the eighty-one-year-old Arthur Bainbridge acting as auctioneer for his forty-ninth successive year. He warmly beckoned me to join the throng and briefly introduced me as the traveller who was passing through. He pointed to a spare seat and I wound my way to it through a maze of excited children who were acting as ushers delivering purchased lots to their recipients. I sat down and looked around the rather tired decor of the room. My eyes were soon fixed on the quantity of produce that very obviously remained to be auctioned. There were fresh fruits and vegetables, tinned fruits and vegetables and numerous other tins containing almost anything imaginable. There was jam and marmalade and chutney and more jam. There were assorted lots of chocolate and other sweets. The year 1998 had indeed seen a very varied harvest. There were so many lots that I had to doubt whether they could possibly ever get to the end – it was after half past seven when I had entered and I wondered if the final lots might not still be coming under the hammer after I was due to arrive in Settle two days hence. However, Arthur Bainbridge maintained a speed that for a man of years was commendable. His eye would catch the very slightest of movement, so much so that if you wanted to avoid buying a lot then absolute stillness was required. His sight was only bettered by his hearing – he would have heard a pin drop at ten paces. I remained as still as possible but even so I ended the evening having paid two pounds for a large tin of cooked ham. I had no use whatsoever for cooked ham, neither had I room for a large tin and wasn't entirely sure what action it had been that had prompted Arthur to bring the hammer down on my apparent bid. The local Women's Institute seemed to understand my bewilderment and took the tin, paying the two pounds into the swelling coffers of the evening's auction takings.

I had a few moments after the proceedings to talk with Arthur Bainbridge but he was more interested in my seeing his model village. I had no idea what his model village actually was but promised that I would call round at his house prior to my departure the following morning. Douglas Birkbeck made himself known to me and we walked back to Hutton Lodge together whereupon I asked him whether he might be able to shed any light on the two ladies who had appeared to run the Black Bull Inn and just who was the old toper referred to as Rowley. He was as fascinated as I was and, having previously heard something of Wainwright's description, promised that he would look through his records to try and put some flesh on the bone. We agreed that we would meet again in the morning prior to my departure and with that we said goodnight. I retired to my room after a most entertaining evening spent at the heart of a thriving community that had welcomed a stranger with open arms. I will long remember Soulby with affection, both for its quiet tranquillity and for the mystery that might have been a figment of my imagination revolving around whether I was correct that there was an acquaintance between the March family and the Wainwrights.

Any mooching experienced at the beginning of my day had been replaced with a revitalised enthusiasm. I carried out my usual nightly practise of note writing, chapter reading and map studying but I did so with my thoughts on other things. I had much to look forward to as I switched out the light, but that would have to keep for tomorrow.

Chapter 10

Soulby to Dent

The rejuvenation of my enthusiasm rendered unnecessary my setting the alarm and I welcomed a return to being awake very early for although I was permanently tired, waking early satisfied me that my appetite for adventure had been rekindled. The past three mornings had seen a blunting of the sharp edge of keenness but on my tenth day I awoke with zeal, relishing the day ahead. The tenth day also saw a return to longer walking – Dent was my goal and lay twenty miles away to the south – and I would end the day's walk following the map on which I had started out. Before I could set out from the delightful Soulby though, I had a busy schedule of appointments to keep, all in the name of investigation. I wanted to know more about the drunken Rowley and a visit to the cemetery might assist, for although the locals had not been entirely sure, they thought that he might have been Roland Fothergill, a member of one of the ancient village families. Being indigenous to the village suggested that his final resting place might be found marked by a gravestone, so my pre-breakfast call was to find the cemetery. I had arranged for breakfast to be taken at eight o'clock in order that at half past I would be able to telephone the television company to ascertain whether they might be able to accommodate me in their schedule. Between breakfast and my continued quest for televisual notoriety I was expecting Douglas Birkbeck to call with any snippets of information that he might have gleaned from his records. My final appointment within the village was to call upon Arthur Bainbridge to view his model village, the pride of his years of retirement and, by all accounts, quite an impressive sight. I had liked Arthur's character very much and even without his village it would have been a pleasure to visit his home. As it was I had been singularly invited for a private showing and it would have been the height of bad manners not to attend. There was, however, an ulterior motive on both sides – I hoped to use his local knowledge and he hoped to raise money for charity because while viewing his work is free, there is a hope that spectators will place money in his charity box. All this and I still wished to be on my way by nine o'clock.

Venturing out into the crisp morning, the weather had deigned to take a turn for the better with a clear sky and a promise of a fine day. A light mist hung over the chilled grass of the low-lying fields so that the trees sprouted from an ethereal grey sea. Cows wandered their pastures legless – a state that, on occasion, I had found myself in, although not so at Soulby, for not a drop had passed my lips. As I entered the church grounds I could not help but feel that the adjacent villagers would be looking out and watching with interest my every move, for they knew of my presence and the vast majority had met me the evening before. 'Ooh, look, it's that walker chap; you know the one who bought the cooked ham.'

There were several engraved memorial stones leaning against the wall of the church – at first sight it seemed that there must have recently been a spate of deaths with stones prepared but services still to be held. Closer inspection revealed that those remembered in the epitaphs had all died long ago and that their stones were being relocated for some reason. The ancientness of the engravings on all the stones suggested that there must have been a more recent burial ground elsewhere and I recalled from the booklet that Mr Braithwaite had loaned to me that there had been additional ground consecrated. I found the new graveyard with some difficulty as it was situated a little way out of the village on the Musgrave Road, a walk in which I was delayed by a herd of cows being guided back to their field after milking. They occupied the complete width of the lane and all I could do was to patiently proceed at their very leisurely pace. It was, I decided, hardly surprising that they moved slowly for I was sure that the female of most species would walk fairly gingerly having just had her teats ravaged by something akin to four vacuum-cleaner suckers. It was, though, all too apparent that their schedule for the morning was not as hectic as mine. The herder, a young man astride a quad bike, greeted me and we passed the time of day while I continued at a snail's (or more accurately a cow's) pace until I reached the large iron gates of the cemetery. I discovered later that it was more than likely that my conversation had been held with the grandson of the remains of the man upon whom I was calling, Roland Brass. Once in the half-full cemetery a parade up and down the rows of stones soon led me to the one that I was seeking. The gravestone, in polished granite, showed that George Roland Brass had died in 1951, his wife living until 1980. Before many minutes the relative chronological mathematics between the ages of man and wife worried me – Wainwright's Rowley had been seventy-eight in 1938, meaning that the internee whose grave I looked upon would have been aged ninety-one when he died. On the proviso that his wife was of a similar age, then for her to live on until 1980 meant that she must have survived to the ripe old age of one hundred and twenty. Acknowledging that country air and country living might well aid longevity, I found it difficult to believe that their combined effects could be so dramatic. I could not be satisfied that my search for Rowley was complete but I found no other stone that might have provided an alternative candidate. There was a second gravestone that was of special personal interest but it is not my intention of relating why because its presence there had been a very painful memory for the person who had told me of it and as I paid my respects I knew that it should remain a confidence.

I walked quickly back to Hutton Lodge, passing the grassed site of the Black Bull Inn, and arrived back to find the table spread with fine cutlery and crockery and adorned with orange juice, cereal and toast. Almost disrespectfully I hurried breakfast in my eagerness for what the day held in promise. There is a saying that pride goes before a fall and my first tumble was to be found in the fact that the schedules of the television company were full. Due to the sudden closure of a large factory in the region their priority was to cover the story and to leave some lone walker to make his own way. My tenth day would be the last during which I would be within their region, so I had missed out on my chance for my fifteen minutes of fame. My second bruising came in the form of a message via

Mrs March that Douglas Birkbeck had not discovered anything conclusive from his records but that he would continue his investigations. As much as I had admired him and was grateful for his efforts, I could not but feel that once my brief sojourn in their company was over I would soon be forgotten. Perhaps that walker sixty years hence will reawaken the village interest in a walker that once passed through. 'You remember, the one who bought the cooked ham.' Things were taking a nosedive as far as discovering village history was concerned but, whatever else, I had the memory of being a part of this fine village, if only ever so fleetingly.

Replete after breakfast, I returned to my room undeterred by the rebuttal of the television company. I was undeterred too by having drawn yet more blanks. Preying more heavily on my mind was the walking that lay ahead of me. If by his ninth day Wainwright was marching purposefully to reach home, then by his tenth he was almost running, having initially started the day by deciding to concede defeat and catch the train from Kirkby Stephen. He had spent interminable hours in torrential rain and storm-force winds and the headline in the morning paper at Soulby told of gales wreaking havoc all across the country. The upshot was that when he finally did stir into action, he had initially decided to make for the station only to change his mind and then follow the fastest route he was able to transport him to Dent. His way led through quiet back lanes to start with but then continued along the Kirkby Stephen to Sedbergh road until finally branching off eastwards up Dentdale, all the way along macadam byways. Had it not been for the clarity of the day, the crispness of the air and the freshness of the slight breeze I would have been downhearted at the thought of twenty miles via such a course. With the weather as it was I retained my humour and set out from Mrs March's with a definite spring in my step. I might have lost the battle for knowledge of my predecessor at Soulby but I could sense overall victory of the war. Arrival in Settle would seal defeat for any that had doubted my ability and would spell the culmination of my triumphal quest.

Within five minutes I arrived at Arthur Bainbridge's cottage – there could be no doubt that it was his by the sight that met me in the front garden. The whole of the sloping lawn had been laid over to provide a scaled-down version of Soulby, albeit that some artist's licence had been used in the positioning of the model houses relative to one another. He must have seen my approach for no sooner had I taken my first glance over the wall than he was out of the house and asking for my opinion. This man's enthusiasm matched both his eyesight and his hearing for intensity and I could only congratulate him on his artistry. Following my tour of his front lawn we adjourned to the workshop to see the next offering in the throes of being assembled and all I could do was to privately marvel at this retired farmer's endeavours. He politely explained that he had raised well over one thousand pounds for charity – cancer research as I recall – and I gladly reached into my pocket to further his fundraising by a further two pounds. I did not begrudge giving to such a cause, although I inwardly smiled when I thought that he had already sold me a tin of cooked ham for two pounds that I had been able to divert elsewhere – he was clearly out to take money from me and had succeeded. I mentioned my trip to the cemetery and my understanding that it had been Roland Brass at the inn when Wainwright had visited, and Arthur immediately disagreed and told me of his own recollections. He was confident that the Rowley referred to in Wainwright's account would have been Rowley Fothergill, an uncle of Roland Brass and a man with a penchant for a drink. Arthur remembered him from his young days as being an elderly and curmudgeonly type who enjoyed a tipple or two and had come to live with in the village staying, he thought, with the Brass family. I also mentioned the ladies of the Black Bull Inn – he deliberated for a moment before proclaiming that their name was Adams and that they moved to Warcop, a village three miles away. The man's memory was as faultless as all his other faculties and I could only hope that if I ever arrived at his age I would possess such an acute mind. Many had suggested that to embark on my journey my mind must have been already slipping which, at barely half his age, I found a little troubling – it is true that I can be told something one minute and forget it the next. Or I can tell of something one minute and have absolutely no recollection of it within minutes.

Or I can tell of something one minute and have absolutely no recollection of it within minutes.

Arthur apologised for not being able to help further but I thanked him profusely because with his help my stay in Soulby had, at the very last moment, revealed more than I might have hoped for. I had a picture of village life and the characters that had all been given more depth by the fact that I had moved among their descendants. Arthur talked briefly of the war that had followed so closely on the heels of Wainwright's visit and how he had been landed on the beaches of Normandy on Dplus2, 7 June 1944. I meant to ask him whether he knew what the 'D' denoted but forgot to and was left with my own definition – 'Damn glad I wasn't there.'

Time, and Arthur's stories, unlike me, was marching on and I had to look for an opportunity to leave without causing offence. I finally found such a chance and, shaking hands, was on my way by half past nine following a narrow road that led into a narrower lane and finally diminished into an even narrower track. Due to the contours of the land I was not far along the track before I was afforded what proved to be my final view of Soulby. It vanished behind the hedgerows that lined the road and I was once again alone on my continued southern travels. Soulby was left behind to return to her tranquil lifestyle free from further rude interruptions from the walker who had muscled in on her age-old traditions and who had disturbed the peace in the early morning by scurrying around her graveyards. It was hard to imagine that such a place could ever have found the passing trade to warrant an inn. It was even harder to reconcile the fact that it had had sufficient trade to merit a second inn, the Exchange Hotel, which had closed in 1935. Village life must have been much more insular sixty years ago with residents living and working much more locally, generating living wages for two innkeepers and their staff. In 1998, while the village appeared not to have reduced in size, it could no longer support any form of commercial business. The grocers had gone, the joiner had gone and the post office had gone, with all such services only now being available in the relative metropolis of Kirkby Stephen. Commercially, Soulby had gone the way of many other rural communities: it had died and would not be revived because small individual enterprise that relied on quality had been irreversibly replaced by bigger business with their eyes on cost and profit. Soulby, perhaps, formed a sad reflection of the nation's ethos: money above all else. The prospect of a journey to the neighbouring towns where larger firms, with their lower costs through economies of scale, would not deter as it once might have done. After all we all have cars and use them as we might once have used our legs. The consequences for our rural communities and for the environment are as nothing when compared to the possibility of the job being just that little bit cheaper. Besides, we justify our choice by the fact that the grocer or the joiner has moved into the larger town in any case. We have developed into a society where the desire to live in the country and the necessity to work in the city has condemned us to a polluted future of choking fumes and choked roads. I had been reminded many times on my travels of what a crime it had been that we had allowed the culling of the railways, for in them lay a means of transport that would have made more bearable so many of the roads along which I had walked. Now we simply build more roads to witness more people sitting alone in their cars wait-ing for the queue to move just a little and cursing the fact that the government hasn't spent enough on its road programme. The principal modes of travel will become blocked perhaps to the extent that we will have no alternative other than to return to the more insular village life simply because to journey anywhere would be intolerable. Perhaps it is more likely that the government will merely pump more and more of our money into new roads. This seemed the more likely proposition for it is only with moving traffic that the government can hope to maintain its vast revenues through petrol and road taxes. While I would not wish to appear cynical, it is clear that if they did not seek to fund more road building then their revenues would reduce drastically as village and town life returned to an ethos centred around the individual community. Wainwright had been able to count on the fingers of one hand the number of vehicles he encoun-tered whereas I would have needed the fingers and toes of many volunteers to carry out the same operation.

I rounded a corner and ahead lay yet another reminder of the death of the branch line. The Eden Valley Railway had closed in 1962 and I passed under a tiny bridge where all that remained were the stone arches. This was home now only to scrub and rough grass with the thought of being able to journey from Kirby Stephen to Bowes a distant memory for a diminishing number of the more elderly residents. Like the village craftsman and the railway they too would die off and we would be left to mourn their passing for once gone they could not return. Strangely, as I approached the bridge I heard, quite distinctly, the noise of an approaching train. There could be no doubt that the rhythmical sound was that of railway carriages, although if this were to be a spectre then the chuff-chuff of the steam locomotive was absent. For a brief moment I thought my mind must be slipping until reference to the map told me that just a little way beyond the bridge lay the Settle–Carlisle line. The train appeared and passed some way away on its journey north. It seemed ironic that the only line that served these parts had found a new lease of life and had been revitalised, and as the gleaning train passed I could see its many charges being carried to their various appointments. The railway I walked under could perhaps have been similarly reborn if only we had not so utterly destroyed it some thirty years previous.

I dwelt on such matters no longer and chose instead to be positive for I had been blessed with weather sufficiently clear to enable a retrospect northwards over to Cross Fell and I could make out the shining structure of the radar station. Fully fifteen miles away, it seemed peculiar that only two days earlier I had scarcely been able to see it from 15 yards and had only been able to find it through worryingly unconvincing map reading. A gentle mist still hung in the vale, held in place by the colder temperatures in the valley bottom. Soulby would still have a chill air to it and the villagers would not be disrobing as I was. Once again I was walking is shirtsleeves and could feel the warm sun on my face. I remembered how, back at Muker, I had hoped for an even tan because for half my trek I would be walking north and west and the other half would be south and east. My wish had not been granted until walking toward Waitby along this idyllic and unused track and it was only a shame that there would be no time for lingering after my late start. I even grew more positive after my earlier disappointment of the television station not being able to rendezvous with me. I had no doubt that they would have delayed me without a thought for my purist schedule of arriving in Dent before evening. I had no doubt that they would have arrived late and been awfully pretentious and neither understood nor cared for my venture. I had no doubt that they would have misinterpreted their report to portray me as a sad and lonely walker with clearly nothing better to do. The only doubts I had were regarding my motives for trying to secure their interest in the first place. I could only conclude that, like most others, I had to recognise and bow to the power of television. It had become a modern-day God with an adoring public reverently staring and listening, motionless, hour after hour to its fashionable gospel. The thirst for its outpourings had become unquenchable and more and more channels had been established to cast the net to an ever-widening audience so as not to miss even the smallest of minority interest groups. Customers flocked around it as moths might be attracted to a light bulb. It would cater for all tastes and would enable a viewer to be endlessly entertained by its presence, only to be separated from its company for calls of nature. It would even allow the viewer to interact with it to be able to remotely take an active part in discussions. There would be nothing that this box could not provide, so much so that any time parted from it would feel as though a part of the body had been amputated. Advertisements and programmes would blend into one long portrayal of how life could be and the desire for that life would fuel the demand for not only a better life, but a better life now. An unceasing and endless diet of such fiction could only serve to enhance that sector of society who seemed to believe that it deserved better and that if their life was not so improved then someone else must be to blame. While television had remained a type of messenger it served a useful purpose, but once it had begun to become a substitute for real interactions with others, its evolution had mutated to that of something overly powerful. If its followers were blind to the dangers of their fictional diets then television would indoctrinate as Hitler had indoctrinated sixty years earlier. In itself television holds no danger until the time when its viewers are unable to differentiate between reality and make-believe. As I walked up the gradual incline out of Waitby I wondered just who was the sadder and the lonelier – me or the viewer watching me on the misinterpreted local news report. At least I knew the truth, for it was happening to me and I was able to experience it first-hand. If television is allowed to do the thinking for the viewer then it becomes not an extension of their minds, but as a replacement. I wagered that Arthur Bainbridge hadn't wasted his time staring aimlessly at a box for the principal source of his entertainment.

My previous two evenings had seen a return to evenings spent away from the invasive influence of television and in the midst of a spirit of family and community life that furnished a stronger bond between the family or community members. At Slakes Farm I had spent a very pleasant hour talking with the Braithwaites about all manner of things, from their way of life to why I was undertaking my walk. The conversation had been enthralling because all the participants spent equal time speaking and listening. There had been a television tucked snugly in the corner of the room but as I returned from the inn I had noticed that it was switched off. It was only as invasive as they permitted it to be and was not left on as though some form of two-dimensional moving sculpture had moved in. At Soulby I had never even noticed a television and could not to this day state whether there was one in my room or not. However, if I were to write my account then I had to decide for whom was I writing it. I could not pretend that I was writing it solely for my own pleasure for it would lie lonely in a sideboard drawer. I sought some modest acclaim as we all do and I knew that if it were to reach the common man in the street then I could not project it unassisted. I needed the media whether I liked it or not because for every Braithwaite family or Soulby community that do not appear to rely on it, there are a hundred others that do.

I passed under the railway bridge carrying the Settle–Carlisle line and as I did so I made way for a farmer herding his sheep down the quiet lane. This was the second time in as many days that I had seen a sight that I had not come across for many years and I stood aside to avoid startling the sheep as they ambled past me. The farmer thanked me and we spent a few polite moments agreeing that the weather was better than of late. I could vouch for that, I thought, casting a rearward glance back toward the high hills of the Pennines that had been so inhospitable forty-eight hours before. A short distance further up from the bridge I came to a waymarked path that indicated the Coast–to–Coast route and for a few hundred yards its way and mine followed one another. It was the Coast-to-Coast path with which Wainwright's name had become even more synonymous than the Pennine Way for he had devised its course from St Bede's Head to Robin Hood's Bay. It came as no surprise to meet other walkers at this point – I had expected a sudden rush because the route between the two coasts has become another where the walker must join a procession undertaking the same task. A first group of four hikers mounted the stile to be quickly followed by a further two and I was more than a little pleased to turn left where they all turned right. Wainwright has received criticism for popularising walking and thus adding to the spoiling and eroding of the countryside with too many people following his documented routes. Perhaps walkers are no better than those who would live by and imitate what they experience from the television in that they sheepishly and blithely trail behind the way set by others. Then again, perhaps Wainwright might have argued that he had only showed the way much as Jesus had shown the way in the Bible – if others, of their own volition, chose to follow then blame not the leader. It is often not just the fact that people follow a master that creates subsequent friction but the manner in which they follow. In the country it is where walkers disperse laterally that the severest of erosion occurs. The same is true of religion, with the disparate beliefs of diverse sects maintaining a friction between the denominations. Throughout history there are numerous conflicts whose root cause was the demand of one sect that another should live by a set of beliefs foreign to them, with refusal being met by force. Although religion undoubtedly lies at the heart of such holy wars, it is never suggested that we should pillory the name of Jesus for we are told that he showed us the way of peace and love. If we are incapable of interpreting the

Bible's guidance and unable to live in unity, then it is clearly inequitable to censure either the co-authors or the subject of their writings. It is equally unjust to castigate Wainwright for we need not have followed and, where we did, we could have ensured that one narrow and clearly defined path was established. My thinking returned for a moment to television and I thought of how equally true it is of those who complain about one thing or another – it is within their power to turn it off. I could only assume that like some fanatical sect they live entirely under its godlike spell and probably aren't aware of where the on/off switch is for it has preached endlessly to them from the very first day they welcomed it into their homes.

Had Wainwright reached the same point and met the farmer with his sheep, their conversation would have been altogether different for they both would have had to shout to make themselves heard and they both would have cursed the foul weather. Although Wainwright had decided to call a halt to his venture while sitting in front of the roaring fire at the Black Bull, once out on the road his account tells of how he had been about to abort when he spied distant fells. They attracted him and gave him renewed enthusiasm despite the continuing howling gale and the rain, and he passed by the station at Kirkby Stephen heading southward without giving it a second thought. He blamed his lethargy on a surfeit of Westmorland Plain and the sight of the hills filled him with a new resolve that was not about to yield to a bit of wind and rain. Their arrival above the horizon turned the rain into no more than a light drizzle and the wind a mere breeze. I have my suspicions that by this stage in the relating of his account he had concluded that he was in need of some intrigue to enliven his story and perhaps over-dramatized his plight with the view of maintaining reader interest. I drew this conclusion from the fact that my first sight of the hills to the south as they began to rise over my near horizon was not one that stopped me dead in my tracks. Yes, they provided a welcome change from the abundance of undulations for which the Vale of Eden was noted, but they were no match for the Lake District hills or the high Pennines that now lay behind me. The hills that rose in front formed the northern extremities of the Howgill Fells with the northernmost uplands and peaks all being part of Ravenstonedale Common. There was, though, something rather fitting about Wainwright's enthusiasm being rejuvenated at a location where his marathon journey intersected with what, many years later, would become the Coast-to-Coast path. Maybe I had spent so much time walking on my own that the vision of other walkers resulted in my feeling hemmed in and distracted me from an appreciation of the nearing hills. It was not far beyond my encountering the six walkers that my perception of them changed and, with their scale and extent beginning to reveal themselves, I too was happy to usher them in as accompaniment for the next step of my journey. They would remain my increasingly impressive companions as I proceeded along the eight miles of the Rawthey valley and would only disappear from my view as I turned eastwards up Dentdale.

First seeing the hills ahead and being relatively unmoved by them caused me to conclude that our appreciation of a subject is affected by our disposition at the time of the encounter. My more usual positive attitude had been dampened by the sensation of being cramped by the other walkers who moved just in front of me. I enjoy walking alone and if I see others in front or behind I soon feel as if I am governing my pace to avoid catching up with them or to avoid them catching up with me. My mood had also been made all the blacker for I was not relishing the prospect of a four-mile walk along the main road connecting Kirkby Stephen and Sedbergh. It was the purist in me that was leading and I was following, possibly foolishly, solely in order to keep to Wainwright's route, however unpleasant. I could not imagine what attractions the main road might have held for the walker in 1938 but, whatever they may have been, they had long since been exhausted and by September 1998 it was the route chosen only by vehicle drivers, not walkers. Walking on the right-hand side of the road I still had to maintain a constant vigil both behind and in front. I could not assume a safe passage just by looking forward because on the numerous straighter sections the sound of a car approaching from the rear would very often herald the imminent arrival of a Vauxhall charging by at break-neck speed. Invariably, on the occasions that I did chance to notice the driver, these were driven by suited gentlemen presumably rushing to their next appointment in their impossibly hectic schedules that might secure their month-end targets. What must the quality of their perception be like, I wondered as another sped by in the direction of Sedbergh. I questioned whether they might possess the ability to perceive anything at all in the light of their kill-or-be-killed attitude in an industry where only the fittest survive. There could be no time to glance at their surroundings for their vision would be blinkered by the necessity to get that next order. They were essentially the possessions of their bosses, who might drop them or promote them on the strength of whether they secured that next deal. They would perceive that next call as a matter of life or death and no one was about to stop them or stand in their way. Nothing else would matter, especially not that walker who had nearly been blown to the wayside.

To enable a full appreciation of one's surroundings, whether in the form of physical objects or comprising relationships with other people, it is first necessary to become attuned to those surroundings. The sales representative could not be expected to meaningfully behold the hills of the Howgills if his mind were to be entirely focused elsewhere, just as my perception of Cross Fell had been influenced by my miserable plight. Appreciation is not dissimilar to radio reception – before any decision can be made as to a particular radio station it is obligatory to switch the radio on and tune into the correct frequency. Only then can a judgement be made. Human relationships and love are no different. Before mutual love can grow both parties have to demonstrate their own propensity to give affection as well as receive it. I could only hope that the sales representative remembered that on his way to Sedbergh, for it is when the kill-or-be-killed ethos spills over into personal relationships that they run into troubled waters. It takes a special kind of woman who would willingly suffer the likes of Wainwright, or perhaps that sales representative, with the old-fashioned hunter-gatherer philosophy without questioning the quality of her existence. In 1938 it may have been more acceptable to bring home the spoils in exchange for dinner being on the table and with sex on a Friday night after the menfolk had been for a drink at the local hostelry. Decisions as to the frequency of sex, and indeed anything else for that matter, would be reserved for the dominant male. Roles were clear, with the female presumably drawing her satisfaction from the fact that the male supplied her with the things that might enable fulfilment of both parties. The underpinning factor was that she was wise enough to know that self-contentment could stem from providing contentment. Sixty years and many divorces later, the perceptions of the roles had changed out of all recognition and it might just as easily have been a woman who nearly ran me off the road. There are no longer any easily identifiable waymarkers within relationships for society has decreed that women and men shall both exist within an environment where only the fittest shall survive. The fittest may very well endure but at considerable human cost: both partners in a relationship may believe themselves to be the dominant one and refuse to yield. The ensuing discord, which is not wholly unlike trench warfare, can only have one ultimate outcome. Single people can survive and flourish in a dog-eat-dog society but only at the expense of others around them. Relationships, where the measure of success is based upon mutual understanding and respect, suffer a failure rate that is directly proportional to the degree by which the parties compete to put their own survival above all else. To strive to put the contentment of those close to you above that of your own will bring its own rewards and will strengthen the commitment that must be present if there is to remain a lasting harmony.

Too many aspects of life have become too easy to casually shrug off and cast aside for pastures new in the belief that they might produce more fruitful outcomes. Maintaining relationships would, perhaps, be given more serious consideration if only people were able to see that there can be no instant fixes as if bought on credit and with never-ending get-out clauses. It is small wonder that marriages break up as though they were made of glass when they are entered into as lightly as some are prone to do and where the get-out clause is so easy to apply. It seems as though marriage is taken on board in the knowledge that, as with most other acquisitions, there is a return-to-base warranty and that at the first sign of dissension all commitment is forgotten and the goods sent packing, leaving both to have another go. If we are upset by our partner then we question less our own behaviour and look to place all blame elsewhere, like a drowning man flailing his arms uncontrollably. I remain convinced that if we first question our own actions and only find fault with others when we are satisfied that our own house is in order we might enjoy more cordial emotional relationships. As I walked I recalled watching one of the increasing genres of holiday programmes that centred on a Dominican Republic wedding and being struck by the superficial nature of those involved. The judge sidled up to officiate in his badly fitting suit and looked generally very blasé about the whole thing. The hotel staff doubled as ushers, groomsmen, waiters, toastmasters, entertainers and looked generally very pissed off about the whole thing (after all this was their third wedding that day and no doubt their umpteenth since the season began). The holiday representative repeated all the judges' mumblings so that the happy couple had some vague clue as to what was actually being said. This was due mainly to the fact that the judge spoke no English. A representative beamed beautifully and even shed a tear from a well-practised eye at the point of pronouncing them man and wife. As a wedding location it might have been idyllic, but as a spiritual altar of sworn commitment to future mutual conduct it was without depth and a sham, typifying the 'modern' perception of the supposed sanctity of marriage and, it seemed to me, most other traditional conventions.

My extensive reflections had carried me, almost without noticing, to the door of the Lamb Inn. The three miles from my joining the road had been both uneventful and uninteresting in roughly equal measure and I did not need very much encouragement to call in and relieve my aching feet. It was twelve o'clock and I had covered seven miles of the twenty required of me in two and a half hours. I deserved a break and, ordering soup and a pot of coffee, decided that thirty minutes rest would still effect my arrival in Dent, thirteen miles to the south, in good daylight. I was the inn's only customer as I entered but gradually one or two other travellers arrived which would at least lend a little more atmosphere for the bar had, until then, been as quiet as the Soulby grave-yard. Even stirring my coffee had seemed louder than usual and once when I had the misfortune to drop my soupspoon I thought I might indeed wake the dead as a great cacophony rang out throughout the bar with no other noise to deaden its impact. Although my fellow travellers' presence was welcome they spoke in frustratingly hushed tones that enabled me to only half-hear the subject of their discussion. I managed to grasp that they had been to Dent and were heading toward Appleby but any other comments were only caught as snippets and meant nothing in isolation. I had little else to divert my attentions because I had no need to study the map as the way was apparent and I had already read Wainwright's account of his tenth day and how he struggled with his boots that were rapidly falling in lumps from his feet. I was pleased that my modern equipment had held out admirably, especially my relatively new boots and very expensive jacket. Had the barmaid from Hexham been serving at the bar I could have found some entertainment and might even have stayed longer than the half-hour that I had allowed myself. The barmaid at the Lamb Inn was an older woman with an altogether more modest taste in clothing for which, in the main, I was quite relieved for she was of buxom build and thoughts of jellyfish rather than slugs would have been at the fore.

Refreshed after my brief halt I was back outside the front door at half past twelve swinging my rucksack over my shoulders, reaffixing my waist bag and checking that I had all other apparatus variously fastened to me. Satisfying my-self that I was short of nothing I re-established my well-practiced left, right, left, right pace that had now carried me nearly one hundred and seventy miles. I had resolved, over lunch, to challenge the puritan in me and leave Wainwright's route where a minor road forked left a mile beyond the inn. I had endured more than enough of passing sales representatives and would take a diversion to seek solace in the quieter back road to Fell End. With purpose in my stride I soon arrived at the fork and bade a thankful au revoir to the cars that had hounded me for the last four miles. It would only be a temporary respite though, for further down the Rawthey valley I would have to rejoin their throng. The noise of the traffic on the main road did not stay with me for long because it dips to lower altitude as quickly as possible, while the road I chose to follow maintained a greater height and a greater panorama of all around – I could look behind and still see the far away hills of the northern Pennines, although they very soon after sank from view below the horizon just as the Howgills had risen above it earlier in the day. As I advanced south-east my views of the Howgills became more and more imposing with their bulk rising on the opposite side of the valley. Their lower flanks were laid out to a random field pattern but the higher ground was left respectfully bare for no commercial agriculture could be deployed on the barren hills that filled my camera's viewfinder more than once during my slow descent of the Rawthey valley. As I gained altitude and the day grew older, the sun burnt off any last lingering haze and the air was sharp and fresh with a brilliance to the light that often follows poorer weather. With the emergent sun had also arrived the need to consider changing into shorts and all the rigmarole that entailed. I shilly-shallied for a full ten minutes until at length I decided that my legs really were becoming uncomfortably warm and would benefit from the additional ten minutes that it would take to change. Boots off and map case, belt and cameras removed, and numerous other bits and bobs retrieved from various pockets and neatly piled ready for re-stowing, I ransacked the rucksack to find my shorts and sun cream. When I packed the sack I had not considered that the day would develop so favourably and had not given any thought to placing the shorts to aid ease of access. The resultant heap of clothes on the verge at the side of the road would all require repacking when I had finally located what I was seeking. Finding them at last I slipped the long trousers off and, stood now in underpants, applied the sun cream before putting on the shorts. This proved to be an unwise ploy for I discovered that the scent of the cream must have been an aphrodisiac for passing insects, and no sooner had I smoothed the cream onto the front of my thighs than I attracted the unwelcome attentions of a large bumble bee. Initially I wafted it away in a relatively calm manner with a flick of my hand, but it became evident that this bee's intentions were serious and it returned for a closer sniff. Bees don't sting without good reason I told myself and tried to ignore its presence. That is all fine and dandy and may indeed be the case, but I defy anyone to remain entirely unruffled with a large insect buzzing busily around your testicles. That bee was very clearly of the misguided opinion that I represented some overlarge flower and it was not about to leave what might be a good source of pollen without a fight. I did manage to elude its advances but not before smartly running across the road then up and down the verge in an attempt to confuse it. These evasive manoeuvres were all carried out in a partially disrobed state of socks and underpants and I was grateful that there were no passing motorists and I could only hope that none of the distant farms had noticed. I returned to my various piles of supplies and, checking that I was alone and listening intently to ensure that there was no nearby drone of the returning bee, quickly dragged on my shorts, packed the sack, fastened the multitude of bits and was on my way again.

The road soon began a steep descent toward its rejoining of the main road at Rawthey Bridge and I was on the lookout for a local of whom I would inquire whether the path shown on the map around Bluecaster Hill was a passable way. If it provided a clear path I would be able to avoid a further two miles of the busy road that was nearing as I descended more and more steeply toward it. As chance would have it, as I approached a small group of farm buildings a lady appeared at the gate about to mount a bicycle and set off down the steep hill. As she emerged from the open gate she was riding scooter-fashion with one foot on the left pedal and propelling herself with her right foot prior to swinging her right leg over to take up the usual bicycle-riding posture. If I did not hail her quickly she would have been gone and as it seemed reasonable that she would know as to whether there existed a navigable path, it was imperative that I stopped her. Still about 10 yards away, I called out to her. Unfortunately my beckoning was at the exact same instant that she swung her right leg over to the right pedal and the incline was very quickly beginning to accelerate her downwards. Midway through swinging her leg she looked round to see from where the call had come and, in so doing, rapidly began to lose control of the bicycle as she tried to put one foot on the ground to stop herself and regain her balance all at the same time. Most of her weight was forward so as she unwisely applied the front brake the rear wheel lifted from the ground and she then looked to be in danger of somersaulting over the handlebars. How she managed to stop without falling off sideways or forwards I will never know but stop she did, and she confirmed that there was a clear path skirting the western flank of Bluecaster Hill to Cautley. I thanked her and apologised for being the cause of her near demise and she remounted and sped off down the hill leaving me to uncharitably chortle to myself at the memory of her ungainly halt.

It was while proceeding along the Fell End road that my way had finally returned to the map on which I had started so many days and miles earlier. I could have, had I chosen, unfolded the map and found Settle. There had been many places in between but it seemed strange to contemplate that in a little over twenty-four hours I would walk passed the end of the road to Horton that had been the start of my journey and my venture would be at an end. Settle was just a vague recollection and it was as though all the days since leaving Sue had merged into one, yet I had walked so very far and would have been away eleven days. In many ways my travels had been a mirror of life with each day holding individual experiences forming a part of the whole. Without the separate component parts there could be no overall sense of fulfilment, yet each of the segments, although relatively insignificant in themselves, had been integral, not so much for their own sake but as important chapters of the full story. Seen in isolation each day in a diary can only ever be as an artist's sketch without structure and colour and only when the entire content is viewed can there be a depiction of the diarist. If the diary were to be a film then entries for individual days would represent single frames. To enable depth and form to be established and to comprehend the diarist's disposition it is necessary to know of the preceding and succeeding entries. While a book cannot be judged by its cover, then neither can it be judged by reading only one page. The recounting of my long journey tramping through the Pennines would give structure to otherwise separate episodes and would reflect my state of mind as it had ebbed and flowed in response to the various high and low points en route. It may be seen as unfortunate that the only way for to appreciate my experiences is to read the account in its entirety. Still, if you have managed to cope thus far then fear not for there is only a little way to go. If, by chance, you are glancing at these very words as you might a single entry in a diary, having not read any previous pages, then decide now whether to turn back to the start or alternatively consign this tome to your car-boot pile, for alone these words will mean nothing. For those who, having read this advice, still insist on reading this current episode in isolation then I can at least give some insight into my mood as I walked along a blissfully quiet path high above the River Rawthey with the dramatic Cautley Spout and Crag opposite. The sun was shining brightly in a sky that was cloudless except for some straggling wisps of high cirrus, the air was calm and birdsong rang out from the fell to my left. The fells that swept up to the west of the valley were so clear that they looked as though they had been modelled and that if photographed would seem unreal, as if made from papier mâché with painted-on fields and scaled-down walls and buildings. I caught my first glances of Whernside, which meant that I was exulting in being if not on the last lap then damn close to it. There could surely be nothing to stop me now from successfully accomplishing my mission. I was also quietly complimenting myself on the rather splendid notion of producing a guidebook so that others might follow where Wainwright had first trodden so many years before. So for those who now believe that there could be nothing to have blighted my way then stop reading because there did exist a concern that had underlain the entire journey. Although a part of me was looking forward to crossing the River Ribble back into Settle, my arrival would mark a return to an unknown future that would more than likely see me at the end of any professional aspirations and at the beginning of something wholly unfamiliar. Whatever pride might stem from becoming a postman, nothing could alter the fact that our lives had been bought on long-term credit and now there would not exist the means to pay for it unless Sue accepted being condemned to a life of continued working. I feared that this would touch on my sense of male pride, which I had only become aware of since contemplating my own perceived inadequacy where being the breadwinner was concerned. Yet another of my turns in life had been found wanting. Still, I would take comfort in the fact that there were many others down the same avenue as I and that it matters more what you are than what you do. I did rather wonder though, for how long such fine sentiments might actually sustain us and keep the creditors from our door.

Sue's sentence to a life of working seemed a far cry from Wainwright's view that women, once married, should never dirty their hands other than through having and tending to babies or doing the housework. Sixty years earlier had not only seen a greater concurrence with Wainwright's outlook but had seen a greater ability of many to live by such a premise. Man's role as bread-winner would mean the whole family were provided for and, if something were required, then cash would be found to acquire it. Hire-purchase was a dirty word, not mentioned in polite society and only whispered in very hushed tones by those of severely limited means. Now, sixty years on, many wives were sentenced to a role that included not only having babies and doing the housework but also to making a major contribution financially to the household in a never-ending struggle to keep the wolves from the door. For most the clearing of life's debts and looking forward to a more prosperous lifestyle would probably be linked to retirement, but by that stage life's tribulations would have taken a heavy toll and drastically reduced the capacity to savour the fruits of their la-bours. In a society where a couple sharing a house could ill-afford to negotiate life's financial obstacle course, it is bewildering as to how so many rejected spouses manage to survive. Having a desire to 'work to live' but being com-manded by circumstances to 'live to work' does not generate the most positive of environments in which to nurture the young borrowers of tomorrow, for bor-rowers they will surely be. There is a saying that warns 'never a lender or borrower be', but the philosophy of a life based on cash purchases is nigh on impossible to contemplate where expectations are so high and failure so easily measured. Borrowers will continue to be the lifeblood of the lenders.

My earlier view of Whernside was short-lived for no sooner had I first no-ticed it than the path began to descend towards the village of Cautley and its bulk sank from view. As I followed the clear path down into the valley, it first became a track, then a lane, and before I knew it I was back among the speeding traffic four miles north-east of Sedbergh. I found myself looking steeply up at the hills that only twenty minutes earlier I had felt equal to as I had looked across at them rather than hopelessly up at them. Now they were dark and brooding monsters with their severe eastern slopes towering over me. They remained the single focus of my appreciation for there was nothing about the road walking to commend it. The verges were typically narrow, the traffic typically rapid, and my feet typically rebelling at the prospect of a further three miles until I could turn off onto the quieter byway that would take me over the spur of Frostrow Fells and into Dentdale. Could my feet have seen the route up Dentdale they would have protested even more for that demanded a final four-mile road walk before Dent village would be reached. My walk along the main road toward Sedbergh had the one saving grace of the sun shining full onto my face and it provided a pleasant warmth to a late-September afternoon. I fairly marched along the side of the road and only very occasionally did I pause to look about me. From time to time when I did I noticed that my lengthening companion, the product of the strong sunlight whom I had not been able to recollect for a number of days, was now following me. I grumbled at him about how busy the road was and implored him to keep up with me, which, to his credit, he did with unerring constancy. Any such grumblings were also short-lived because before I reached my exit from the road at the foot of Garsdale intermittent clouds had appeared and the sun's presence became more and more infrequent. These were dark and threatening clouds that held a promise of inclemency and I could only hope to reach Dent before their threats were realised for I did not relish the hassle of changing back into walking trousers. I certainly did not relish the thought of changing alongside the main road for if I were to again be assaulted by a maverick insect, my embarrassment would be extreme. It is one thing to skip about in underwear on a quiet byroad but quite another where one's antics would be viewed by so many passers-by.

I knew that I must be somewhere approximately on the same latitude as Wensleydale when a Tornado jet screamed overhead heading eastwards. In only a matter of seconds a walker in Askrigg would be looking up while all the locals continued about their business unmoved by the noisy interruption. To the pilot the hills opposite, which now looked even more forbidding without sunlight as friendly illumination, would have lost all sense of majesty. His perspective would flatten their height and his perception of them would be so different to mine as he looked down on them and I up at them. Also he did not have the luxury of time to appreciate them as I had: in a matter of seconds they would be gone from his vision while I had had hours in which I could come to feel I knew every nook and cranny. He might see more of the world but he would not have time to treasure any of it for he saw it all as nothing but a blur. If you don't, won't, or can't take in what is around you then it is barely worth looking in the first place.

It is not only the pilot of the Tornado who travels so fast that appreciation is impossible, although in his case it was the actual speed that marred his vision. Most people, salesmen in Vauxhalls particularly, live every day at such a virtual mental speed that much of life passes them by unnoticed. The majority of time is spent in an isolated world of emails and faxes where even communication over the telephone has decreased as part of normal day-to-day routine. We live increasingly in a world where all that we require is a 14-inch monitor sitting atop a clever box of tricks with never a need to speak to another living soul. Former loved ones may have moved out; work involves sitting in a car alone all day, exaggerated by sitting hunched at a computer screen sending detached messages to others whose loved ones have moved out, ad infinitum. It is folly to believe solely that working on the computer is bad for posture – it is even worse for the soul and must slowly and surely damage relationships. Or are we to find love on the Internet as well? No doubt I will receive a long list of sad websites where I might care to look if only I ever had the time or the inclination.

My reward for having endured the road for so long was the enchanting hamlet at Garsdale Bridge that I came to a few minutes after leaving the road and proceeding down a quiet backwater. I stopped for a few moments and rolled a cigarette, which I then smoked looking over the parapet wall of the bridge at the ancient and picturesque mill that lay 100 yards upstream. The sun had returned,

I was off the main road, I was having a cigarette and I was enjoying the last of the water from my bottle. I could think of nothing more bucolic as I watched the Clough River dance and sparkle where the sun caught it as it played over the stony riverbed just upstream of the bridge. Although I could have stayed longer – in fact I could quite easily have moved into one of the delightful cottages and remained stationary forever – I set off again at four o'clock for the final few miles through Millthrop, round into Dentdale and on to Dent. I knew Millthrop from an earlier visit when I had walked the Dales Way and I was pleased to make its acquaintance again for it too is a most agreeable hamlet that only lacks a welcoming inn. I entered without difficulty but my exit was less fortunate for after I wound my way along its only street a lack of both concentration and signs contrived to see me walking on the wrong road. I had intended to follow the Dales Way path for a mile or so to spare my feet the uninviting task of following the road around via Catholes but somehow managed to miss the track that would provide a more direct and less tiresome route. I realised my error only after seeing signs for the nearby golf course and could not face the half-mile walk back to pick up the correct path. My only consolation was that once beyond the entrance to the golf course there was a marked reduction in both the amount (and quality) of cars – I had been passed by several BMWs and other executive marques making their way for an evening's nine holes.

The road remained sufficiently busy to present some difficulty in relieving a personal problem that was growing with every stride. The lack of verges or suitable gate openings tied with either the high hedgerows that lined the road or the field walls that were built tight against the roadside prevented me for some distance from attending to a call of nature. I would listen intently for the sound of approaching cars but each time I thought that all was clear I had no sooner begun to tuck myself as best I could into some small breach than a line of cars would appear around the next corner. I would then wait for some seconds before deciding to move on in the hope of a more suitably modest place of concealment further along the road. All was quiet again and I took up the position with anticipatory eagerness only to be thwarted by the sight of three girl hikers striding in silence around the corner just a few yards in front of me. Adjusting myself with some rapidity I made as though I had been unfastening my map case for close scrutiny and we passed the time of day for a few moments as they walked by where I was stood. As the road behind me was as straight as these dales roads can be, and was fairly long, the girls remained in sight long enough for me to again decide to move on and hope for better fortune elsewhere. Finally, and much to my relief, I came upon a small lay-by that was home to a most judiciously placed pile of gravel (which is now washed gravel) and my sense of pleasure was heightened still further by pausing for a cigarette before tackling the last three miles to Dent.

I had walked along roads for the full length of yesterday's walk and much of today's and my feet and legs had tired to the extent that it took all my effort just to complete the distance. My memories of Dentdale remained scant and in my hurry, more than once I misread the map thinking that I was nearer to my goal than I actually was. The breeze that had sprung from nowhere and whistled from behind me up the valley chilling me on its passage intensified this frustrating end to the day. The clouds had now blotted out the last of the sun and the hills ahead had lost the clarity of earlier – their summits now hung in a light veil of grey mist. I suspected that they also may have blotted out any thoughts I might have had as to enjoying my final day accompanied by fine and sunny weather. I had not seen a forecast but I did not need to be an accomplished meteorologist to know that these clouds had begun to gather with a permanency that did not bode well for day eleven. The rest in the lay-by had done nothing for my tired limbs which ached abominably, and the prospect of the further twenty-one miles of predominantly road walking on the final leg of my journey did nothing to help.

As with all things, whether they are good or bad, they must pass, and my suffering finally ended at a quarter to six as I entered the village of Dent. The village may have held an impression for Wainwright of great antiquity with an expectation of squalor, but now it is a tourist Mecca, especially for hikers and enthusiasts of caravanning and camping. Approaching from the west, Dent appears to be a temporary home for thousands of refugees with the fields adjacent to the road littered with tents and caravans and signs advertising camping with all manner of facilities. There is something rather out of keeping with an otherwise sleepy village. There is no sense of Dent slowly dying for want of custom for it is more like Buckden, having secured a definite place on the tourist rounds. Although I have nothing against tents or caravans, to see them hemmed in so close to the village detracts from the more usual village qualities that I had prepared myself for as I had made my weary way along the valley road. Since my euphoric high of the path approaching Cautley I seemed to have received nothing but disappointments and I was to receive one last one in the form of my desire for a swift drink not being realised. The two village inns were both closed as I arrived so I dejectedly made my way, following my hosts' instructions, to their guest house, the Old Vicarage. Greeted by Mr Neal on the front doorstep of his very sizeable and impressive detached house, I was courteously shown to my room, with him insisting on porting my rucksack, which I had removed to take off my boots before entering. It would have been very rude to enter such a magnificent home clomping all the way on his fine carpeted hall and stairs.

I found the room to be just as I would have expected based on the other aspects of the house: spacious and beautifully decorated, with en suite bath and shower and windows to both sides of the corner room that overlooked an enormous rear garden. The old vicar certainly had enjoyed an abode that was a cut above the quaint but run-of-the-mill cottages that typified the majority of the village. The outlook to the rear was only spoiled by the modern development that had crept up the hillside away from the village centre and had impinged somewhat on what must have once been a grand open view of the fells. Luxuriating in these splendid surroundings, I hurriedly threw my clothes to the floor and equally hurriedly threw myself into the shower. No time for a bath tonight I thought, for my preference was for food and drink. With only the minimum of delay I was dressed and sitting on a bar stool at the Sun Inn as close to the nearest beer pump I could find in order that I might save as much unnecessary walking as possible. Almost before the change from my first drink was given to me I was requesting a second. The locally brewed beer was very good and it seemed promising that something of local origin had survived without being absorbed by some huge conglomerate. The barmaid had recommended that I try Dent Brewery beers and I was only too happy to oblige. In turn I might also recommend Dent Brewery – they brew a fine pint of beer that is most gladly received after a long day's walk. I could have very easily been tempted by the barmaid's persuasive charms to overstay my welcome but my willpower remained intact and I made my exit and found my way back to the Old Vicarage at nine o'clock.

There was no sign of life downstairs so I retired immediately to my room whereupon switching on the light I was greeted by a buzzing from near the ceiling pendant uplighter in the centre of the room. At first I feared that I had been followed by the bee that had shown such an ardent desire back on the Fell End road, but, on looking up, I noticed that there were two bluebottles flying excitedly round and round the lit bulb. First there were two, then three, then another and another until a dozen or so had been aroused by the light. Not content with remaining near the light source, they would in turn fly on reconnoitring sorties around the room and, more exasperatingly, around my head. There was no chance of my settling down to write any notes amid the distraction, so, armed with folded map, I assaulted them with great gusto but to little effect. Drowsy they may have been but their avoidance tactics were eminently more effective than my slightly drunken swatting. I was left no alternative other than to seek out Mr Neal and request assistance. Finding him in the family's front room, he followed me to my room with a large can of insect spray which he then proceeded to spray liberally toward the lampshade. However perfumed the manufacturers make a can of fly spray, the smell is still revolting and lingers annoyingly for hours afterwards. Not so annoying, though, as a dozen half-crazed bluebottles flying faster and more erratically than ever, caring not what they crash into. Telling myself that their aerobatics would be only temporary, I began making my notes for the day while reclining on the bed. Every few moments I would be joined by a bluebottle as one would crash-land onto the pillow beside me allowing me the opportunity to reduce the enemy by one. Six landed within map-swatting range while the others all met their end noisily and frantically buzzing against the material of the uplighter that amplified their agony acting as a drum skin.

Finally silence reigned and I was left in peace with only the scent of fly spray for company. Notes finished, and a quick check to make sure that there were no stray bits of insect next to me, I lay back on the bed and reflected. For ten days I had walked and now had only twenty-one miles remaining. Checking again, I pulled back the covers and climbed into bed very satisfied with myself. Sleep should have come quickly but I found that I was climbing back out of bed soon after to pay a call of nature that was, at least, far less problematical than my earlier efforts had been on the Dent road.

Chapter 11

Dent to Settle

Being late to bed after having done battle with the plague of blue-bottles and no doubt having been anaesthetised by a cocktail of Dent Brewery beer and fly spray, it was the alarm that stirred me into action, the first of which was to lumber over to the window to survey the weather. The second action was to remove the squashed bluebottle that I trod on from the sole of my bare foot. Lifting my foot up was an awkward exercise of more than a little discomfort because my leg and ankle simply did not want to be bent. I successfully achieved it by perching on the edge of the bed and bodily lifting and then resting one leg on the other. My observation of the weather revealed generally what I had expected: the clouds were down lower than the evening before and the fells were hidden above a grey ceiling that was spread full across the valley. Although not actually perceptibly raining the stone flagged paths of the garden were wet and provided vague reflections of a very drab and uninspiring scene. The weather matched my underlying mood, for however jubilant I felt about my imminent success I could not disguise the fact that the joy of my adventure's culmination would also witness the sadness of it marking the end of my liberty. Making sure that the carpet was clear of further bodies I crossed the room to the bathroom to shower and shave and make myself presentable for the tumultuous hordes that would line the streets of Settle to welcome home the explorer. Well, whoever else might or might not be there, I knew that Sue would be and I knew that she would welcome me home – it's always gratifying if even one person is glad to have you about the place.

I had arranged with Mr Neal to breakfast at eight o'clock to enable an early start for I had planned to arrive in Settle at half past five. I was surprised to see

293

him as I entered the dining room for I had assumed that it would be Mrs Neal who would preside over breakfast. Please note that this was not because I am a male chauvinist pig; it was simply that I had guessed that if it were he who ushered in the guests in the evening and tended to their bluebottles then her workshare would be to see to breakfast needs. He showed me to the solitary place setting at the large table – I had neither seen nor heard any other guests and the sight confirmed that I was the only customer – a fact that did not intrigue me at the time for the tourist season was nearing its end. Nevertheless, my aloneness in the large room made me feel rather as I had at the Lamb Inn where even the slightest sound seemed as though amplified a thousand times. I took care not to drop the jam spoon or to spill scrambled egg on the carpet for there was no one else at whom the finger could be pointed. I could just spy Mr Neal through the open door sat on a stool in the kitchen waiting a polite interval between courses so as not to hurry my breakfast. His judgement was excellent for as soon as I had nicely finished a course he would appear to clear away surplus dishes and then return with the next course, or with fresh toast. At the end of breakfast, and accepting his offer of fresh coffee, I was left alone to look around the dining room with its grand bay window and ornately plaster-decorated and coved ceiling. I wrote out a cheque for my lodgings and picked up the visitors' book with a view to trying to find some original comment to make. I was bemused to see so few entries for 1998 and assumed that previous guests must have been as stumped as I was to enter something suitably meaningful, and simply hadn't bothered. I was equally bemused, though, by the fact that if I were the only guest then why should the 'No Vacancies' sign that I had noticed as I had trudged up the drive the evening before have been hanging in the window.

I made an entry in the book – the content of which was so startlingly witty that I have completely forgotten it – handed my cheque to Mr Neal and, as usual, asked whether his local knowledge might be able to help with my seeking information of my predecessor. He explained that he had lived in the village for only five years and was soon to be moving out as the house was on the market and that I was to be the last paying guest. I had telephoned many months earlier, having spoken to Mrs Neal, and reserved my accommodation; he had felt duty-bound to honour the booking. There was still no mention of Mrs Neal or explanation of her whereabouts and I was not about to pry, but I detected an air of some sadness about the place that remained a mystery even as I walked down the drive at half past eight. The sale of the house explained the no vacancies sign and also the sparse entries in the visitors' book. This was the second guest house on my travels where I had stayed as the final customer. Perhaps that spoke volumes for the state of trade for the old-fashioned bed and breakfast establishment – guests now demanded the more regal services offered by the plush hotel chains, another example of the large company squeezing the last drop of blood out of small business, just as I had done to the bluebottle – I trod on yet another when I returned to my room to finish packing.

I was to visit yet another cemetery before setting out toward Ingleton. Visiting graveyards was becoming something of a slightly morbid fascination, but I had received on good authority that Wainwright's hosts now lay at the village church. My evening at the Sun Inn had not just been a beano of food and drink for I had met an elderly lady by the name of May who had resided in Dent all her life and, I was told, if anyone knew of Wainwright's hosts, she would. He had found accommodation at the home of Mr and Mrs Mason, he a wheelwright with a workshop under the house and she a keen knitter who was seldom without needles clicking busily. Beyond that I knew nothing of the couple who fed and watered Wainwright on his last doleful evening as he looked forward with loathing to the life to which he had to return so very soon. May had not been in the bar when I initially inquired but the barmaid assured me that she would arrive in due course and that she would introduce me. She entered not long after and made her way to the bar to order her usual. From my position around the corner of the bar I could not hear the barmaid's words but I could see the aged lady cast an inquisitive glance in my direction. Compared to May I counted as young and I was sure that she must have been intrigued as to why a young man might wish to buy her a drink – I had paid for a drink for her before she had arrived. An elderly woman, who must have been all of eighty, she appeared to have faculties similar to those of Arthur Bainbridge. It was with eyes as bright as buttons that she looked me over and I smiled and moved toward her to clarify my motives. It did not surprise me to learn that she recalled the Masons and believed their names to be Jack and Judith, although she wasn't sure. She also recalled their house, no more than just a few yards from the inn, and she recalled that they were buried in the churchyard. It soon became my turn to outline to her my reasons for wanting to glean the information from her and I detected a look of even greater inquisitiveness as I explained my presence in Dent.

On my way to look for the graves I had walked by the three-storey house that May had indicated had been the Masons' home. The Masons may be long gone but, renamed Little Oak, the sign hanging outside the house advertised that bed and breakfast could still be secured for travellers. The veranda, which sixty years earlier had provided access to the first-floor living quarters of their home above the workshop, was still intact, although it was now formed from ornate wrought ironwork decorated with tastefully planted flower tubs and hanging baskets. Leaving the house and entering the cemetery, fifteen minutes scouring through the sea of gravestones rewarded me with sight of the one that I sought. May had not been entirely sure as to the Masons' Christian names and she had been right to doubt her memory for the only stone I could find commemorating Mason bore the inscription Joseph and Phyllis. Although I had not checked the parish records the ages coincided with Wainwright's account and I was confident that I was paying my respects to the wheelwright and his wife. Seeing their last resting place on earth may not have achieved anything in a material sense but it provided a firmer connection between Wainwright and myself. I would like to think that the walker in 2058 will gain a sense of greater accomplishment by seeking out the places that I had stayed, but I doubted whether he or she would be able to find the graves of my hosts. The majority of us are so transitory in respect of our domicile that it seemed very unlikely that my hosts' remains would rest forever in the villages in which I had found shelter. For most of my journey I had lodged with residents who themselves had been incomers. I doubted whether their dependants would continue the family lines in the various villages after their demise and their temporary stay would soon be forgotten other than by checking of the records of local residents. Largely gone are the days of generation after generation continuing to live in the same village as their ancestors for there is less and less opportunity to continue the trade of their parents, and slowly but surely families fragment through the seeking of independence and their own ways of earning a living. The Masons were, no doubt, no exception to this and I imagine that had I been in need of a wheelwright in Dent on that Wednesday morning I would not have been able to find one.

At nine o'clock I left the Masons in continued peace and, passing the Sun Inn, found my way onto the start of the road that would lead me into Deepdale. I called at the post office to buy rations because my next chance would not arise until I reached Ingleton, eleven miles away up Deepdale, over the pass at White Side Moss and down Kingsdale. The post office doubled as a purveyor of general provisions, selling everything from snacks, food, maps and guidebooks, stationery and, I suspected almost anything else that I might have cared to mention. Dent is not so unlucky as many of the other rural villages I had visited for it still retains a number of shops along its narrow streets, although these mainly cater for the tourists who swarm during the summer months. In the 1930s there had been twenty or more shops with three banks and, apparently, five inns, but most of these have gone just as the old families have gone. In their place, to satisfy the summer multitudes, are guest houses and car parks that must seem eerily quiet during the winter months. Much of the traditional farming had been replaced, as far as I could see, by camping and caravan sites and, as if to confirm the point, I walked by yet another as I left the village having stowed my provisions.

With the higgledy-piggledy wet Yorkshire-stone-slated rooftops of Dent falling below me as I gained altitude, I looked over to the north to a dismal scene. The earlier drabness of the day had given way to a more ominous diffused light emanating from the low cloud base that was nearer to brown than any other shade. Just as I was having serious doubts as to whether I would see this day out without receiving a severe soaking the rain started, blown by a freshening wind that was stronger than yesterday and had a far greater malicious intent to it. I found some limited shelter behind a tree and quickly pulled my waterproof leggings from my waist bag. With my right leg partly in the leg of the trouser the left leg flapped madly in the wind and rendered the donning of them a most difficult and irksome task. I finally managed to get my left leg partway in also, only to find that I could not pull them up over my boots. Tugging and pulling at them did nothing to help – such actions only succeeded in my losing my balance and falling backwards into the hedgerow while cursing the weather for its sudden turn for the worse. Pulling myself firstly out of the hedge and secondly out of the trouser legs, it was only then that I noticed the lower part of both legs were equipped with zips that I had not previously detected. Unfastening them effected an altogether far more straightforward exercise and I was soon back on the road again, zipped and buttoned up against the elements. Wainwright would have walked beside me with his cycle cape whipping about his head, his flat cap dripping rainwater annoyingly onto his glasses and his body odour vying with other natural smells for the rural pungency award.

Even on a clear day Dent would have been receding from view, but today it had disappeared completely in the first of the frequent squally showers that seemed to match my speed for they stayed with me all the way up Deepdale. With their arrival came a chill wind that was channelled from behind me up this steep-sided tributary valley of the River Dee. I was fortunate to be heading south for at least the worst of the elements were beating against my back. As quickly as they would start the squalls would cease and the wind drop and I very quickly became too warm as I proceeded up the steady incline of the by-road that had, thus far, been almost entirely free of cars. Although Wainwright had, for a fourth day in succession, chosen to make his way via what are now hard paved roads, I was pleased that on this occasion the intervening years had seen only a modest increase in traffic and I ascended without undue disturbance. As I climbed I came to a farm where a barking dog emerged from an open gate heading at alarming speed directly toward me. While not wishing to tarnish all farmers as owning savage dogs, I had seen plenty shackled and snarling, straining at the end of a long metal chain so taut that it might snap at any moment. I observed this animal's approach with some trepidation. I found myself practicing my 'good boy' line again, but as it emanated from my lips it did so in little more than a whimper that was clearly unlikely to persuade the beast to consider me its pack leader. I need not have worried for as it neared its tail began to wag so furiously that its whole back end followed and, by the time it had reached me, its back was bent almost doubled round on itself looking for some attention. Although I was not about to indulge in any form of heavy petting, I did oblige the collie with a warm greeting and friendly patting as it curled around my legs and hindered any form of forward motion. A young farmer appeared at the gate and bade me good morning, calling the collie off at the same time. As quickly as he had arrived the dog scurried away and disappeared back through the gate to his master. I was left to smile wryly to myself, slightly discomforted by what I had thought might have resulted in my downfall on my final day – to have come this far only to be maimed by a dog that could well have arrested any further progress would have been a crushing irony.

During a lull in the vicious weather, when the wind and rain had abated sufficiently to enable the rolling of a cigarette, I paused at the small but beautifully formed Gastack Beck waterfall and took out the now battered copy of *A Pennine Journey*. It would be one of the last times that I would refer to its pages to guide me on my travels and I tried to gauge from my predecessor's account his frame of mind in the final chapter as he neared the final stretch of the final hill. Did he believe that he had achieved anything, I wondered, and did he feel a growing euphoria as he neared his goal. He described his trip as a truancy that was nearly over and of having to return to a normality that would once again, very soon, include the renewed threat of war. It was during Wainwright's escapade that Neville Chamberlain had posed augustly upon disembarkation with his infamous piece of paper and many breathed a sigh of relief at the man's powers of diplomacy. Wainwright would have certainly been one of them for he admitted that he would have hated being a soldier, although he omitted to specify exactly why. As I looked to the pass between Deepdale and Kingsdale I had no such worries for the world would surely not dare to enter into any form of combat lest such skirmish lead to all-out war. There would be no six-year struggle now, just a few seconds of button pushing followed by a series of blinding flashes as cities vaporised in a conflagration where there could only be losers. No, I satisfied myself, the diplomats and politicians would save us from such a fate and I was happy for I too would have hated to be a soldier. A very limited rugby-playing career facing opposition who had wished only minor injury upon me had been bad enough. I couldn't possibly imagine how I might have coped pitched against an opponent with a loathsome desire to inflict severe pain through the indiscriminate use of a bayonet or some other gruesome instrument. Perhaps I, and many others who have felt that life has, on occasion, dealt them a poor hand, ought to think themselves very fortunate that their life's path had never led them down the avenue of having to face such an enemy. For Wainwright, his worst fears were realised – there was a war but he would, presumably, have been relieved not to have been required to take an active part. For me, I hoped too that I would also be excused service for I would be just too plain old, so if the diplomats and the politicians did get it wrong then I would be off with my map and cigarette looking for that most likely targeted epicentre.

Toward the end of his account Wainwright made a reference to himself as a thwarted genius, which, when related to his general malaise, suggests that he had longed for something that he might have perceived as being of greater consequence than his post at Blackburn Council. He must have approached the final pass with a burgeoning belief that his Pennine Campaign (as he initially dubbed his journey) was about to set him on a new road that would blossom and launch him into fame and fortune. He surely desired something other than the existence he referred to in his closing paragraphs as being the sorry business of living. I was rather glad we had not been walking together for we would have dwelt on depressing matters too long and not long enough on the aspects of life that had given pleasure. It is all too easy to take a perspective on life and pronounce that the only type of fortune to come one's way has been lamentable ill luck with associated intermittent setbacks ranging in severity from minor to cataclysmic. The better experiences are more easily passed off as just being a part of life's plan and are forgotten for, as they are absorbed, they are also taken for granted. If you must take a rearward view, recall all experiences or otherwise your account is both unbalanced and bloody boring because no one wants to hear incessant bad-luck stories or tales of what might have been. Remember too that it is the bad times that make the good times seem good for pleasure is a relative sensation and that without bad times life would be an endless series of successes. To only experience success inevitably generates conceit – to be humble in triumph is to have known how the vanquished feels at the moment of defeat. Without that sentiment the victor is not an entire being for he is unable to display humility in victory and grace in failure.

Notoriety was a long time coming and any aspirations Wainwright might have held of achieving fame only materialised years later – and not as the product of the story of his eleven days spent in the Pennines. His account lay undisturbed for over forty years and was only published for public consumption after his reputation was established as a guidebook writer. While his guides may be a series of instruction manuals for journeying from one place to another, it is his eleven-day autobiography that provides a more profound portrait of a man walking alone and feeling the essence of that oneness. He described more than once the delight of walking unaccompanied and it is true that the innermost emotions are best experienced alone for in company conversation hinders the purest of self-investigation.

My thoughts were rudely interrupted by the return of the wind and the rain, so stubbing my cigarette out on the wall beside me, I set off once more up the road that was becoming ever steeper as I began to traverse the contours in earnest. The head of the valley in front of me withdrew into the squall and the precipitous-looking flank of Whernside also vanished from view while the shower persisted. My field of vision was further restricted by the fact that I had sought the protection of my hood and was shrouded as best I could against the elements. The road as far as Gastack Beck had been largely devoid of anything akin to a verge and was tightly lined with hedgerows to either side, but a little way beyond the beck a gate marked the end of relative civilisation and the start of open and wild moorland. Turning to close the gate I could see that better weather was chasing the rain out of the valley and as I arrived at the steepest part of the road the scene was suddenly flooded in sunlight that very soon had me peeling off my leggings and stowing my very expensive jacket. The wind had dropped and I foolishly believed that I might see out my final day bathed not only in glory but in glorious sunshine also. My legs were rapidly tiring and I was very glad to reach the flatter watershed area of White Shaw Moss. I was pleased too to be walking on the road for all around were squelching bogs and peat hacks that would try to suck loosely fastened boots off. Surrounded by such a quagmire I recalled my crossing of Foxup Moor ten days earlier and won-dered whether the couple had finally found their way off the moor or whether she might still be there splashing about and blaming him for her predicament. My reaching the watershed was something of a milestone for it marked the last of any strenuous uphill walking and it meant that I was at the beginning of the last dale in which I would walk, Kingsdale. Only seventeen miles remained between my position stood aloft above Deepdale and Settle that nestled on lower land and sheltered by fells to the north and east. Essentially it was now all downhill and it was with a growing sense of achievement that I strode along the firm grass verge on the upper reaches of this strange dale.

Wainwright had noted Kingdale's peculiarities with its channel-like qualities that gave the impression that it had been excavated by man rather than formed by the forces of nature. He had noted that everything about the dale was of such regularity as to render it almost unreal and more than a little uninteresting as a result of its uniformity. Nothing has changed in the intervening sixty years. The dale, unlike any other, seems to comprise of only straight lines. The river and road lie parallel to one another, both as straight as though the Romans had built them for want of something to do on their way northwards to the wall. The field walls that run both laterally and longitudinally across and down the dale are as direct in their intent as the road and river. Even the walls that cross the valley appear to have been erected at a spacing that is so regular as to defy belief short of seeing them first-hand. There are still only two outlying farms as there were in 1938 and both are supplied by telegraph lines that are strung between poles that never veer from their arrow-like course up the opposite side of the flat valley floor. The whole dale gives the impression that it was constructed by some Germanic race with an eye for neatness and efficiency but with absolutely no heart for imagination. In their design they had forsaken any particular detail to the sides of the dale, simply finishing them with a few trees scattered about among an otherwise barren but uniformly shaped profile. Whoever had built the riverbed, though, had forgotten to insert the butyl liner for it is not until the far southern end of the valley that it holds any water. It exists as a dry pebble-strewn canal bizarrely spanned by one or two bridges where perhaps once water flowed and presumably still does, but only after heavy rain. As if to confirm that limestone country had been re-entered the water suddenly sprang forth and within a matter of yards what had been a dry bed had turned into a healthy beck in readiness for its grand spectacle down the falls on its course to Ingleton. I finally left the road to make my way along a track that would lead to a footbridge across the river and as I did so I looked back up the valley to see that my amiable weather-window looked as though it was to be only temporary. I was being followed by a bulking mass of cloud that was moving almost imperceptibly toward me giving a stormy backdrop to the scene north-east up the dale. It was as impressive as it was ominous and did not bode well for a fair afternoon unless it had the decency to change direction.

It was noon as I reached the narrow bridge and, as I suspected that there might be more sightseers at the Ingleton Falls than when Wainwright had had the place to himself, I decided to rest awhile in peace sitting on the stone steps next to the bridge. I couldn't help but return to my thoughts of Wainwright as he anticipated his return to the rat race and the pushing and shoving and jockeying for position. I tried to picture his mood had he been returning to that same rat race sixty years on and I wondered whether he might be able to cope with the vastly increased bureaucracy that would undoubtedly now exist. I thought also of the hotel guests at Hexham as they had shared their high-power breakfast with me and I wondered what Wainwright might have made of their apparent refusal to cease their work even over breakfast. Although never quite sure whether fortunate is the correct definition, I have, nevertheless, been fortunate enough to be employed in a number of roles ranging from quantity surveying through to shelf-stacker at Sainsbury's. These varying roles have given an insight into differing management styles and provided me with my own opinion of the one that will, without any doubt, kill off any last vestiges of enthusiasm within the workforce. It is where employers talk of empowering the workforce that I have generally encountered a heightened sense of friction between managers and workers. The management, in furthering its wish to be seen to be adopting some form of proactive style and securing official but meaningless certification to the effect, looks to embrace a modern management ethos that has been heralded as the modern leadership philosophy. It is more than probable that some well-meaning management mumbo-jumbo consultant has advocated such empowerment (and earns a fine commission for instilling such modern thinking). The truth of the matter is that hierarchical talk of employees being empowered often falters at the point of letting go of the reins, ultimately only relinquishing the mundane or the risk-laden aspects. The only manner in which management feels that it can maintain control is to define in great detail all job roles, duties, rosters, work patterns, targets and a thousand other minutiae that all contrive to impede the performance of actually carrying out the role. So complex does the structure become that there evolves a need to provide ongoing training so that the staff might have even the vaguest of ideas as to what their roles are. This bureaucratic structure without any doubt killed stone dead any motivation that I had retained, other than the obvious drive to ensure that a copy of the Thursday *Yorkshire Post* appointments section was to hand to check the job market. A colleague best likened such levels of bureaucracy at the time as similar to wading through knee-deep mud with a pair of flippers on. I have, conversely, worked in an environment at the other end of the spectrum where the only guidance was to 'do the job' – the prime motive being to make money, for nothing else mattered beyond profit. The unfortunate fact was that the job role would change daily from its original unwritten definition, which, when added to the fact that the role was never originally defined anyway, generated a sensation of wading through knee-deep mud with a pair of flippers on and blindfolded. Whether the management is autocratic or bureaucratic, I had my doubts that Wainwright would have been a happy man in an office environment in 1998 and that his yearning for something more meaningful would only have been more profound.

I left the bridge and ascended the track for a short distance in search of the path leading sharply down to the right that would steer me to Ingleton via the falls that I had never before visited. Finding it, I also found that any prospects of being alone as Wainwright had been were immediately dispelled by the sight that greeted me as I turned right through the gate onto the well-trodden path. Below me, at the head of the steep-sided gorge, were seemingly hundreds of bodies all swarming along the paths and rocks to either side of the river. I had grown accustomed to being alone and could only imagine that these hordes had all climbed the ravine from Ingleton. There would not be the quiet contemplative thoughts that Wainwright had enjoyed as I joined the thronging crowds as they milled back and forth. If a detour had existed I might well have forgone my wish to follow Wainwright and struck out on my own – to follow my own star as he might have said. During my journey I had thought often of his comments as to others following their own routes and not necessarily sheepishly following his and I had concluded that it was generally prudent to explore alternatives only when the original was comprehended. In my days as a surveyor I had not sought to carry out a role in any different manner to that that had been established until I was able to substantiate my reasons for varying a tried and tested procedure. Too many things in life have been made the subject of change for change's sake and few, if any, have ever benefited from needless change. Educational authorities have been allowed to follow their own star and a right old pig's ear they've made of it, having turned the system on its head so that the pupils now control the masters. Criminal authorities have acted, as their name suggests, with an authority that has been close to criminal and which has allowed lawbreakers to act almost with impunity in the knowledge of the meek penalties that exert little or no deterrent. It sometimes seems that regardless of whether an aspect of society has been proved to be effective over a long period there is a principle edict that states it will be subjected to fundamental change simply as a function of its length of service. If I was adjudged to be sheepishly following Wainwright then I did so with good reason – it was only with the knowledge of his itinerary that I might be able to ascertain a more suitable route to best accommodate modern wayfarers.

I have to confess to not loitering while descending the riverside paths around the falls. At every turn there were parties of schoolchildren and parties of hikers and just parties of others. There were people shouting to one another, or sitting eating their sandwiches among this general hullabaloo and there were even those who were talking on mobile phones. Crowds swarmed over every avail-able nook and cranny, which wasn't actually that many because most had been fenced off. There was a strict path to be followed and throughout its length on the upper part of the falls the rock had been polished over the years due to scrambling visitors. Partway down the polished path there was an unsightly, corrugated, green metal snack bar formed from what looked like a redundant freight container which sold a variety of drinks and snacks including such local delicacies as Pot Noodles. Why these people couldn't buy their rations at some outlet at the base of the falls and then manage to carry them up was beyond me. Perhaps the authorities had deemed the hut necessary to provide a stopping point in an attempt to avoid there being litter. I recalled how on Sleightholme Moor I had seen the old railway carriage that had been given a new lease of life and I had applauded its reuse. Here, though, in a place that should have held such beauty, such a sight was only notable for its incongruity. Here it was, the crowning anathema amid the hordes of trippers that were bad enough without the addition of such a commercial eyesore. No, I had no desire to linger and found my way quickly down the gorge passing, at intervals, various groups of schoolchildren whom all appeared to be measuring the volume of the water flow for some inexplicable reason. Why they had to make so much noise while engaged in their activities I did not pause to inquire. Instead I resigned myself to the fact that my days of isolation seemed to have done little for my toleration of others. Probably when I was a schoolchild I would have made just as much noise so long as the teacher was safely out of earshot. The difference now seemed to be that these clamorous children could do exactly as they wished regardless of their teachers' proximities. I will move off the subject smartly for fear of being deemed a killjoy and return to my speedy escape from the pandemonium…

On a quiet day, if the ravine could be had to oneself (sometime around dawn I would imagine), it would be a spectacular place of tumbling falls and rushing water as the River Twiss battles its torturous way between sheer enclosing walls to either side. Only when Swilla Glen is reached does the changed geology allow its rate of descent to slow leaving it to enjoy a more tranquil passage to its confluence with the River Doe in Ingleton. How things had changed in the intervening years between our visits. Wainwright had savoured the falls in splendid isolation with the only interruption being the sound of trains emanating from the railway and the blare of a factory hooter. Neither I nor anyone else would ever hear the railway again for it, like so many others I had encountered, is long dead and the viaduct stands high over the village as a grand memorial to commemorate its passing. Neither would anyone hear the sound of the factory hooter for it had been silenced just as it had silenced the sound of the 'knocker-up' before it. I would not have considered the railway or the hooter as great an interference as I had done the crowds for they had trespassed on my sense of anticipation as they squeezed passed me throughout the length of the gorge. If you relish peace and harmony and wish to come to the falls then do come early, very early. If it is your heart's desire to spend your days in the melee of Blackpool or Morecambe then come here just after midday as I had done.

The one consolation that I had been granted was that any threat of worsening weather had held off and as I walked downstream at Swilla Glen I did so with sunlight filtering through the canopy of trees that enclosed the valley. Their cover was only broken as I approached the car park near the bottom of the glen where the riverbank opened out onto a wide grassy expanse of picnic seating and I sat for a few minutes having escaped the crowded narrow confines of the ravine. Sitting next to a timber-framed and covered rubbish bin, I retrieved what waste had accumulated in my rucksack and waist bag and emptied the varied collection into it. As I did so I noticed the front cover of a glossy journal that had been discarded and a closer inspection revealed it to be a copy of what Wain-wright would have termed a nudist magazine. He admitted to something of a predisposition to such literature and I have to confess that I swept my rubbish from the face of the front cover and rather surreptitiously rescued the magazine from its resting place. My pulling it from the bin was no different to the sign in a fish and chip shop that warns of the range being hot – there is a sudden urge to feel just how hot and touch it with tentative fingers. I recalled such publications as *Parade* from when I was younger and admit that there had been occasions when I had plucked up the courage to try to look older than my years and pur-chase a copy. My recollection was of images of inartistically posed ladies in various states of partial (or sometimes even full) undress with camerawork that was of dubious technical quality, and the overall impression being one of rela-tively innocent naughtiness. The fact that the artistry was lacking and the photographer of limited skills did not especially detract from the end result and only mirrored what, in reality, had indeed been the subject of the brush for hun-dreds of years previously. I have for years held a keen interest in photography and acknowledge that the photographic press relies heavily on containing a fair sprinkling of reasonably tastefully exposed ladies' parts to help boost sales. While the feminists may not be pleased at such an affront on the nature of the males' view of women, at least the quality of the images could not be faulted. It was in a state of some nostalgia that I flicked open the magazine at a random page. What met me from the page was neither of artistic merit nor of photo-graphic quality. I flicked again and while the hair and the skin colour were different and clearly of separate models, the picture was essentially a view of the woman's genitalia exposed as if undergoing an unbelievably close personal examination while in a mood, it seemed, of some arousal. Again I opened a page at random and again was met by a similarly extraordinary pose only this time the model squeezing her breasts so hard that they looked as though had they been balloons they would have burst at any moment. One last time I turned the pages and, by chance, happened upon the page purporting to contain letters from avid readers. Did I really have to share the same world with deviants and miscreants so deranged as these who would apparently write such utter filth, I wondered. I turned back to the front cover to find that this was not the pornography of seedy backstreet shops whose products leave the premises in brown paper bags but was top-shelf material of high-street sellers. Perhaps I really was becoming intolerant of others and maybe I was out of step and that these images really did represent the way in which men should view women. Or perhaps I was developing feminist tendencies in my advancing years and felt that they were indeed an insult to womanhood. Bugger all that, it was just far more likely that I had maintained a level of general decency that this exceptionally sad publication had affronted. I considered whether it might just be me taking the moral high ground, but I concluded that there was no moral high ground as far as these pictures and words were concerned. Everywhere was of greater moral altitude than them. Initially, on seeing the magazine, I had been intrigued that someone should discard it in such a public place. The only intrigue after my brief skim through its pages was why I had bothered in the first place – I should have lived with my innocent nostalgia of the dirty mags of my past and left this pornography well alone.

Tossing the magazine (now, less of it) back into the bin, refastening my various buttons and zips (now, I've told you once...) I sauntered toward the tollbooth to see what my hour of hustle and bustle was to cost. In 1938 Wainwright had not bothered to wake the sleeping gate man as he dropped a sixpence onto the step. I paid a pound to the alert uniformed man and we chatted for a couple of minutes, during which it transpired, by a strange coincidence, that his first visit to the falls as a child had been in 1938. It was one o'clock as I left the steward as he moved to relieve the next carload of their fare and I made my way in the shadow of the huge viaduct up the hill into the centre of the village. The paths that Wainwright had followed had, for the most part, been confidently discernible, but his account of his route walked from Ingleton to Settle was far less so and I decided to retire for a swift pint to have a final check of my assumptive route. His description revealed only that he passed over Newby Common in such a way that took him via Clapham Station. I resolved to follow the old road toward Clapham, imaginatively called 'Old Road' as far as Newby Cote where I would turn to Newby and cross over the main road and walk to the station. Beyond the station the route, according to my estimation, passed through Eldroth and via a maze of back roads until finally passing Giggleswick School before going on into Settle itself. My excursion would be completed as a grand circular tour just a few yards beyond the bridge over the River Ribble at the junction with the Horton road.

With my route determined, I sat and drank and smoked looking out at a scene that was now bereft of sun and, judging by the way people were walking, had welcomed a freshening wind. From my table I could not see the sky but I guessed that the weather that had muddied the far end of Kingsdale as I had left it had finally eased its way down the valley and was about to do its worst. With eleven miles left to walk on my eleventh and last day, I left the inn at half past one, allowing myself only minimal time for rests during the afternoon. I could see little on the map that might hold my interest and arrest my progress and my sole objective was now to reach Settle. The crowds at the falls had brought me back down to earth. I had been reminded that I still lived in the fast world of 1998 where people would elbow their way up the ladder of progress in the same way as they had been unwilling to give way at any point on the narrow paths around the falls. I might be viewed as weak but I generally give way to someone who is much older than myself or to a woman – with others the right of way just establishes itself at the appropriate time. I was taught to respect my elders and believed that it was of common courtesy to permit a lady to pass first. The problem with both these principles is that they are both of such an age to have become largely scornfully neglected and have suffered the same demise as many other aspects of tradition that have been crushed in the stampede called progress. In the case of gallantry toward women it is, to some degree, they themselves that have demanded that such practises should cease. With the loudly hailed clamour for equality had come an attitude where some would look with disdain upon the man that held a door open or invited them to pass first. As with most things it is so often the few which spoil it for the remainder and the contempt shown for those who would offer courtesy soon eroded any last token gestures of gentlemanliness. Wainwright left his last lambasting of the liberation seekers until his last few miles of walking. He very obviously respected women on the proviso that they understood and accepted that their place was elsewhere than what he perceived as the male domain. Perhaps, sixty years on, there are those women who might, after all, wish that their sisters had not made such deep incursions into what was seen as male territory for they are now saddled with responsibilities that are not so attractive when experienced first-hand. As for the elderly, they appear to be treated as though they have just become an unavoidable liability, a product of advances in medicine whereby they don't die off quite so early. Oh, dear, my cynicism was regrouping; I must be approaching a return to the real world, I thought as I placed my empty glass back on the bar and made for the front door of the inn.

Standing outside the inn the increased chill of the wind that whipped along the street had me putting my jacket on before I had walked even 50 yards. The sky overhead was dark and forbidding with an appearance that threatened dire consequences for any who chose to venture out under it. The clouds hurried on their way and had blocked out any last brightness so that the sun of just an hour earlier, filtering through the trees at Swilla Glen, was but a distant memory. I strode out briskly for there was nothing to be gained now by dawdling and after a few hundred yards turned right onto the road to Clapham. Presently the road began to climb surely and steadily and, having left any sheltering influence of Ingleton, I was battered by a wind that was strengthening by the minute and insisted on blowing from a whole variety of directions. Sometimes, had I been wearing roller skates, I could have ceased walking and have been almost blown along by it, while at other times it veered and made any progress at all up the continuous incline very hard work. After a mile or so the wind was joined by a light drizzle that grew in persistence until it was a steady and stinging rain from which there was very little effective refuge for it was propelled by strong gusts. With jacket fastened, hood tightened around my face and waterproof trousers on, I could not gain any better protection, so I resigned myself to walking without rest until I reached Clapham Station. I had never previously called at the station and had the idea that perhaps there might be a café or other refreshment available. I had also formed the fanciful notion that, on victorious arrival at Settle, the streets would be lined with bunting and flags and painted with words of warm welcome, full of people greeting the great crusader. Children would be waving their paper flags on sticks and straining for a better view as I walked in triumph the last few yards. I can't recall where I had formed such an idea but, somewhat like having had the television company show an interest in my venture, I found the prospect of a modest degree of hero-worship rather appealing.

There is little to relate of the next four miles for they were singularly uninteresting with the possible exception of seeing the old Ingleton railway. Even disused railways held little attraction on such an afternoon for I had seen so many and this was just another. You grow used to death if you are around it long enough. It came as great relief to see Clapham Station because the wind was even stronger and rain even harder and I would seek the haven of the station and wait until the worst of it had passed. It became apparent that I was not about to secure any form of refreshment at the station – all that remained was a husk of an original building that now provided the only shelter. It had been emptied of all internal fittings except for the tubular steel vandal-proof benching. I entered to see the customary graffiti adorning the walls and the usual discarded wrappers and tin cans scattered about the floor and again I pondered on what might motivate a person to simply cast aside their waste without thought for others. I thought back to the volunteers of the South Tynedale Railway and could only marvel at their persistence and energy in the face of such crass stupidity and indolence. I might not normally have tarried at the station but

I was out of the rain and was thankful for the chance of a cigarette. Hand rolling cigarettes and howling gales and rain are not good bedfellows, so I was glad of the temporary respite. After ten minutes it became abundantly clear that I was enjoying what would prove to be a temporary reprieve from the weather – if anything the elements outside grew fiercer as I watched. I was to experience the type of weather that had dented Wainwright's enthusiasm and had caused him to take a more direct southerly route than he otherwise might have done. For the final four days he walked on roads, which for a man who loved the wild hills so much must have been more like a sentence than a holiday. Then again, any break that tested the mettle was always looked back on with some degree of fondness once the memory of the more grim parts had faded slightly. In 1938, as Wainwright made his journey, he might have appreciated it more acutely than in 1998 for we have become accustomed to taking regular holidays, apparently regardless of cost.

As I sat I recalled that I had, or more than one occasion, heard people tell of the holiday they had just had or were planning and in the same breath tell also of their plans to consolidate all their debts into one large pot on the advice of the bank manager. It seems extraordinary to me that regardless of the ability to pay for something, we still believe that we can attain it almost as our right. Although this applies to many purchases, the more usual reasoning in terms of the holiday is that it is deserved and needed. Deserved and needed it may appear to be, but any recuperative benefits enjoyed while partaking in the dream would surely be more than cancelled out by the waking up to the fact that the debt of the holiday is only going to increase. By 'eck, better plan the next holiday, all this debt is stressful. The philosophy has largely been brought about by the lenders themselves who have increasingly been willing to lend ever-larger wads of cash. I recalled that within my lifetime the family holiday had, when I was young, comprised of a week in Filey in a modest B&B (my father being a relatively successful self-employed shop owner. In those days what you couldn't afford to pay for you didn't have – there appeared to be a greater ability to entertain oneself, accept one's lot and make the best of a bad job. Now, the demand is to be entertained on a wholly grander scale with the sights set considerably further afield than Filey. There must be others who share my logic in believing that nothing has changed from the 'can't afford-can't have' philosophy, but where are they? I have come across very few. That something has changed is all too apparent – it is the attitude of the borrowers that has changed, with indoctrination-by-advert leading to the belief that there is such a thing as a free lunch and that you can (nay, should) have something now regardless of its expense. At the end of the day why worry, for if the easy terms become too much to handle a return trip to the bank manager will see the consolidation of this year's debt and tag it onto last year's – the sad fact is that last year's included part of the year before, and so on, ad infinitum. Still, there's always next year's holiday to look forward to and, according to the adverts, the terms get easier and easier. Surely, the deciding factor in whether something is deserved or not is whether there exists the wherewithal to fund it – perhaps the interpretation of need has been mistaken for want?

Sitting at the station waiting for an improvement in the weather was beginning to prove futile for the wind lashed the rain and there was nothing for it other than to set out again and accept my lot. If Noah had seen this weather he would have been out looking for a reliable source of timber. I had waited until half past three and, with six miles still to walk, could wait no longer if Settle were to be my goal by half past five. The remaining miles were spent cursing the weather and wondering whether Wainwright himself had had a heavenly hand in making sure that I would not forget my last day too quickly. I had visions of him viewing my progress angelically but with a devil sitting on his shoulder persuading him that no one should successfully be allowed to follow his journey without a struggle. Even my very expensive jacket was letting water in at the seams and the fronts of my legs were cold and damp for the wind had decided to concentrate its efforts in one direction – namely, head-on – and my overtrousers were proving to be not so waterproof. Shielding my face from the rain was also proving impossible and the vision through my glasses was as though painted by an impressionist pointillist. When not cussing the weather I, like Wainwright had done, reflected on my days of liberty, which were so nearly at an end. The conclusions of my musings were strangely similar to those of Wainwright's. Perhaps even after sixty years things hadn't changed so much after all – well at least relative to one other in any case. Buckden was still beautiful albeit that it had, in itself, changed dramatically from being a working village to an attraction to be gaped at by a thousand tourists. Blanchland could only ever be almost as it was sixty years earlier for it had been excluded from change and now had the air of a working model town fit for a museum. As for the rest, there had been much devastation to the rural way of life in the intervening years which had seen the influx of rich townsfolk arriving at their weekend retreats that they had bought and renovated themselves. There had been an equally great influx of commercially-minded businessmen who had bought cottages and let them out to those who could not afford their own retreat. At the same time, the indigenous inhabitants had seen their traditional livelihoods wither and die and have had to adapt if they were to remain. With their incomes falling and the associated supply and demand for property heralding huge increases in value, the local population was changing so that the countryside was fast becoming the playground for the wealthy. After all it would only be the wealthy that might be able to afford the fuel prices in another sixty years and they certainly would not wish to be seen boarding public transport when the four-by-four could transport them so much more efficiently. My despondency at returning was generating such pessimism that I changed the focus of my thinking and addressed whether I had learned anything on my travels. I had learned a little about Hadrian's Wall; I had learned a little about Wainwright; I had learned a little about places that I had never before visited; I had learned a little about life. More than these, though, I had learned volumes about myself.

Squelching along in boots that I now realised were also letting water in, I thought back to Douglas Adams being convinced in The *Hitchhiker's Guide to theGalaxy* that the answer to life, the universe and everything was forty-two. I was forty-two and had decided that I had found the answer in that there was no absolute answer. Life is as an indeterminate and unspecific question, and many labour under the misapprehension that there must be a definite answer and that if they cannot find it their lives will remain unfulfilled. I concluded that life's question cannot be answered successfully because it is written in a language that most do not understand. Finding an acceptable answer is similar to old school examinations – marks were awarded for showing calculations in the margin at the side of the page. Although a wrong answer might actually be finally arrived at, the master would still recognise the quality of the workings-out. The answer was not the be-all and end-all of the question. So it is with life, where each day or week or year is an individual episode for which new and independent levels of consciousness are required, not in finding the answer but in best deciphering the question. It is not so much what we achieve; it is how we achieve it along the way.

I trudged manfully on with the cold – which I have not mentioned for days – causing me to sniff incessantly rather than remove my hands from snug pockets and reach into to retrieve a damp handkerchief. After crossing the bypass that has so reduced Settle's traffic I was faced with one last interminable hill that seemed to rise forever. As I finally crested its highest brow I could see the famous dome of the chapel at Giggleswick School. I knew that my destination was near and I could detect a spring in my step as I fairly raced down the hill into the village itself. I was now in the lee of the hills to the east of Settle and my worst exposure to the elements had ended, allowing me a greater sense in which to savour my triumphal entry.

Incredibly, on the stroke of half past five I crossed the bridge over the River Ribble and looked ahead up the long straight stretch of road toward the town centre where I had looked back eleven days earlier having said to Sue that I wouldn't. I was bemused for there was no bunting, no flags, no paint and no children shouting. All there was was rain and wind and cold and the thought that perhaps the wind had blown away the bunting and the flags, and the rain had washed the paint from the road, and that the chill had resulted in the mothers keeping their offspring safe in the warm. Perhaps there never was any bunting or flags or paint or children, and perhaps the only person really concerned about my return from my journey was me. Well, so be it, for I was the most important; it had been I who had fulfilled my dream and it is rare indeed for others to share the same dream, or at least in the same way. I have to admit, though, to being more than a little pleased when a local chap out walking his dog did trouble to greet me. He wished me good afternoon and commented that it was not a nice day for a walk. I agreed and quickly looked down at his dog for I swore that it had eyed me with a knowing glance as I passed.

I had arrived and felt no smaller than Wainwright had done sixty years previously. The greatest difference between us was that I did not smell quite so unheavenly as he must have done. Other differences were, I suspected, marginal for we had both walked two hundred miles in eleven days and we had both walked it alone. I also suspected that Wainwright had learned a lot as I had done and had been able, during his days of freedom, to clear his mind of extraneous troubles, be they the fear of war or the boredom of the incessant coverage of the American president's misdemeanours. There is no experience quite like that of testing yourself and rising to the challenge; seeking and finding your goal and overcoming all that might be thrown at you. I had started my walk in a state of some depression at a future that seemed to have been steered by previous errors of judgement, but in finishing it would stand forever as something that worked out as planned. If you ever feel that you have got your back to the wall then I could do no better than to recommend that you do as I do and go back to the wall.

Acknowledgements

Although this book has not been written to provide anything other than the merest study of social history, there have been a number of people to which I owe a debt of gratitude or to publications that have been particularly helpful. A general thanks is due to all those who gave me accommodation.

Buckden

Angela Falshaw for her tolerance of my calling upon her cold, and for her letter to me after my return.

Muker

Margaret (surname unknown) for her help in directing me to the Harkers' house and grave.

Romaldkirk

Joyce Hughes for her personal letter to me and for her detailed knowledge of Romaldkirk. She is the caretaker and deputy churchwarden at St Romald's Church.

Blanchland

Blanchland – A Short History. The late G. W. O. Addleshaw MA. BD. FSA (Formerly Treasurer of York Minster and Dean of Chester).

Alan Murray for his personal letter to me in trying to identify the Elliott family.

Alston

Jo and Sam Pester for trying to find out something of the Richardson family.

Knock

Christine Braithwaite for the loan of the booklet outlining Soulby's social history (her father-in-law had been the vicar and her husband had lived there as a child).

Soulby

Douglas Birkbeck for his efforts in trying to identify the two Black Bull ladies.

Arthur Bainbridge for no other reason than just being Arthur – a fine man.

Dent

May (surname unknown) for her help at the Sun Inn regarding the Mason family.

I also acknowledge the Hunter Davies volume *Wainwright – The Biography*. Reference to it has helped me to get to know the man who, by the end of the journey, perhaps I know well enough to refer to as AW. No, I could not be so presumptuous.

ABOUT THE AUTHOR

Yorkshire-born author A Walker's writing centres around the earlier works of Alfred Wainwright, particularly his *Pennine Journey,* which he had undertaken in 1938. Walker retraced the route and found it became the inspiration for *Back to the Wall*, a personal reflection that uses the walk as a microcosm of life's journey. Walker's interpretation of his 1998 trek takes the form of a rambling account that compares and contrasts with Wainwright's original book using his own views and opinions as the basis of a thought-provoking and amusing yarn. Walker also wrote his historically based guide to the walk published as *In Wainwright's Footsteps: The Pennine Journey.*

Lightning Source UK Ltd.
Milton Keynes UK
UKHW041305250620
365560UK00001B/98

9 780995 604339